Separa
Powers—
Does It
Still Work?

D0792841

Separation of Powers— Does It Still Work?

Robert A. Goldwin
and Art Kaufman
editors

American Enterprise Institute for Public Policy Research
Washington, D.C.

This book is the fourth in a series in AEI's project "A Decade of Study of the Constitution," funded in part by a Bicentennial Challenge Grant from the National Endowment for the Humanities. The first book in this series was *How Democratic Is the Constitution?* the second was *How Capitalistic Is the Constitution?* the third was *How Does the Constitution Secure Rights?* All three books were edited by Robert A. Goldwin and William A. Schambra.

Library of Congress Cataloging-in-Publication Data

Separation of powers—does it still work?

    (AEI studies ; 446)
    Contents: To form a government / Lloyd N. Cutler—
Political parties and the separation of powers / James
Q. Wilson—The renewal of American constitutionalism /
Donald L. Robinson—[etc.]
    1. Separation of powers—United States. I. Goldwin,
Robert A., 1922-   . II. Kaufman, Art. III. Series.
JK305.D64 1986   320.473   86-14083
ISBN 0-8447-3606-6 (alk. paper)
ISBN 0-8447-3607-4 (pbk.: alk. paper)

1 3 5 7 9 10 8 6 4 2

AEI Studies 446

© 1986 by the American Enterprise Institute for Public Policy Research, Washington, D.C. All rights reserved. No part of this publication may be used or reproduced in any manner whatsoever without permission in writing from the American Enterprise Institute except in the case of brief quotations embodied in news articles, critical articles, or reviews. The views expressed in the publications of the American Enterprise Institute are those of the authors and do not necessarily reflect the views of the staff, advisory panels, officers, or trustees of AEI.

"American Enterprise Institute" and   are registered service marks of the American Enterprise Institute for Public Policy Research.

Printed in the United States of America

Contents

The American Enterprise Institute for Public Policy Research, established in 1943, is a nonpartisan, nonprofit research and educational organization supported by foundations, corporations, and the public at large. Its purpose is to assist policy makers, scholars, business men and women, the press, and the public by providing objective analysis of national and international issues. Views expressed in the institute's publications are those of the authors and do not necessarily reflect the views of the staff, advisory panels, officers, or trustees of AEI.

Council of Academic Advisers

Donald C. Hellmann, *Professor of Political Science and International Studies, University of Washington*

D. Gale Johnson, *Eliakim Hastings Moore Distinguished Service Professor of Economics and Chairman, Department of Economics, University of Chicago*

Robert A. Nisbet, *Adjunct Scholar, American Enterprise Institute*

Herbert Stein, *A. Willis Robertson Professor of Economics Emeritus, University of Virginia*

Murray L. Weidenbaum, *Mallinckrodt Distinguished University Professor and Director, Center for the Study of American Business, Washington University*

James Q. Wilson, *Henry Lee Shattuck Professor of Government, Harvard University*

Executive Committee

Willard C. Butcher,
  Chairman of the Board
Paul F. Oreffice, *Vice Chairman*
Paul W. McCracken, *President*

John J. Creedon

Richard M. Morrow

Richard D. Wood

Robert J. Pranger, *Vice President, External Affairs*

James F. Hicks, *Vice President, Finance and Administration*

Thomas F. Johnson,
  Director, Economic Policy Studies

Howard R. Penniman,
  Director, Political Processes Studies

James W. Abellera, *Acting Director, International Studies*

William A. Schambra,
  Director, Social Policy Studies

Edward Styles,
  Director of Publications

Periodicals

AEI Economist, Herbert Stein, *Ed.*

AEI Foreign Policy and Defense Review,
  Evron M. Kirkpatrick, Robert J. Pranger, and Harold H. Saunders, *Eds.*

Public Opinion,
  Seymour Martin Lipset and
  Ben J. Wattenberg, *Co-Eds.,*
  Everett Carll Ladd, *Sr. Ed.,*
  Karlyn H. Keene, *Mng. Ed.*

The Editors and the Authors

ROBERT A. GOLDWIN is resident scholar and director of constitutional studies at the American Enterprise Institute. He has served in the White House as special consultant to the president and, concurrently, as adviser to the secretary of defense. He has taught at the University of Chicago and at Kenyon College and was dean of St. John's College in Annapolis. He is the editor of *A Nation of States* and coeditor of *How Democratic Is the Constitution? How Capitalistic Is the Constitution?* and *How Does the Constitution Secure Rights?*

ART KAUFMAN is currently acting director of educational programs at the Commission on the Bicentennial of the U.S. Constitution. He is former assistant director of constitutional studies at the American Enterprise Institute, former program officer at the Institute for Educational Affairs, and former assistant editor of *The Public Interest* magazine. He has taught constitutional law at the Catholic University of America.

ANN STUART ANDERSON was assistant director of legal policy studies at the American Enterprise Institute. She has taught American political thought and constitutional law at Claremont-McKenna College, Rockford College, Yale University, and Georgetown University. She is the author of articles published in *The Political Science Review* and *Publius* and of "Decent, Even Though Democratic," in *How Democratic Is the Constitution?* Robert A. Goldwin and William A. Schambra, editors.

JAMES W. CEASER is associate professor of government and foreign affairs at the University of Virginia. He is the author of *Presidential Selection* and *Reforming the Reforms* and coauthor of *Proportional Representation in the Presidential Nominating Process* and *American Government —Origins, Institutions and Public Policy.*

LLOYD N. CUTLER is an attorney in Washington, D.C., and was counsel to President Carter, 1979–1980. Mr. Cutler is cochairman of the Committee on the Constitutional System.

WILLIAM B. GWYN is professor of political science at Tulane University. He is the author of *Democracy and the Cost of Politics in Britain* and *The Meaning of the Separation of Powers* and coeditor of and contributor to *Perspectives on Public Policy* and *Britain: Progress and Decline*.

CHARLES M. HARDIN is professor emeritus of political science at the University of California, Davis. He was professor of political science at the University of Chicago and associate director of the Rockefeller Foundation. He has been a visiting professor at the University of Colorado, Boulder, at Pennsylvania State University, and at Texas A&M University and a visiting fellow at the Center for the Study of Democratic Institutions, Santa Barbara, California.

DONALD L. ROBINSON is professor of government and director of American studies at Smith College. He is the editor of *Reforming American Government: The Bicentennial Papers of the Committee on the Constitutional System* and the author of *Slavery in the Structure of American Politics, 1765–1820*, as well as numerous articles on the presidency.

L. PETER SCHULTZ is assistant professor of politics at the Catholic University of America. Currently he is on leave working for the National Endowment for the Humanities. His specialty is constitutional law, and he has written on the presidency, the separation of powers, and the Constitution in professional journals. His article "The Court, the Constitution and Presidential Immunity: A Defense of *Nixon* v. *Fitzgerald*" appears in the Spring 1986 volume of *Presidential Studies Quarterly*.

JAMES Q. WILSON is the Shattuck Professor of Government at Harvard University and the Collins Professor of Management at UCLA as well as a member of the AEI Academic Advisory Board. He is the author or coauthor of ten books, most recently *Crime and Human Nature* (with Richard J. Herrnstein), *Watching Fishes: Life and Behavior on Coral Reefs* (with Roberta Wilson), and *American Government: Institutions and Policies* (3rd edition). His previous writings on political parties include *Political Organizations* and *The Amateur Democrat*.

Preface

This book examines the widespread criticism that the structure of government in the United States is seriously flawed. The authors address the allegation that the constitutional separation of the executive and legislative powers makes it difficult, if not impossible, for the government to make and carry out policies to sustain our domestic prosperity, to conduct a sound foreign policy, and to sustain a strong national defense.

The separation of powers is distinctly American. Other Western democracies do not separate the legislature and the executive in our fashion, achieving a much closer coordination of the two, with little apparent loss of liberty for their people. The American doctrine grew out of a fear of tyranny. As James Madison put it, "the accumulation of all powers, legislative, executive, and judiciary in the same hands . . . may justly be pronounced the very definition of tyranny." There was general agreement on this principle then, especially among severe opponents of the Constitution, who thought there wasn't enough separation in the Constitution. Madison replied that some combining of the branches and sharing of the powers was necessary to enable each branch to check the others and thus sustain the separation.

The controversy over separation of powers continues steadily, although with interesting changes, as the years go by. In the nineteenth century, Woodrow Wilson called for closer cooperation between legislative and executive, but with an inclination toward congressional leadership, or "congressional government." Today it is more common to hear calls for diminishing the separation in order to allow greater presidential leadership, to make it possible for a newly elected president "to form a government." But either way, the underlying analysis is the same, that the separation of powers works too well, to the detriment of effective government. And the hope is the same, that by diminishing or eliminating the separation of the two branches we will lessen their disruptive rivalry and increase their cooperation, coordination, and accountability.

The essays in this volume address these issues and in doing so attest to the complexity of the question posed, whether the separation of powers still works. How can we judge whether it is working? What are the criteria? If the liberties of the people are safeguarded but the operations of government are confused or inefficient, is separation working? And can we judge efficiency in government? Further, is it true that the policies of the parliamentary democracies are wiser and their implementation more effective than ours? And, after all, how applicable is their experience to our situation? And what about the word "still"? How much must we be guided by two-hundred-year-old intentions? Now we are a superpower in a hostile world, with allies and adversaries who need to know what our stand is and that we will act sensibly and consistently and that we will do as we say when action is called for. These were not dominant concerns when we were a small, primarily agricultural, out-of-the-way, developing country. Must we consider present necessities without concern for old principles—or can it be both?

Finally, there is the question of practicality. Can fundamental structural change be brought about in the ways we constitute ourselves after two hundred years of experience and habit? Must we contemplate such change, nevertheless, if the dangers are as great as contended, posing a threat not only to our domestic well-being but to our leadership role in the affairs of the world?

This volume, like the others in AEI's series on the Constitution, has two distinguishing characteristics. The first is that it is a book of controversy; that is, the authors have been deliberately chosen because they disagree with one another in fundamental and interesting ways. We sought most of all authors who are authoritative masters of the facts but who interpret those facts in opposing fashion. The essays have been ordered so that almost every one is followed by another dealing with the same or a very similar topic but employing a significantly different analysis to reach a different conclusion. In arranging the book in this way, we had very much in mind its utility for classroom use, to provoke discussion and facilitate instruction. Our aspiration was to leave attentive readers no choice but to think for themselves.

The second distinguishing characteristic is that this is a book about the Constitution itself, first of all, and only secondarily about constitutional law. This important distinction has been given little or no thought in recent decades, with the result that study of the Constitution has been almost completely absorbed and lost in the study of constitutional law. Our hope is to encourage serious attention to the great issues posed by the Constitution itself.

The editors selected the essays in this volume, presented by spokesmen as authoritative, thoughtful, and instructive as could be found, to give the reader a wide range of views on these questions. The reader should be able to make up his or her own mind, therefore, with the assurance that many reasoned arguments have been presented, and with little fear of simply succumbing to the unchallenged views of a partisan.

ROBERT A. GOLDWIN
ART KAUFMAN

1

To Form a Government

Lloyd N. Cutler

[On May 10, 1940, Winston Churchill was summoned to Buckingham Palace.] His Majesty received me most graciously and bade me sit down. He looked at me searchingly and quizzically for some moments, and then said: "I suppose you don't know why I have sent for you?" Adopting his mood, I replied: "Sir, I simply couldn't imagine why." He laughed and said: "I want to ask you to form a Government." I said I would certainly do so.

WINSTON S. CHURCHILL
The Gathering Storm *(1948)*

Our society was one of the first to write a constitution. This reflected the confident conviction of the Enlightenment that explicit written arrangements could be devised to structure a government that would be neither tyrannical nor impotent in its time and to allow for future amendment as experience and change might require.

We are all children of this faith in a rational written arrangement for governing. Our faith should encourage us to consider changes in our Constitution—for which the framers explicitly allowed—that would assist us in adjusting to the changes in the world in which the Constitution must function. Yet we tend to resist suggestions that amendments to our existing constitutional framework are needed to govern our portion of the interdependent world society we have become and to cope with the resulting problems that all contemporary governments must resolve.

A particular shortcoming in need of a remedy is the structural inability of our government to propose, legislate, and administer a balanced program for governing. In parliamentary terms one might say that under the U.S. Constitution it is not now feasible to "form a

This article is adapted from the Strasburger Lecture delivered at the University of Texas Law School in April 1980. It is reprinted from *Foreign Affairs* (Fall 1980).

government." The separation of powers between the legislative and executive branches, whatever its merits in 1793, has become a structure that almost guarantees stalemate today. As we wonder why we are having such a difficult time making decisions we all know must be made and projecting our power and leadership, we should reflect on whether this is one big reason.

We elect one presidential candidate over another on the basis of our judgment of the overall program he presents, his ability to carry it out, and his capacity to adapt his program to new developments as they arise. We elected President Jimmy Carter, whose program included, as one of its most important elements, the successful completion of the SALT II negotiations that his two predecessors had been conducting since 1972. In June 1979 President Carter did complete and sign a SALT II treaty, which he and his cabinet regarded as very much in the national security interests of the United States. Notwithstanding subsequent events, the president and his cabinet continued to hold that view—indeed they believed the mounting intensity of our confrontation with the Soviet Union made it even more important for the two superpowers to adopt and abide by explicit rules about the size and quality of each side's strategic nuclear arsenal and how each side can verify what the other side is doing. Because we do not form a government, however, it was not possible for President Carter to carry out this major part of his program.

Of course the constitutional requirement of Senate advice and consent to treaties presents a special situation. The case for the two-thirds rule was much stronger in 1793, when events abroad rarely affected this isolated continent and when "entangling foreign alliances" were viewed with a skeptical eye. Whether it should be maintained in an age when most treaties deal with such subjects as taxation and trade is open to question. No parliamentary regime anywhere in the world has a similar provision. But in the United States—at least for major issues like SALT—there is merit to the view that treaties should indeed require the careful bipartisan consultation essential to win a two-thirds majority. This is the principle that Woodrow Wilson fatally neglected in 1919. But it has been carefully observed by recent presidents, including President Carter for the Panama Canal treaties and the SALT II treaty. For each of these there was a clear record of support by previous Republican administrations, and there would surely have been enough votes for fairly rapid ratification if the president could have counted on the total or nearly total support of his own party—if, in short, he had truly formed a government, with a legislative majority that took the responsibility for governing.

Treaties may indeed present special cases, and I do not argue here for any change in the two-thirds requirement. But our inability to form a government able to ratify SALT II is replicated regularly over the whole range of legislation required to carry out any president's overall program, foreign and domestic. Although the enactment of legislation takes only a simple majority of both houses, that majority is very difficult to achieve. Any part of the president's legislative program may be defeated or amended into an entirely different measure, so that the legislative record of any presidency may bear little resemblance to the overall program the president wanted to carry out. Energy and the budget are two critical examples. Indeed, SALT II itself could have been presented for approval by a simple majority of each house under existing arms control legislation, but the administration deemed this task even more difficult than achieving a two-thirds vote in the Senate. This difficulty is of course compounded when the president's party does not even hold the majority of the seats in both houses, as from 1946 to 1948, from 1954 to 1960, and from 1968 to 1976—or almost half the duration of the seven administrations between 1946 and 1980.

In such a case the Constitution does not require or even permit the holding of a new election, in which those who oppose the president can seek office to carry out their own program. Indeed, the opponents of the various elements of the president's program usually have a different makeup from one element to another. They would probably be unable to get together on any overall program of their own or to obtain the congressional votes to carry it out. As a result the stalemate continues, and because we do not form a government, we have no overall program at all. We cannot fairly hold the president accountable for the success or failure of his program, because he lacks the constitutional power to put that program into effect.

Compare this system with the structure of parliamentary governments. A parliamentary government may have no written constitution, as in the United Kingdom. Or it may have a written constitution, as in West Germany, Japan, and Ireland, that in other respects—such as an independent judiciary and an entrenched Bill of Rights—closely resembles our own. Although it may have a ceremonial president or, as in Japan, an emperor, its executive consists of those members of the legislature chosen by the elected legislative majority. The majority elects a premier or prime minister from among its number, and he or she selects other leading members of the majority as members of the cabinet. The majority as a whole is responsible for forming and conducting the government. If any key part of its program is rejected by the legislature or if a vote of no confidence is carried, the government must resign, and either a new government must be formed out

3

of the existing legislature, or a new legislative election must be held. If the program *is* legislated, the public can judge the result and can decide at the next regular election whether to reelect the majority or turn it out. At all times the voting public knows who is in charge and whom to hold accountable for success or failure.

Operating under a parliamentary system, Chancellor Helmut Schmidt formed a West German government with a majority of only four, but he succeeded in carrying out his overall program. In 1979 Margaret Thatcher won a majority of some thirty to forty in the British Parliament. She had a very radical program, one that could make fundamental changes in the economy, social fabric, and foreign policy of the United Kingdom. There was room for legitimate doubt whether her overall program would achieve its objectives and, even if it did, whether it would prove popular enough to reelect her government at the next election. There was not the slightest doubt, however, that she would be able to legislate her entire program, including any modifications she made to meet new problems. In a parliamentary system it is the duty of each majority member of the legislature to vote for each element of the government's program, and the government possesses the means to punish members if they do not. Each member's political and electoral future is tied to the fate of the government his majority has formed. Politically speaking, he lives or dies by whether that government lives or dies.

President Carter's party had a much larger majority percentage in both houses of Congress than Chancellor Schmidt or Prime Minister Thatcher had. But this comfortable majority did not even begin to ensure that he or any other president could rely on that majority to vote for each element of his program. No member of that majority had the constitutional duty or the practical political need to do so. Neither the president nor the leaders of the legislative majority had the means to punish him if he did not. In the famous phrase of Joe Jacobs, the fight manager, "it's every man for theirself."

Let me cite one example. In the British House of Commons, just as in our own House, some of the majority leaders are called whips. In the Commons the whips do just what their title implies. If the government cares about the pending vote, they "whip" the fellow members of the majority into compliance, under pain of party discipline if a member disobeys. On the most important votes, the leaders invoke what is called a three-line whip, which must be obeyed on pain of resignation or expulsion from the party.

In our House a Democratic majority whip can himself feel free to leave his Democratic president and the rest of the House Democratic leadership on a crucial vote if he believes it important to his constituency and his conscience to vote the other way. When he does so, he is not expected or required to resign his leadership post; indeed he is back a few hours later whipping his fellow members of the majority to vote with the president and the leadership on some other issue. All other members are equally free to vote against the president and the leadership when they feel it important to do so. The president and the leaders have a few sticks and carrots they can use to punish or reward, but nothing even approaching the power that a British government or a German government can wield against any errant member of the majority.

I am hardly the first to notice this fault. As Judge Carl McGowan has reminded us, that "young and rising academic star in the field of political science, Woodrow Wilson—happily unaware of what the future held for him in terms of successive domination of, and defeat by, the Congress—despaired in the late 19th century of the weakness of the Executive Branch vis-à-vis the Legislative, so much so that he concluded that a coalescence of the two in the style of English parliamentary government was the only hope."[1]

As Wilson put it, "power and strict accountability for its use are the essential constituents of good Government."[2] Our separation of executive and legislative power fractions power and prevents accountability.

In drawing this comparison, I am not blind to the proven weaknesses of parliamentary government or to the virtues that our forefathers saw in separating the executive from the legislature. In particular, the parliamentary system lacks the ability of a separate and vigilant legislature to investigate and curb the abuse of power by an arbitrary or corrupt executive. Our own recent history has underscored this virtue of separating these two branches.

Moreover, our division of executive from legislative responsibility also means that a great many more voters are represented in positions of power, rather than as mere members of a "loyal opposition." If I am a Democrat in a Republican district, my vote in the presidential election may still give me a proportional effect. If my party elects a president, I do not feel—as almost half the voters in a parliamentary constituency like Oxford must feel—wholly unrepresented. One result of this division is a sort of permanent centrism. While this means that no extreme or Thatcher-like program can be legislated, it also means fewer wild swings in statutory policy.

This is also a virtue of the constitutional division of responsibility. It is perhaps what John Adams had in mind when, at the end of his life, he wrote to his old friend and adversary Thomas Jefferson that "checks and ballances, Jefferson, . . . are our only Security, for the

5

progress of Mind, as well as the Security of Body."[3]

These virtues of separation are not without their costs. I believe that the costs have been mounting in the past half-century and that it is time to examine whether we can reduce the costs of separation without losing its virtues.

During this century other nations have adopted written constitutions, sometimes with our help, that blend the virtues of our system with those of the parliamentary system. The Irish constitution contains a replica of our Bill of Rights, an independent Supreme Court that can declare acts of the government unconstitutional, a figurehead president, and a parliamentary system. The postwar German and Japanese constitutions, which we helped to draft, are essentially the same. Although the Gaullist French constitution contains a Bill of Rights somewhat weaker than ours, it provides for a strong president who can dismiss the legislature and call for new elections. But it also retains the parliamentary system and its blend of executive and legislative power achieved by forming a government out of the elected legislative majority. The president, however, appoints the premier or first minister.

The Need to Govern More Effectively

We are not about to revise our own Constitution so as to incorporate a true parliamentary system. We do need to find a way, however, of coming closer to the parliamentary concept of forming a government under which the elected majority is able to carry out an overall program and is held accountable for its success or failure.

For several reasons it is far more important in the 1980s than it was in 1940, 1900, or 1800 for our government to have the ability to formulate and carry out an overall program.

1. The first reason is that government is now constantly required to make a different kind of choice than was common in the past, a kind for which it is difficult to obtain a broad consensus. That kind of choice, which may be called allocative, has become the fundamental challenge to government today. As a newspaper article put it:

> The domestic programs of the last two decades are no longer seen as broad campaigns to curb pollution or end poverty or improve health care. As these programs have filtered down through an expanding network of regulation, they single out winners and losers. The losers may be workers who blame a lost promotion on equal employment programs; a chemical plant fighting a tough pollution control order; a contractor who bids unsuccessfully for a government contract, or a gas station owner who wants a larger fuel allotment.[4]

This is a way of recognizing that, in giving government great responsibilities, we have forced a series of choices among those responsibilities.

During the second half of this century, our government has adopted a wide variety of national goals. Many of these goals—checking inflation, spurring economic growth, reducing unemployment, protecting our national security, ensuring equal opportunity, increasing social security, cleaning up the environment, improving energy efficiency—conflict with one another, and all of them compete for the same resources. There may have been a time when we could simultaneously pursue all these goals to the utmost. Even in a country as rich as this one, however, that time is now past. One of the central tasks of modern government is to make wise balancing choices among courses of action that pursue one or more of our many conflicting and competing objectives.

Furthermore, as new economic or social problems are recognized, a responsible government must *adjust* its priorities. In formulating energy policy, the need to accept realistic oil prices had to be balanced against the immediate effect of dramatic price increases on consumers and affected industries and on the overall rate of inflation. To cope with the energy crisis, earlier objectives of policy had to be accommodated along the way. Reconciling one goal with another is a continuous process. A critical regulatory goal of 1965 (automobile safety) had to be reconciled with an equally critical regulatory goal of 1970 (clean air) long before the safety goal had been achieved, just as both those critical goals had to be reconciled with 1975's key goal (closing the energy gap) long before either automobile safety or clean air had lost its importance. Reconciliation was needed because many automobile safety regulations increased vehicle size and weight and therefore increased gasoline consumption and undesirable emission and also because auto emission control devices tend to increase gasoline consumption. Moreover, throughout this fifteen-year period, we had to reconcile all three goals with another critical national objective—wage and price stability—when in pursuit of these other goals we made vehicles more costly to purchase and to operate.

In 1980 we found our automobile industry at a serious competitive disadvantage vis-à-vis Japanese and European imports, making it necessary to limit those regulatory burdens that aggravated the extent of the disadvantage. A responsible government must be able to adapt its programs to achieve the best balance among its conflicting goals as each new development arises.

For balancing choices like these, a kind of political triage, it is almost impossible to achieve a broad consensus. Every group will be against some part of the balance. If the losers on each item are given a veto on that part of the balance, a sensible balance cannot be struck.

2. The second reason is that we live in an increasingly interdependent world. What happens in distant places is now just as consequential for our security and our economy as what happens in Seattle or Miami. No one today would use the term "Afghanistanism," as the opposition benches did in the British Parliament a century ago, to deride the government's preoccupation with a war in that distant land. No one would say today, as President Wilson said in 1914, that general European war could not affect us and is no concern of ours. We are now an integral part of a closely interconnected world economic and political system. We have to respond as quickly and decisively to what happens abroad as to what happens within the portion of this world system that is governed under our Constitution.

New problems requiring new adjustments come up even more frequently over the foreign horizon than over the domestic one. Consider the rapid succession of events and crises after President Carter took up the relay baton for his leg of the SALT II negotiations in 1977: the signing of the Egyptian-Israeli peace treaty over Soviet and Arab opposition, the Soviet-Cuban assistance to guerrilla forces in Africa and the Arabian peninsula, the recognition of the People's Republic of China, the final agreement on the SALT II terms and the signing of the treaty in Vienna, the revolution in Iran and the seizure of our hostages, the military coup in Korea, the Soviet-supported Vietnamese invasion of Kampuchea, our growing dependence on foreign oil from politically undependable sources, the affair of the Soviet brigade in Cuba, the polarization of rightist and leftist elements in Central America, and finally the Soviet invasion of Afghanistan and the added threat it posed to the states of Southwest Asia and to the vital oil supplies of Europe, Japan, and the United States.

Each of these portentous events required a prompt reaction and response from our government, including in many cases a decision about how it would affect our position on the SALT II treaty. The government must be able to adapt its overall program to deal with each such event as it arises, and it must be able to execute the adapted program with reasonable dispatch. Many of these adaptations—such as changes in the levels and direction of military and economic assistance—require joint action by the president and the Congress, something that is far from automatic under our system. When Congress does act, it is prone to impose statutory conditions or prohibitions that fetter the president's discretion to negotiate an appropriate assistance package or to adapt it to fit even later developments. The congressional bans on military assistance to Turkey, any form of assistance to the contending forces in Angola, and any aid to Argentina if it did not meet our human rights criteria are typical examples.

Indeed, the doubt that Congress will approve a presidential foreign policy initiative has seriously compromised our ability to make binding agreements with nations that form a government. Given the fate of SALT II and lesser treaties and the frequent congressional vetoes of other foreign policy actions, other nations now realize that our executive branch commitments are not as binding as theirs, that Congress may block any agreement at all, and that at the very least they must hold something back for a subsequent round of bargaining with the Congress.

3. The third reason is the change in Congress and its relations with the executive. When the Federalist and Democratic Republican parties held power, a Hamilton or a Gallatin would serve in the cabinet but continue to lead rather than report to their party colleagues in the houses of Congress. Even when the locus of congressional leadership shifted from the cabinet to the leaders of Congress itself in the early nineteenth century, it was a congressional leadership capable of collaboration with the executive. This was true until very recently. The Johnson-Rayburn collaboration with Eisenhower a generation ago is an instructive example. But now Congress itself has changed.

There have been well-intended democratic reforms of Congress and an enormous growth of the professional legislative staff. The former ability of the president to sit down with ten or fifteen leaders in each house and agree on a program those leaders could carry through Congress has virtually disappeared. The committee chairmen and the leaders no longer have the instruments of power that once enabled them to lead. A Lyndon Johnson would have a much harder time getting his way as majority leader today than when he did hold and pull those strings of power in the 1950s. When Senator Mike Mansfield became majority leader in 1961, he changed the practice of awarding committee chairmanships on the basis of seniority. He declared that all senators are created equal. He gave every Democratic senator a major committee assignment and then a subcommitee chairmanship, adding to the sharing of power by reducing the leadership's control.

In the House the seniority system was scrapped. Now the House majority caucus—not the leadership—picks the committee chairmen and the subcommittee chairmen as well. The House parliamentarian has lost the critical power to refer bills to a single committee selected by the Speaker. Now bills like the energy bills go to several committees, which then report conflicting versions to the floor. Now markup sessions take place in public; indeed, even the House-Senate joint conference committees, at which differing versions of the same measure are reconciled, must meet and barter in public.

The conference committees on the Synthetic Fuels Corporation and the Energy Mobilization Board, for example, were so big and their procedures so cumbersome that they took six months to reach agreement, and then the agreement on the board was rejected by the House. All this means that there are no longer a few leaders with power who *can* collaborate with the president. Power is further diffused by the growth of legislative staffs, sometimes making it difficult for the members even to collaborate with one another. From 1975 to 1980 the Senate alone hired 700 additional staff members, an average of seven per member.

Party discipline and the political party itself have also declined. Presidential candidates are no longer selected as Adlai Stevenson was, by the leaders or bosses of their party. Who are the party leaders today? There are no such people. The party is no longer the instrument that selects the candidate. Indeed, the party today, as a practical matter, is no more than a neutral open forum that holds the primary or caucus in which candidates for president and for Congress may compete for favor and be elected. The party does not dispense most of the money needed for campaigning, as European and Japanese parties do. The candidates raise most of their own money. To the extent that money influences legislative votes, it comes not from a party with a balanced program but from a variety of single-interest groups.

We now have a great many diverse and highly organized interest groups—not just broad-based agriculture, labor, business, and ethnic groups interested in a wide variety of issues affecting their members. We now have single-issue groups—environmental, consumer, abortion, right to life, pro- and anti-SALT, pro- and anti-nuclear—that stand ready to lobby for their single issue and to reward or punish legislators, both in cash and at the ballot box, according to how they respond on the single issue that is the group's raison d'être. On many specific foreign policy issues involving particular countries, exceptionally strong voting blocs in this wonderful melting pot of a nation exert a great deal of influence on individual senators and representatives.

Why the Structure Sometimes Works

It is useful to compare this modern failure of our governmental structure with its earlier classic successes. There can be no structural fault, it might be said, so long as Franklin Roosevelt could put through an entire antidepression program in 100 days or Lyndon

Johnson could enact a broad program for social justice three decades later. These infrequent exceptions, however, confirm the general rule of stalemate.

If we look closely, we will find that in this century the system has succeeded only on the rare occasions when an unusual event has brought us together and created substantial consensus throughout the country on the need for a whole new program. Roosevelt had such a consensus in the early days of the New Deal and from Pearl Harbor to the end of World War II. But we tend to forget that in 1937 his court-packing plan was justifiably rejected by Congress—a good point for those who favor complete separation of the executive from the legislature[5]—and that as late as August 1941, when Roosevelt called on Congress to pass a renewal of the Selective Service Act, passage was gained by a single vote in the House. Johnson had such a consensus for both his domestic and his Vietnam initiatives during the first three years after the shock of John Kennedy's assassination brought us together, but it was gone by 1968. Carter had it for his responses to the events in Iran and Afghanistan and to the belated realization of our need for greater energy self-sufficiency, but he did not hold it for long. Yet the consensus on Afghanistan was marred by the long congressional delay in appropriating the small amounts needed to register nineteen- and twenty-year-olds under the Selective Service Act—a delay that at least blurred the intended effect of this signal to the world of our determination to oppose further Soviet aggresssion.[6]

When the great crisis and the resulting large consensus are not there—when the country is divided somewhere between 55–45 and 45–55 on each of a wide set of issues and the makeup of the majority is different on every issue—it has not been possible for any modern president to form a government that could legislate and carry out his overall program.

Yet modern government has to respond promptly to a wide range of new challenges. Its responses cannot be limited to those for which there is a large consensus induced by some great crisis. Modern government also has to work in every presidency, not just in one presidency out of four, when a Wilson, a Roosevelt, or a Johnson comes along. It also has to work for the president's full time in office, as it did not even for Wilson and Johnson. When they needed congressional support for the most important issue of their presidencies, they could not get it.

When the president gets only half a loaf of his overall program, it is not necessarily better than none, because it may lack the essential quality of balance. Half a loaf leaves both the president and the public in the worst of all possible worlds. The public—and the press—still expect the president to govern. But the president cannot achieve his overall program, and the public cannot fairly blame the president because he does not have the power to legislate and execute his program. Nor can the public fairly blame the individual members of Congress, because the Constitution allows them to disclaim any responsibility for forming a government and hence any accountability for its failures.

Of course the presidency always has been and will continue to be what Theodore Roosevelt called "a bully pulpit"—not a place from which to bully in the sense of intimidating the Congress and the public, but in the idiom of Roosevelt's day a marvelous place from which to exhort and lift up Congress and the public. All presidents have used the bully pulpit in this way, and this is one reason why the American people continue to revere the office and almost always revere its incumbent. Television has probably amplified the power of the bully pulpit, but is has also shortened the time span of power; few television performers can hold their audiences for four consecutive years. In any event, a bully pulpit, though a glorious thing to have and to employ, is not a government, and it has not been enough to enable any postwar president to form a government for his entire term.

Finally, the myth persists that the existing system can be made to work satisfactorily if only the president will take the trouble to consult closely with the Congress. During the period between 1947 and 1965 there were indeed remarkable cases, at least in foreign policy, where such consultation worked to great effect, even across party lines. The relations between Senator Arthur Vandenberg and Secretaries George Marshall and Dean Acheson and between Senator Walter George and Secretary of State John Foster Dulles come readily to mind. But these examples were in an era of strong leadership within the Congress and of unusual national consensus on the overall objectives of foreign policy and the measures needed to carry them out.

Even when these elements have not been present, every president has indeed tried to work with the majority in Congress, and the majority in every Congress has tried to work with the president. When there was a large consensus in response to the crises in Afghanistan and Iran, a notable achievement was a daily private briefing of congressional leaders by the secretary of state and weekly private briefings with all Senate and House members who wanted to attend —a step that helped to keep that consensus in being. Another achievement of recent times is the development of the congressional budget process, exemplified by the cooperation between the congressional leadership and the president in framing the 1981 budget.

The jury is still out, however, on how long such a large consensus will hold. Except on the rare issues where there is such a consensus, the structural problems usually prove too difficult to overcome. In each administration it becomes more difficult to make the present system work effectively on the range of issues, both domestic and foreign, that the United States must now manage even though there is no large consensus.

Changing the Structure through Constitutional Amendment

If we decide we want the ability to form a government, the only way to get it is to amend the Constitution. That, of course, is extremely difficult. Since 1793, when the Bill of Rights was added, we have amended the Constitution only sixteen times. Some of these amendments were structural, such as the direct election of senators, votes for women and eighteen-year-olds, the two-term limit for presidents, and the selection of a successor vice president. But none has touched the basic separation of executive and legislative powers.

The most we can hope for is a set of modest changes that would make our structure work somewhat more in the manner of a parliamentary system, with somewhat less separation between the executive and the legislature than now exists. There are several proposals. Here are some of the more interesting ideas.

1. We now vote for a presidential candidate and a vice-presidential candidate as an inseparable team. We could require that in presidential election years voters in each congressional district vote for a trio of candidates, as a team, for president, vice president, and member of Congress. This would tie the political fortunes of the party's presidential and congressional candidates to one another and give them some incentive for sticking together after they are elected. Such a proposal could be combined with a four-year term for members of the House of Representatives. This would tie the presidential and congressional candidates even more closely and has the added virtue of giving members greater protection against the pressures of single-issue political groups. This combination was the brainchild of Representative Jonathan Bingham of New York.

In our bicameral legislature the logic of the Bingham proposal would suggest that the inseparable trio of candidates for president, vice president, and member of Congress be expanded to a quintet including the two senators, who would also have the same four-year term. But no one has challenged the gods of the Olympian Senate by advancing such a proposal.

2. Another idea is to permit or require the president to select 50

13

percent of his cabinet from among the members of his party in the Senate and the House, who would retain their seats while serving in the cabinet. This would be only a minor infringement on the constitutional principle of separation of powers, but it would require a change in Article I, section 6, which provides that "no person holding any office under the United States shall be a member of either house during his continuance in office." It would tend to increase the intimacy between the executive and the legislature and add to their sense of collective responsibility. The 50 percent test would leave the president adequate room to bring other qualified persons into his cabinet, even though they did not hold elective office.

3. A third intriguing suggestion is to provide the president with the power, to be exercised not more than once in his term, to dissolve Congress and call for new congressional elections. This is the power now vested in the president under the French constitution. It would provide the opportunity that does not now exist to break an executive-legislative impasse and to let the public decide whether it wishes to elect senators and representatives who *will* legislate the president's overall program.

For obvious reasons, the president would invoke such a power only as a last resort, but his ability to do so could have a powerful influence on congressional responses to his initiatives. This would of course be a radical and highly controversial proposal, and it raises a number of technical difficulties relating to the timing and conduct of the new election, the staggering of senatorial terms, and similar matters. But it would significantly enhance the president's power to form a government.

The experience of presidents—such as Nixon in 1970—who sought to use the midterm election as a referendum on their programs suggests that any such dissolution and new election would be as likely to continue the impasse as to break it. Perhaps any exercise of the power to dissolve Congress should automatically require a new presidential election as well. Even then, the American public might be perverse enough to reelect all the incumbents to office.

4. Another variant on the same idea is that in addition to empowering the president to call for new congressional elections, we might empower a majority or two-thirds of both houses to call for new presidential elections. This variant was scathingly attacked in a series of conversations between Professor Charles Black of the Yale Law School and Representative Bob Eckhardt of Texas, published in 1975, because they think that such a measure would vitally diminish the president's capacity to lead.[7]

5. Another proposal that deserves consideration is a single six-

year presidential term, an idea with many supporters, among them Presidents Eisenhower, Johnson, and Carter, to say nothing of a great many political scientists. (The French constitution provides a seven-year term for the president but permits reelection.) Of course, presidents would like to be elected and then forget about politics and get to the high ground of saving the world. But if first-term presidents did not have the leverage of reelection, we might institutionalize for every presidency the lame duck impotence we now see when a president is not running for reelection.

6. It may be that one combination of elements of the third, fourth, and fifth proposals would be worthy of further study. It would be roughly as follows:

• The president, vice president, senators, and representatives would all be elected for simultaneous six-year terms.

• On one occasion each term the president could dissolve Congress and call for new congressional elections for the remainder of the term. If he did so, Congress, by majority vote of both houses within thirty days of his action, could call for simultaneous new elections for president and vice president for the remainder of the term.

• All state primaries and state conventions for any required mid-term elections would be held 60 days after the first call for new elections. Any required national presidential nominating conventions would be held 30 days later. The national elections would be held 60 days after the state primary elections and state conventions. The entire cycle would take 120 days. The dissolved Congress would be free to remain in session for part or all of this period.

• Presidents would be allowed to serve only one full six-year term. If a midterm presidential election were called, the incumbent would be eligible to run and, if reelected, to serve the balance of his six-year term.

Limiting each president to one six-year term would enhance the objectivity and public acceptance of the measures he urges in the national interest. He would not be regarded as a lame duck, because of his continuing power to dissolve Congress. Our capacity to form a government would be enhanced if the president could break an impasse by calling for a new congressional election and by the power of Congress to respond by calling for a new presidential election.

Six-year terms for senators and representatives would diminish the power of single-interest groups to veto balanced programs for governing. Because any midterm elections would have to be held promptly, a single national primary, a shorter campaign cycle, and public financing of congressional campaigns—three reforms with independent virtues of their own—would become a necessity for the midterm election. Once tried in a midterm election, they might well be adopted for regular elections as well.

7. One final proposal may be mentioned. It would be possible, through constitutional amendment, to revise the legislative process in the following way. Congress would first enact broad mandates, declaring general policies and directions and leaving the precise allocative choices, within a congressionally approved budget, to the president. All agencies would be responsible to the president. By dividing tasks among them and making the difficult choices of fulfilling some congressional directions at the expense of others, the president would fill in the exact choices, the allocative decisions. Then any presidential action would be returned to Congress, where it would await a two-house legislative veto. If not so vetoed within a specified period, the action would become law.

If the legislative veto could be overturned by a presidential veto —subject in turn to a two-thirds override—this proposal would go a long way toward enhancing the president's ability to form a government. In any event, it should enable the elected president to carry out the program he ran on, subject to congressional oversight, and end the stalemate over whether to legislate the president's program in the first instance. It would let Congress and the president each do what they have shown they now do best.

Such a resequencing, of course, would turn the present process on its head. But it would bring much closer to reality the persisting myth that it is up to the president to govern—something he now lacks the constitutional power to do.

Conclusion

How can these proposals be evaluated? How can better proposals be devised? Above all, how can the public be educated to understand the costs of the present separation between our executive and legislative branches, to weigh those costs against the benefits, and to decide whether a change is needed?

One obvious possibility is the widely feared constitutional convention—something for which the Constitution itself provides—to be called by Congress itself or two-thirds of the states. Jefferson expected one to occur every generation. Conventions are commonplace to revise state constitutions. But Congress has never even legislated the applicable rules for electing and conducting a national constitutional convention, even though more than thirty states have called for one to adopt an amendment limiting federal taxes and expenditures. Because of the concern generated by this proposal, any idea of a national constitutional convention on the separation of powers is probably a nonstarter.

A more practicable first step would be the appointment of a bipartisan presidential commission to analyze the issues, compare how other constitutions work, hold public hearings, and make a full report. The commission could include ranking members of the House and Senate, or Congress could establish a parallel joint commission of its own.

The point of this article is not to persuade the reader of the virtue of any particular amendment. I am far from persuaded myself. But I am convinced of these propositions:

- We need to do better than we have in forming a government for this country, and the need is becoming more acute.
- The structure of our Constitution prevents us from doing significantly better.
- It is time to start thinking and debating about whether and how to correct this structural fault.

Notes

1. Carl McGowan, "Congress, Court, and Control of Delegated Power," *Columbia Law Review*, vol. 77, no. 8 (1977), pp. 1119–20.

2. Woodrow Wilson, *Congressional Government: A Study in American Politics* (Boston and New York: Houghton Mifflin, 1913), p. 284.

3. Adams to Jefferson, in *The Adams-Jefferson Letters*, ed. Lester J. Cappon (Chapel Hill: University of North Carolina Press, 1959), vol. 2, p. 134.

4. Quoted from Carl P. Leubsdorf, "Contemporary Problems Leave U.S. Political System Straining to Cope," reprinted in the *Congressional Record*, October 31, 1979, pp. S15593–94.

5. The mention of this example may strike some readers as sharply impairing the general thesis of this article in favor of disciplined party voting in the Congress. But one can readily envisage a category of issues—analogous to mutual defense treaties—where an administration would not be entitled to apply party discipline. (In Britain, for example, votes on such issues as capital punishment have traditionally not been subject to the party whip.) Any measure amending the Constitution or affecting the separation of powers (as the 1937 Court plan did) should probably be exempted, as well as any issue of religious conscience, such as legislation bearing on abortion.

6. Similarly, the belated consensus on energy self-sufficiency did not restrain the Congress from overriding, by one of the largest margins in history, the president's unpopular but necessary oil import fee order.

7. Bob Eckhardt and Charles L. Black, Jr., *The Tides of Power: Conversations on the American Constitution* (New Haven, Conn.: Yale University Press, 1976).

2

Political Parties and the Separation of Powers

James Q. Wilson

The chief criticism of the separation of powers is that it inhibits the capacity of the government, especially the president, to enact policies that are bold, timely, and comprehensive and reduces the ability of the citizenry to hold the government—again, especially the president —accountable for those policies. Among the possible remedies for these difficulties is a party system that can overcome the separation of powers by bringing together under informal arrangements what the founders were at pains to divide by formal ones. James MacGregor Burns has argued that the constitutional system has given rise to a four-party system—Democratic and Republican presidential parties and Democratic and Republican congressional parties. The solution, he suggested, is to consolidate the presidential and congressional wings of each party:

> The presidential parties must singly and jointly overcome the arrangements that thwart political competition, that prevent them from broadening their electoral support, and keep them from dealing with way-of-life issues that increasingly dominate the nation's future. This means that each presidential party must convert its congressional party into a party wing exerting a proper, but not controlling or crippling hold on party policy.[1]

Neither the diagnosis nor the remedy is new. In the nineteenth century Lord Bryce quoted the lament of a critic of the American separation of powers:

> Will not a scheme, in which the executive officers are all independent of one another, yet not subject to the legislature, want every condition needed for harmonious and effective action? They obey nobody. They are responsible to nobody. . . . Such a system seems the negation of a system, and more akin to chaos.[2]

The solution was suggested in 1900 by Henry Jones Ford: "The explanation of this mystery is that the scattered powers of government are resumed by party organization, and this concentration of power carries with it a public responsibility that may be enforced."[3] Party machinery, according to Ford, was created to meet the need for a means "to establish a control over the divided powers of government. . . . It is a necessary evil."[4] He was not under illusions about the character or motives of the men who had fashioned this machinery (they were running a "business pursuit" for "personal gain"). Unlike many of his Progressive contemporaries, however, Ford fully appreciated what he believed that machinery had achieved: its capacity for creating a measure of public accountability and political efficiency was "the true glory of our political system."[5]

The claims of Ford and the hopes of Burns have not been realized. The parties have not overcome the separation of powers, at least to the degree critics of the separation would like. And to judge from the essays in this volume that argue for constitutional rather than party remedies for the alleged defects of the separation of powers, the earlier optimism about the prospects and possibilities of "party government" seem to have abated. To see why, it is necessary to review the recent history of parties within Congress, to understand the ways in which parties have and have not become weaker, and to consider the circumstances under which stronger legislative parties might emerge and the effects, if any, of such stronger parties on the separation of powers.

The Decline of Party Voting in Congress

When Ford wrote (1900), Thomas B. Reed of Maine had just resigned as Speaker of the House, a post he had filled—and transformed— off and on since 1889. During his tenure party voting in the House was commonplace. In 1896 over half the roll-call votes in the House saw 90 percent of the Democrats voting against 90 percent of the Republicans; nearly 80 percent of the votes saw at least half the Democrats opposing at least half the Republicans.

Nor was the House displaying this party unity only with respect to minor matters. In the Fifty-first Congress the Force Bill, providing for federal supervision of elections in the South, came before the House Republican caucus. Many key Republicans opposed it, including some of Speaker Reed's own lieutenants. After it was finally endorsed by a slim majority of the caucus, Reed's men united behind it when it came to the floor.[6] Under the Reed regime the House passed not only the Force Bill but also the McKinley tariff, the Sherman

Antitrust Act, a new pension law, a bankruptcy act, and a meat inspection law.

Party unity in the House began to disappear almost from the day Reed resigned; by the time of the Sixty-fifth Congress in 1917–1919, only about one-tenth of the roll-call votes pitted 90 percent of the Democrats against 90 percent of the Republicans, and less than half saw at least 50 percent of the Democrats oppose 50 percent of the Republicans. Although there were brief upsurges in party voting in the House during the early 1920s and again during the early New Deal years, the present pattern of weak party influence over roll-call votes was evident by the time Woodrow Wilson was in his second term as president. In the Seventieth Congress (1927–1929), when only one of every fourteen House votes pitted 90 percent of one party against 90 percent of the other, over nine out of ten votes in the British House of Commons were party votes by this definition.[7] There are other ways to measure party voting, but no matter which is used the result is the same—the House is less consistently partisan in its voting behavior today than it was at the turn of the century.[8] Not once since 1948 have as many as 10 percent of House roll-call votes pitted 90 percent of the Democrats against 90 percent of the Republicans; only in a very few years have half the roll-call votes seen 50 percent of the Democrats opposing 50 percent of the Republicans.

In fact, the decline may be even greater than is suggested by examining all roll-call votes taken together. Separating important from trivial votes and dividing the former into specific policy areas reveals sharper declines in party voting on important than on trivial issues; moreover, party voting has recently declined on many matters that for much of the first half of the twentieth century had retained a partisan character. In the Seventy-fourth and Seventy-fifth congresses, which convened during Franklin Roosevelt's first and second terms (1935–1939), a great deal of party voting occurred on issues of economic management, social welfare, and agricultural assistance. By the time of Dwight Eisenhower's second term (1957–1961), party voting on these issues had become much less common. In neither era was there much party voting on civil liberties and civil rights. By the 1970s party voting in most of these policy areas had declined even further.[9]

The consequences of lessened party voting can be seen in many aspects of congressional affairs. The sharp rise in the number of specialized caucuses reveals a need on the part of congressmen to create ad hoc affiliations around particular issues rather than to join more general coalitions assembled by party leaders in ways that cut across policy areas. In 1959 there were only four such caucuses; by the early 1980s there were more than seventy, including the Steel Caucus, the Mushroom Caucus, the Shipyard Coalition, and the Roller- and Ball-Bearing Coalition.

Given this apparent fragmentation of the Congress, some observers have claimed that when an issue comes to a vote, a new coalition supporting it must often be assembled from scratch. Anthony King has described this process as akin to "building coalitions in the sand."[10] Douglas Arnold and Barbara Sinclair, among others, have looked hard at the evidence to see if those claims are correct.[11] Sinclair finds that during the 1970s the split in the House between northern and southern Democrats became more acute on economic management and that northern Democrats became less cohesive on both economic and foreign aid issues; the Democrats in this period continued, however, to back social welfare legislation and became a bit more unified on civil rights issues, owing to growing support from southern Democrats. On various key votes, President Jimmy Carter suffered from the defection of northern Democrats to a much greater extent than President John Kennedy had. Sinclair will not go so far as to say that new coalitions must be built from scratch, but she does find plenty of evidence that coalition building has become more difficult and has had less predictable outcomes. Freshman representatives are "vigorously courted," the whip system has been greatly expanded, and more effort is devoted to persuasion and negotiation.

No one has yet been able to show that the weakness of party in Congress has contributed to the extraordinary and often remarked increase in the number of interest groups based in Washington, but it is not unreasonable to suppose that there may be a connection. If party becomes weaker, other sources of information and pressure—such as interest groups—ought to become stronger. Kay Schlozman and John Tierney discovered that 70 percent of all the groups now represented in Washington established their offices there after 1960 and nearly half opened their doors after 1970.[12] Now, there are reasons having little to do with party why such groups should proliferate. The increased scope of governmental activity—for example, the growth of governmental regulation of the environment—would stimulate the creation of interest groups to cope with that activity whether or not parties were strong. The heightened consciousness of racial and feminist groups in society as a result of civil rights laws and changes in popular attitudes might facilitate group formation. Easier access to the courts, caused by changes in the rules governing standing and class action suits, would create more opportunities for group activity. But we cannot rule out the possibility that the fragmentation of authority in the national government, manifested in the decline of party voting in Congress, has created more points at which interest group intervention might succeed and thus caused more group efforts to intervene.

Causes of the Decline in Legislative Partisanship

The decline of legislative partisanship and the apparent rise in interest group activity are sometimes attributed to the decline of party generally. Parties are weak in Congress because they are weak in the nation as a whole. Therefore, if parties could be reinvigorated generally, party control of the legislature would increase. I am skeptical of this explanation. To see why, it is first necessary to understand the different ways in which a political party might be said to be strong or weak.

A party can be strong in one or more of at least three ways. First, it may be strong as an organization because it has the ability to control, centrally and by plan, who receives its nominations for office. Second, a party may be strong in the electorate because many voters staunchly identify with it and regularly vote for its candidates. Finally, it may be strong because it can induce its members in a legislature to vote together all or most of the time and thus, if it is the majority party, to determine the outcome of legislative struggles.

Parties and Nominations. The parties have become indisputably weaker, both in the states and in the nation, as organizations able, by plan, to control access to nominations for office. Their weakness has largely been a result of the spread of the direct primary, a procedure —virtually unique to the United States—that removes a candidate's access to the general election ballot from the hands of party leaders and gives it to whatever voters take the trouble to enroll and vote in a primary. With the steady relaxation of rules defining party membership, it is now possible in many states for voters to decide at the moment they walk into the polling place which party's primary they wish to vote in. As a result, people who have every intention of supporting a Republican in the general election may vote in the Democratic primary, or vice versa. Voters in primary elections are unusual in other respects as well. In general, they tend to have more schooling, to come from higher-status occupations, and to contain a larger proportion of whites than voters in the general election. There is also some reason to believe that they are ideologically more extreme than the average general election voter.

Some consequences of the parties' having lost, except in a few localities, control of nominations for office are plain. Elected officials cannot be punished, by denying them renomination, for failing to support the party leadership. Other consequences are more conjectural: parties unable to control their nominations may lose the ability to offer ethnically and regionally balanced tickets to the electorate; they may come to back candidates who are ideologically more extreme than the average voter; they may find that candidate selection is heavily influenced by skill at using the media (especially television); and they may become preoccupied with issues that excite the activists but are not those of greatest concern to the general voters.

Parties in the Electorate. Although it is clear that American parties have lost control over the nomination process, it is not at all clear that they have lost their influence with the voters. A decline has occurred in the extent to which voters identify themselves with one or the other party, but that decline is often exaggerated. Partisan identification is still quite strong and still influences, often greatly, how people vote. Although many people say they are independents and identify themselves with neither party, many of them regularly incline toward either the Democrats or the Republicans. The number of true independents is much smaller than survey data sometimes suggest. The percentage of persons describing themselves as Democrats is about the same today (around 40 percent) as it was in 1945, and the proportion of voters describing themselves as Republicans has increased (about 30 percent today, less than 20 percent in 1950).[13]

Of course, voters may cast their ballots in ways not dictated by their professed inclinations. Split-ticket voting has increased sharply since 1920, when it scarcely existed. By the 1950s about one-fourth of the congressional districts were carried by candidates of a party other than the party that won the district's vote for president. By 1972 over 40 percent of the districts were carried by congressional and presidential candidates of different parties.[14] But at least in presidential elections, and possibly in congressional ones as well, party identification still remains a powerful predictor of how people will vote.

Parties in the Legislature. The ability of parties to organize and dominate the legislatures of the nation has weakened, but unevenly; in the Congress the weakening began so long ago as to call into question whether it is the result of any recent (say, post–World War II) decline in parties generally. Congressional leaders were able to count on about as much party voting in the Ninety-sixth Congress (1979–1980) as they had in the Seventy-seventh (1941–1943). In the Ninety-seventh Congress, which convened during Reagan's first term, party voting rose dramatically, but the Ninety-eighth witnessed a decline to more customary levels. What has changed, without a doubt, is the extent to which congressional leaders must invest scarce resources in achieving some measure of party unity. What once the Speaker and majority leader could achieve in the House almost unaided now requires an army of whips and assistant whips, aided by staffers and computers.

But a high level of party voting persisted in many state legislatures long after it had become a historical relic in the Congress. In Massachusetts the percentage of party votes (that is, a majority of Democrats against a majority of Republicans) was "for several decades well over 80 percent"; it has declined in recent years, but as late as 1965 it was 72 percent. Comparably high levels of party voting have been found in Connecticut, New York, Kansas, Michigan, and Vermont.[15] By contrast, very low levels of party voting occur in such states as Kentucky, New Mexico, Idaho, Montana, and Utah.[16]

The notion that party voting in legislatures has declined with the general decline in party identification is refuted not only by the great differences among the states but also by the increase in partisanship in recent years in some state legislatures. Party voting in California, for example, increased between 1953 and 1969.[17]

In fact, these statistics underestimate the influence of party in many state legislatures. The legislative leaders of the parties in some states are sufficiently strong to prevent matters they oppose from coming to a vote at all and to shape the contents of those measures that do reach the floor in such a way as to make the final roll call vote relatively unimportant. In Massachusetts the speaker of the house and the president of the Senate exercise extraordinary control over the timing, contents, and outcome of proposed legislation.

The power that Speaker Reed exercised over the House was indeed great, but we must carefully specify its source before we conclude that it represented in some general sense the power of party or that its loss can be attributed to the decay of party. In 1890 Reed acquired the authority to refuse to entertain dilatory motions and to count nonvoting members as present in ascertaining a quorum. He named the members and chairmen of all committees (seniority was a secondary consideration) and served as chairman of the Rules Committee. He could reward and punish House members, decide who would be allowed to speak, and control the agenda of legislative business.[18]

Reed resigned from the House one year before Ford's book appeared, and he had no real successor. David B. Henderson of Iowa was not up to the job; Joseph G. Cannon, who assumed the post in 1903 determined to wield the same power as Reed, discovered that this power was less durable than he had supposed. Within a few years a revolt against Cannon was under way; by 1910 it had succeeded. Liberal Republicans joined with the Democrats to adopt a new set of rules that removed the Speaker from the Rules Committee and permitted a bill to be discharged from a committee that had bottled it up and brought to the floor for a vote. The next year the Democrats took control of the House, reaffirmed these changes, and added more of their own. Chief among them was the creation of a Committee on Committees, chaired by someone other than the Speaker, which would make committee assignments. This stripped the Speaker of his right to appoint the members or chairmen of committees.

Parties became weaker in Congress because the members of Congress chose to make them weaker. The history of Congress during much of the twentieth century can be understood as a general and persistent effort to democratize and decentralize authority in that institution.[19] Authority once held by the Speaker was given to the Rules Committee and to the Committee on Committees. As the latter body struggled with the task of allocating committee chairmanships in a way that would least disturb the interests of the party's members in Congress, it came to rely almost exclusively on the seniority rule. Any other principle—party loyalty or individual merit—meant choosing among contenders for a chairmanship, and it was precisely to avoid such choices and the power that the chooser would inevitably wield that gave to the seniority system its great appeal. (Lord Melbourne would have found in the seniority rule the same value he found in the British Order of the Garter—there was no damned merit about it.)

In time the Rules Committee and the seniority system came to be seen as limitations on the power of the individual member, and so they, too, were challenged. The challenge became possible when a majority of the Democratic caucus was ideologically opposed to the leadership of the Rules Committee and to the rule of many, if not most, committee chairmen. The House Democratic caucus adopted rules designed to enhance rank-and-file power. When the caucus refused to reelect a few key chairmen, they and others quickly got the message that these new rules were to be taken seriously. Some backing and filling has taken place throughout this process—from time to time, the rules have been modified to enhance slightly the power of the Speaker or of the Rules Committee—but the modifications have never amounted to a general retreat from the principle that the representatives would be as free as possible to vote their convictions (or those of their constituents or allied interest groups).

Many state legislatures chose not to follow this path, at least to the same degree. Party voting in those states remains much stronger than it is in Congress and is achieved with far less expenditure of energy—not because political parties as a whole are "strong" in New York, Massachusetts, or Pennsylvania but weak in the country as a whole but because the rules that democratized and decentralized the Congress were not adopted by these and other state legislatures. In Massachusetts, for example, the speaker of the house appoints all committee members and committee chairmen and controls the order of business, much as Speaker Reed once did in Washington. A committee chairmanship in many state legislatures is a prized job, not simply because of the power over legislation that it confers but also because of the tangible benefits—higher salaries, better offices, more lavish expense budgets—attached to it and also, alas, because of the opportunities for corruption that these centers of power create.

If we would like to see Congress organized in a more hierarchical fashion to minimize the capacity for individual obstruction, we need not pine for the days when political parties in the country at large were stronger as organizations or sources of political identification; we need only reform the reforms and return to the rules under which Reed and Cannon once operated. Such a return is, of course, no simple matter. The power of Speaker Reed rested in the first instance on the rewards and punishments he controlled, but that control required the consent of his fellow partisans in the House. Whatever powers the Speaker enjoyed ultimately depended on his ability to get his party to vote in favor of the rules in which those powers were embedded. Whether the "unreforming" of Congress is politically feasible is a matter to which I shall shortly return.

Parties and the Separation of Powers

If political parties are to overcome the separation of powers, they must be able to control their own nominations. They can become more popular in the electorate, but that will have few consequences for governance owing to the inclinations (carefully nurtured by constitutional arrangements) of each branch of government to resist the incursions of the others. They can equip their legislative leaders with greater authority so as to affect the kinds of legislation that get passed, but that will have only a marginal effect on the separation of powers. The crucial test of the party government hypothesis is whether at the time party voting was strong in Congress it enabled the president to get his way in Congress by virtue of party discipline.

The evidence on this question is almost nonexistent; there was in those days no "presidential program" the fate of which could be measured against roll-call votes, but we do know that the national parties were divided. Reed resigned from the House because he disagreed with his own party's president, McKinley, over American policy toward Cuba and Hawaii, and the revolt against Speaker Cannon was made possible by the defection of Republican congressmen who were willing to vote with the Democrats. The Democrats were divided between those who had supported William Jennings Bryan in 1896 and those who had opposed him; the Republicans were divided between Theodore Roosevelt's reformers and the party stalwarts. The president used his patronage for political ends, but even in those days of abundant political jobs and legions of jobseekers, he was by no means able to enforce his will on fellow partisans in Congress. Far from the president's being able to use jobs to influence congressmen, congressmen—and their state party allies—dictated to the president whom he should appoint to what post. It was, as Morton Keller has observed, the era of organizational politics,[20] but the organizations that existed did not so much coordinate the separate branches of national government as, fleetingly, organize one part of it—the legislature—and seek to cash in on the rest. Henry Jones Ford's rejoinder to Lord Bryce was a statement about the role of parties that, at least at the national level, was supported by no evidence. It included a lone footnote quoting two senators to the effect that parties dominate the affairs of Congress and a brief reference to the ability of the Democratic party in 1896 to force its national platform on dissenting state parties; otherwise, only argumentation.[21]

If not much evidence indicates that party had overcome the separation of powers in the national government, a great deal shows that it had unified many state and local governments. At the turn of the century, political machines had come to power in countless cities and many states. The rise and influence of the machine is well known, although some scholarly disputes remain about the reasons for its success (and, just as important, the reasons for its failure to appear in some places). New York, Chicago, and Philadelphia, among other places, were governed by party organizations that controlled the executive, the legislative, and (to a large degree) the judicial branches of government. They sent representatives to Congress who were beholden to (or sometimes the leaders of) the local machines.

The advent of the civil service cut back on the patronage these organizations could dispense, the scrutiny of the media inhibited the freedom with which sweetheart contracts could be awarded, and the nationalized welfare system begun by the New Deal gave needy voters an alternative source of financial help. Party machines suffered from these changes, but they were not wholly destroyed by them. The Cook County regular Democratic organization persisted in Chicago well into the 1970s, when racial and ethnic conflict, not political reform, broke it asunder.

As long as the city and county machines were intact, they were able to unite the executive and legislative (and sometimes the judicial) branches of local government. They did so chiefly because they controlled nominations for office; patronage and other kinds of favoritism played a lesser role.

It is not clear, however, whether the governors of states with highly partisan legislatures do any better in creating stable coalitions of lawmakers than the president does with Congress. A Democratic governor of Illinois can wield more influence with the Democratic members of the legislature if he can ally himself with the leaders of the Cook County Democratic organization than he can if he ignores them. There are probably other states where strong parties knit together governors and legislators. But it is quite obvious that in many states where the legislature votes regularly along partisan lines the governor's influence is not, by that fact, greatly enhanced. Certainly Democratic governors of Massachusetts have had about as much trouble with the Democratic-controlled legislature as Kennedy and Carter had with Democratic congresses.

Sarah Morehouse analyzed the success of governors with their legislative programs and found evidence that they may wield influence over the legislature (at least when the same party controls both the legislature and the governor's office) in some of the states where party voting in the legislature is frequent. That influence seems to result from the governor's leadership of the political party outside the legislature. "If the governor has been successful in building a coalition to support him in the primary and general election, he is also successful in building a coalition within the legislature to pass his legislation."[22] But the existence of a correlation between a governor's popularity in the electorate and his or her success with his party in the legislature is a highly general finding that says little about the precise means—or even the direction—of influence.

Even if we assume that strong parties make it easier for the governor to do business with his or her legislature, it is not at all clear that the same result would occur if party voting were more common in Congress. State party leaders may have some ability to influence who is nominated for office and to direct the flow of money with which to finance campaigns. National party leaders have not in this century had the ability to influence who is nominated for Congress, and (owing to campaign finance laws) they have lost much of their ability to direct the flow of political cash. (They are energetically exploring every loophole in those laws, however.) There are virtually no examples of presidents controlling congressional nominations (everyone remembers Roosevelt's ill-fated purge in 1938); since the death of the congressional caucus in the 1830s, there have been few (if any) examples of congressmen controlling presidential nominations.

Short of controlling nominations, the mere existence of strong party leadership in a legislature might make it easier for an elected executive to do business with lawmakers. It stands to reason that it would be easier for a governor or a president to deal with three or four powerful legislative leaders than with several dozen committee chairmen or several hundred individual legislators. The former pattern has often been the case, as when Presidents Franklin Roosevelt and Harry Truman dealt with the House through Speaker Sam Rayburn or President Eisenhower with the Senate through Lyndon Johnson and Everett Dirksen. This method saves energy and alters the kinds of coalitions that can be formed. But it does not so much overcome the separation of powers as simplify the capacity for managing that separation on the basis of a working—but wary—partnership.

Why Do We Have Any Party Voting at All?

Given the radically decentralized and individualistic ethos of Congress, what is astonishing is that we should see any signs of party voting at all. What can explain the fact that, even today, the single best clue to how a congressman will vote is his or her party affiliation? One reason is that congressmen do not join a party for random or accidental reasons; they do so, in most cases, because their outlook on politics has more in common with that of one party than with that of the other. Democrats are more liberal than Republicans, and so liberal congressmen are more likely to be Democrats than Republicans.

Indeed, there is some reason to think that the ideology of a congressional party is more consistent today than formerly. Jerrold E. Schneider has supplied evidence that Senate voting can be described in ideological terms, although his analysis is disputed by others.[23] There is little doubt that southern Democrats have declined in numbers and influence in the House, thereby making Democrats ideologically more alike than they once were; at the same time Republicans in Congress have become more consistently conservative, so much so that some observers speak of liberal Republicans as an endangered species. William Schneider has calculated the percentage of the members of each party in Congress who cast liberal votes in three areas and finds that only on social issues, such as abortion or school prayer, are as few as 75 percent of Senate Democrats liberals (see table 2–1). On all other issues at least 80 percent of the Democrats

29

TABLE 2–1
MEMBERS OF CONGRESS VOTING ON THE LIBERAL SIDE OF ISSUES,
BY PARTY, 1983
(percent)

	Senate		House	
Kind of Issue	Democrats	Republicans	Democrats	Republicans
Economic	85	8	93	7
Social	75	27	91	18
Foreign and military policy	82	9	85	7

SOURCE: *Baron Report*, May 7, 1984. Data compiled by William Schneider.

and no more than 9 percent of the Republicans vote on the liberal side.

Party voting can lead to party control of much of the congressional agenda when one party (in recent decades almost invariably the Democrats) has a massive majority in Congress. The upsurge in party voting in the 1930s reflected the temporary ideological cohesion of the huge Democratic majorities that came to power with President Roosevelt. The lopsided Democratic majorities after the crushing electoral victory of President Johnson in 1964 meant that the northern Democrats in the House could outvote the combined forces of Republicans and southern Democrats; hence we got such programs as Medicare and the rest of the Great Society legislation.

David W. Brady has found evidence that critical or realigning elections create the conditions necessary for strong party government in the House.[24] The realignments associated with the elections of 1896 and 1932 brought into the House many new members who disrupted the established order and provided consistent party support for new policies. This support, in turn, enhanced the power of the House leadership. Thus the power of party leaders in Congress is, to a degree, linked to events in the electorate. The dominance of Speaker Reed and the high level of party voting during his regime reflected a degree of ideological unity among the Republicans that, as events proved, did not last.

In the past two decades the Democrats have not enjoyed massive majorities; and, as the research of Barbara Sinclair suggests, some northern Democrats have defected from the traditional liberal positions on some issues. The Republicans, by contrast, have become ideologically more unified, although the so-called gypsy moth Republicans have been staging a rear-guard action.

Can the Parties Overcome the Separation of Powers?

One of the great ironies in the recent history of scholarly argumentation about parties is that, to a degree the proponents probably never imagined, the recommendations of the "party government" school have been adopted. But the adoption has made the reality of party government even more remote than it once was. In 1950 the Committee on Political Parties of the American Political Science Association, chaired by E. E. Schattschneider, issued its well-known report "Toward a More Responsible Two-Party System." The committee called for parties that were ideologically more consistent and organizationally stronger so that, when in office, they could enact a coherent program and, when out of office, they would supply a coherent alternative. Political scientists often suppose that the recommendations of the committee were ignored; in fact, I am struck by how many were adopted, especially by the Democrats.

Consider the specific recommendations of the committee: party platforms should clearly state the differences between the parties; government financing should be provided for elections; parties should become internally more democratic; the seniority rule in Congress should be relaxed; biennial party conferences should be held; the emergence of two-party systems should be encouraged in such one-party areas as the South; party rules and procedures should be published; congressional districts should be made equal in population; congressional committees should have bigger staffs; and professors should participate more in politics. To a substantial degree, all these things have happened. So far as I can tell, only two major recommendations of the committee have not been adopted—a four-year term for members of the House of Representatives and a modification of the electoral college so as to reduce, in some unspecified fashion, the winner-take-all rule that is in effect in most states.

By any ordinary standards, this record should be hailed by the advocates of party government as a great victory. Yet no cheers resound. Why? Because the policies designed to produce responsible party government did not, when adopted, produce it. Advocates of becoming more like the British have not abandoned the effort, of course, but they have shifted the locus of their hopes from party reform to constitutional revision. It is as if they were determined to make one last assault on the American system by taking up and enlarging on the two recommendations of the Schattschneider committee that fell by the wayside. For reasons given by James Ceaser and others in this volume, I doubt that these changes, if adopted, would have the desired effect either.

Why did the Schattschneider plan not produce its intended effect? One answer has already been given: the separation of powers in the federal government cannot be overcome by political parties because the essential means for uniting the executive and legislative branches—control by one branch over nominations to office in the other branch—has not existed since the days of Andrew Jackson and can no longer be made to exist, except perhaps for a fleeting moment in the aftermath of a major electoral realignment. Greater party voting could, in principle, be produced in Congress by undoing the "reforms" of the past seventy-five years. Even if that were to occur, however, there is little reason to think that more party voting in Congress would lead to greater cooperation between the president and Congress except when the president and his party have come to power in a moment of crisis (the 1930s) or at a time of optimism and apparent national consensus (the mid-1960s). In ordinary times the advantages to congressmen of a decentralized and fragmented Congress are too great—the fragmentation permits them to pursue their desire for reelection (not their only goal, but obviously an important one) with a minimum of party or presidential constraints.

Another reason why the Schattschneider plan did so little to increase the extent of party governance is that the two assumptions on which that plan rested were inconsistent. In the United States we can have ideologically more coherent parties or organizationally stronger parties, but it is not clear that we can have both. The ideologically most coherent parties (various Marxist third parties excepted) have been organizationally weak in the sense that they have lacked the capacity for sustained action under the direction of some central leadership group. The factionalism of the Democratic party as it began in 1972 to become more consistently liberal is well known. Greater ideology has been infused into the Democratic party precisely by making it weaker organizationally—by removing from the control of party leaders the ability to decide who gets nominated and how money is spent. This was done in the name of greater grass-roots democracy, but whether it is the grass roots or a cadre of activists that has taken power is another question. The strongest parties organizationally have ordinarily been those, such as city and county machines, that cared scarcely at all about ideology.[25]

Can We Achieve More Party Control of Congress?

Even if we conclude that parties will not overcome the separation of powers, we might still wish to see more party control of the House and the Senate to facilitate bargaining between the president and

Congress. We have plausible anecdotal evidence of how Truman dealt with Richard Russell or Eisenhower with Lyndon Johnson and how that pattern of negotiation made managing the policy agenda a good deal easier than is possible when a staff of White House legislative liaison specialists must round up votes from scores of subcommittee chairmen and hundreds of congressmen. I am not certain how much weight to attach to biographical and journalistic accounts of the extent to which the decentralization of Congress has made policy coordination more difficult. But I am inclined to prefer a system in which a president can make a deal with a group of congressional leaders small enough to be seated comfortably around the president's breakfast table, in the reasonable expectation that the deal will stick and that the rank and file in Congress will fall into line.

In the light of the early history of Congress and the present behavior of many state legislatures, it is not difficult to specify institutional arrangements that will facilitate such a process. Give to the Speaker (and to the majority leader in the Senate) the power to name committee chairmen and assign members to committees. Arrange the perquisites of office so that members will be eager to get and retain committee chairmanships. Abolish the recorded teller vote and the electronic roll-call vote, which make it so easy to force members to take positions publicly on a bill and thus so hard to vote (by anonymous ayes and nays) for the leadership in ways that are contrary to the interests of the members' constituencies. Reduce the number of subcommittees, and restore the power of committee and subcommittee chairmen to control agendas. Repeal rules that require virtually all committee sessions to be held in public, where the temptation to play to the media and to interest group representatives is often irresistible. Reduce the capacity of individual senators to introduce dilatory or nongermane motions or to filibuster.

What all these changes have in common is a reduction in the rights and privileges of the individual member of Congress—a lessening, as it will be perceived, of the degree to which Congress is a "democratic" institution. No one can say that such changes are impossible, but one can say that there are very few examples in American history of people who possess certain rights voting to give them up or voting to have less democracy rather than more. The decentralization and democratization of institutions are, in the main, irreversible. Some changes are possible, and various senators and representatives are contemplating them. But any change great enough to empower the congressional leaders to induce members to vote along party lines (or in accordance with the leaders' wishes on a particular issue) is likely to be, at best, temporary and contingent. It may have a large effect on small matters and occasionally a small effect on large ones; but if the power is not used with great circumspection, it will simply be taken away. Speaker Reed once defended his power in the House by pointing out, rightly, that the members could at any time vote to replace him. In effect, they did just that with one of his successors, Joe Cannon.

The likely congressional resistance to any serious effort to restore party voting is but one measure of the degree to which the American constitutional order values rights over responsibilities and encourages citizens and politicians alike to think of policy making in essentially adversarial terms. The preeminence of a philosophy of rights can be found throughout our political institutions, though nowhere to a greater degree than among the activist courts. (It is strange, as others have remarked in this volume, that people who urge constitutional reform so that policy making may become more coherent never offer proposals to curb the power of the courts to make policy in ways quite at variance with the intent of Congress.) The separation of powers reflects and magnifies the disposition (evident since at least the Revolutionary War) to think of politics as a process whereby rights are defined and defended.

How then can we explain the existence of high levels of party voting in American state legislatures despite the separation of powers and the existence of a distinctive American political culture? If we knew that, we would know a great deal. My conjecture is that legislative politics in certain states have been insulated, perhaps by their low visibility, from the process of decentralization and democratization that has affected Congress. Of course, we would want to know why that insulation occurred. I am not aware of much research that bears on the question. If I am correct, however, we should see state legislatures slowly emulating the congressional pattern as the insulation—whatever it is—breaks down.

We sometimes look longingly at other nations, notably Great Britain, in search of ways whereby our political system can more easily adopt comprehensive solutions to national problems. For reasons stated elsewhere I am skeptical that other nations, including Britain, do a better job of making policy than the United States or that the conditions of life in this country would have been better if our Constitution had made it easier to formulate and enact "coherent" policies (by which is usually meant policies favoring the growth of government).[26] Even if other nations were rightfully envied and our policies desperately needed more coherence, it is far from clear that political parties could be made stronger in ways that would achieve those ends.

For one thing, there is not much evidence that it is the parliamentary system as such that causes strong parties to emerge. Julius Turner noted over thirty years ago that the formal powers of a prime minister, such as the ability to dissolve parliament and call for new elections, cannot explain party cohesion in those parliaments.[27] That cohesion depends as much on strong partisanship among the voters and the ability of party leaders to control access by candidates to the party label (in short, no nonsense about primary elections) as it does on the structure of the constitution. Moreover, if a parliamentary system, or some approximation of it, were installed in a nation as heterogeneous as the United States, we might get more party cohesion only at the price of multiplying the number of parties, so that although the parties might be more cohesive, public policy would be less so. There is no reason to assume that any constitutional or party changes we make will move us closer to Great Britain; given our political culture and the issues that divide us, France or Italy seems to be more likely as a model that we may, no doubt without intending it, come to emulate.

Where Have the Party Government Enthusiasts Gone?

James MacGregor Burns, writing in 1963, was quite candid about who was to gain from stronger parties—it was the president. "Each presidential party must convert its congressional party into a party wing exerting a proper, but not controlling or crippling hold on party policy."[28] But the clear evidence of a century of American political history is that when party becomes stronger in the making of national policy, it is the congressional party, not the presidential one, that is strengthened. Roosevelt and Johnson may have been helped by brief periods of strong congressional leadership, but they by no means dominated that leadership. When national party leaders have become powerful, it has been in Congress and toward congressional ends that their power has been exercised. The president has gained, if he has gained at all, only in having fewer congressional leaders to persuade. But persuasion it has been, and rarely much more. The hopes that party government would, in the context of American politics, mean presidential government have proved vain.

All that is left to try, then, is to alter that context by reducing, through constitutional amendment, the separation of powers that strong parties were once supposed to overcome. If strong parties fail to discipline—that is, bend to the president's will—congressional leaders, then strengthened parties can no longer be the instrument of reform. There is a case for improving congressional procedures and

35

strengthening congressional leadership, but that case must rest on grounds other than the alleged defects of the separation of powers. Many of the supporters of a strong presidency have finally acknowledged that party government—for decades their rallying cry—will not serve their ends. And so they have turned to a different means—constitutional amendment. But it is a more risky strategy. We could learn from experience about the role of parties without having to make fundamental changes in the regime. To learn from experience about constitutional "reform," we will have to take a precipitous leap into the dark.

Notes

1. James MacGregor Burns, *The Deadlock of Democracy: Four-Party Politics in America* (Englewood Cliffs, N.J.: Prentice-Hall, 1963), pp. 325–26. See also E. E. Schattschneider, *Party Government* (New York: Farrar and Rinehart, 1942).

2. James Bryce, *The American Commonwealth*, 3d ed. (New York: Macmillan, 1909), vol. 1, p. 530.

3. Henry Jones Ford, *The Rise and Growth of American Politics* (London: Macmillan, 1900), p. 300.

4. Ibid., pp. 297–98.

5. Ibid., pp. 325, 310.

6. George Rothwell Brown, *The Leadership of Congress* (Indianapolis, Ind.: Bobbs-Merrill, 1922), p. 100.

7. Julius Turner, with Edward V. Schneier, Jr., *Party and Constituency: Pressures on Congress*, rev. ed. (Baltimore: Johns Hopkins University Press, 1970), p. 16.

8. David W. Brady, Joseph Cooper, and Patricia A. Hurley, "The Decline of Party in the U.S. House of Representatives, 1887–1968," *Legislative Studies Quarterly*, vol. 4 (1979), pp. 381–407.

9. Melissa P. Collie, "Policy Dimensional Analysis and the Structure of Voting Patterns: The U.S. House of Representatives in Three Periods" (Paper presented to the 1983 annual meeting of the American Political Science Association). See also Aage Clausen, *How Congressmen Vote* (New York: St. Martin's Press, 1973).

10. Anthony King, "The American Polity in the Late 1970s: Building Coalitions in the Sand," in Anthony King, ed., *The New American Political System* (Washington, D.C.: American Enterprise Institute, 1978), pp. 371–95.

11. R. Douglas Arnold, *Congress and the Bureaucracy: A Theory of Influence* (New Haven, Conn.: Yale University Press, 1979), p. 210; and Barbara Sinclair, "Coping with Uncertainty: Building Coalitions in the House and Senate," in Thomas E. Mann and Norman J. Ornstein, eds., *The New Congress* (Washington, D.C.: American Enterprise Institute, 1981), pp. 178–220. See also Barbara Sinclair, *Congressional Realignment, 1925-1978* (Austin: University of Texas Press, 1982).

12. Kay Lehman Schlozman and John T. Tierney, *Organized Interests and*

American Democracy (New York: Harper & Row, 1985), p. 76.

13. *Public Opinion* (April/May 1984), p. 32.

14. James Q. Wilson, *American Government: Institutions and Policies*, 2d ed. (Lexington, Mass.: D. C. Heath, 1983), p. 185.

15. Samuel C. Patterson, "American State Legislatures and Public Policy," in Herbert Jacob and Kenneth N. Vines, eds., *Politics in American States: A Comparative Analysis*, 3d ed. (Boston: Little, Brown, 1976), pp. 178–82; and Malcolm E. Jewell and Samuel C. Patterson, *The Legislative Process in the United States*, 3d ed. (New York: Random House, 1977), table 16.1, pp. 384–85, 389. See also Duane Lockard, *New England States Politics* (Princeton, N.J.: Princeton University Press, 1959).

16. Patterson, "American State Legislatures," p.180.

17. Ibid., p. 181

18. Congressional Quarterly, *Guide to Congress*, 3d ed. (Washington, D.C.: Congressional Quarterly, 1982) pp. 49–50.

19. Samuel P. Huntington, "Congressional Responses to the Twentieth Century," in American Assembly, *The Congress and America's Future* (Englewood Cliffs, N.J.: Prentice-Hall, 1973), pp. 6–38.

20. Morton Keller, *Affairs of State* (Cambridge, Mass.: Harvard University Press, 1977), chap. 7.

21. Ford, *Rise and Growth*, p. 295, fn 1, and p. 332.

22. Sarah McCally Morehouse, "The Governor as Political Leader," in Jacob and Vines, *Politics in American States*, p. 232; and Sarah P. McCally, "The Governor and His Legislative Party," *American Political Science Review*, vol. 60 (1966), pp. 923–42.

23. Jerrold E. Schneider, *Ideological Coalitions in Congress* (Westport, Conn.: Greenwood Press, 1979); and Collie, "Policy Dimensional Analysis."

24. David W. Brady, "Elections, Congress, and Public Policy Changes: 1886–1960," in Bruce A. Campbell and Richard J. Trilling, eds., *Realignment in American Politics: Toward a Theory* (Austin: University of Texas Press, 1980), pp. 176–201. See also David W. Brady, *Congressional Voting in a Partisan Era: A Comparison of the McKinley Houses to the Modern House* (Lawrence: University of Kansas Press, 1973).

25. Whether this tension between ideology and organization exists to the same degree in the Republican party is a matter on which the evidence is not clear. It is worth some scholarly inquiry.

26. James Q. Wilson, comments in AEI Public Policy Forum, published under the title "President versus Congress" (Washington, D.C.: American Enterprise Institute, 1981).

27. Turner, *Party and Constituency*, pp. 29–33. See also Leon D. Epstein, "The Cohesion of British Parliamentary Parties," *American Political Science Review*, vol. 50 (1956), p. 364.

28. Burns, *Deadlock of Democracy*, p. 326.

3

The Renewal of American Constitutionalism

Donald L. Robinson

There is growing evidence that the problems confronting the American constitutional system are outstripping its capacity. Our industrial plants are no longer competitive with those of Japan, France, South Korea, or Brazil, yet our government cannot decide whether to remove regulations or to impose more coordination and incentives. Our southern border is defenseless against illegal immigration, but our government cannot decide whether to fortify it or to negotiate a comprehensive agreement with our Latin neighbors. We are spending a dangerously high proportion of our substance on weapons that we must never use; yet our government cannot reach an agreement with the Soviet Union to stop at present levels, much less to begin to dismantle existing stockpiles.

Perhaps the most revealing example of the impotence of our system is its inability to live within its means. In 1983 the federal government spent $190 billion more than it raised. In 1984 the annual deficit was even greater, and it is expected to stay near $200 billion for the foreseeable future.* According to the Reagan administration's economic report, the cumulative federal debt will soon exceed $2 trillion. At rates of 10 percent, interest payments thereafter will consume at least the first $200 billion of revenue each year.

The opposition party always deplores deficits. No one was more adept at charging Democrats with "fiscal irresponsibility" than Ronald Reagan in his pundit days. Now Reagan is president, Republicans control the Senate, and it is the Democrats who rage that the defense

---

*It may be years before we can assess the effects of the Gramm-Rudman-Hollings bill. As Jonathan Rauch put it in the *National Journal*, January 4, 1986: "The New Balanced Budget Act may, as intended, help end the standoff between Congress and the President, but the untested statute could just as easily make matters worse than ever and perpetuate the deadlock."—EDS.

buildup and tax cuts will pile up huge debts that will constitute the first claim, probably a preemptive one, on future revenues. Democrats have their own priorities, but they will have little chance to implement them. The nation's resources will be devoted to paying the interest on Reagan's debt.

Even apart from these partisan quarrels, however, a deficit of the current proportions poses profound dangers for the nation. First, a large deficit drains resources from other sections of the economy. Because revenues are insufficient to cover expenditures, the Treasury must borrow huge sums to pay the government's bills. Its borrowing forces up interest rates, crowds out private borrowers, undermines industries that depend on credit, such as housing, automobiles, and agriculture, and discourages capital investments in industrial plants and public works (roads, bridges, airports, harbors). Alternatively, the Federal Reserve Board could purchase the federal bonds, which would create new money and prevent crowding out in capital markets. But that would rekindle inflation.

A second danger arises from the fact that domestic sources of credit can no longer meet the demand for borrowing. In 1983 the American economy needed $280 billion in new funds to cover the public and private debt. Net domestic savings available for borrowing totaled only $250 billion. The difference of $30 billion had to be obtained from foreign sources.

The year 1982 was the first since the Civil War in which foreigners invested more in America than American companies, banks, and individuals invested or lent abroad—$8.3 billion more. In 1983 this negative balance grew to $32.3 billion, and in 1984 it exceeded $100 billion. Sometime in 1985, according to Martin Feldstein, former chairman of the Council of Economic Advisers, Americans will owe more to foreign creditors than they owe to us. In that situation national independence depends on the ability of the government to raise enough taxes to meet its interest payments plus any scheduled retirements of principal or to arrange new loans. New York City's difficulty along these lines in 1975 led to its having to accept the dictates of bankers concerning its spending priorities and level of indebtedness. Poland in 1982 had to restructure its budget before creditors would grant new loans. Mexico and Argentina, among other developing nations, have been similarly at the mercy of their creditors.

The American economy is not yet in a condition of vulnerability comparable to New York City's in 1975 or Poland's in 1982. If the trend in deficits continues, however, American taxpayers will owe the first fruits of their labors to foreign creditors.

These implications of the deficit are well known in Washington. Everyone knows that it is ominously large. Everyone deplores it. Everyone has a plan for reducing it. The trouble is that, under our constitutional system, no one—no individual in office, no party—is able to do anything about it, and the electorate cannot hold anyone responsible for the inaction.

Defects of Our Constitutional System Today

A government is an organism with work to do. It must be judged according to its fitness to perform the tasks we assign to it. A horse is fit to pull a carriage, but it cannot take a man to the moon.

When the Constitution was framed two centuries ago, only a few crucial tasks required a national government. National security was one: Americans needed to define a common policy toward foreign powers and to cooperate in implementing it. To this end the Constitution gave Congress the power to regulate foreign commerce, levy tariffs, define and punish piracy, raise an army and a navy, and declare war; it made the president commander in chief of the armed forces and empowered him, with the consent of the Senate, to make treaties and appoint ambassadors; and it prohibited the states from entering into treaties or alliances with foreign powers.

The second major function of the national government was to establish a common market among the states. For this purpose the Constitution gave Congress the power to regulate interstate commerce, establish uniform laws on bankruptcies, coin money, punish counterfeiting, fix weights and measures, and issue patents and copyrights. States were forbidden to coin money, issue paper currency, impair the obligation of contracts, or tax imports or exports for their own benefit.

In support of these two broad areas of governance, the Constitution assigned certain other functions to Congress: to enact a uniform rule of naturalization, to establish post offices, to provide for organizing and training state militias and for calling them into the national service, to establish a national system of courts, and to govern territories and "exercise exclusive legislation" over the nation's capital city.

This list of powers and prohibitions, contained mostly in Article I, sections 8, 9, and 10, and Article II, section 2, of the Constitution, gives a good clue to the framers' notion of the role of the national government.[1] It focused essentially on foreign relations, national defense, and the regulation of commerce, both foreign and domestic.

Performing these functions required energetic administration, and the leading framers did not hesitate to provide it. They knew that the nation, its economy, and its social structure would not always be primitive. Believing that they were building a Constitution for a great empire and for the ages and having read Blackstone and Hume on the growth of ministries in Britain, they were at least dimly aware that the executive would grow as the nation grew, and particularly as the nation came into contact with other nations that posed a threat to its security.[2] Even the boldest spirits, however, did not foresee—indeed, could not have foreseen, any more than Blackstone and Hume did— the modern welfare-garrison state. They did not foresee a world in which even the proponents of limited government, modern disciples of Adam Smith, would campaign for the presidency in 1980 on a platform that pledged support for federal subsidies and incentives for health care, education, housing, transportation, environmental protection, and even assistance for workers left unemployed by "technological obsolescence or imports."[3]

A government that decides in a few days to allocate billions of dollars to a road-building program, partly to alleviate unemployment, must be set up differently from one that frets for decades about whether it has constitutional authority to build a road joining the coastal areas to the interior. A government that monitors and adjusts the amount of money in the system virtually daily requires a different structure from one that debates for decades whether it needs a national bank and, if so, whether it has constitutional authority to set one up. A government that might have to decide in minutes whether to return nuclear fire must be structured differently from one that does not learn for several weeks whether its envoys have been able to buy the Louisiana Territory.

Richard Neustadt has called attention to the fact that the framers of the Constitution, in adopting the separation of powers, gave it an important twist. They provided, says Neustadt in a famous phrase, a system of "separated institutions sharing powers."[4]

Neustadt's formula deserves its renown. It calls attention to the importance of checks and balances in our constitutional scheme. It may, however, obscure a crucial distinction: *the shares of power were not randomly or casually distributed.* They were carefully related to the capacities of each branch, to its constituency, and to its intended role in the system.

From the beginning the theory of our Constitution has been that Congress writes the laws that determine rights, define crimes, authorize public enterprises, and appropriate funds, while the president, as chief executive, preserves public order, conducts foreign relations, commands the armed forces, and administers public services as directed by law. This division of responsibility reflects the composition of the bodies. Congress, by its size and close ties to the communities of the nation, ensures that the popular will directs what the government undertakes; the presidency, centering on a single individual, ensures that the government uses its resources efficiently in the service of that will.

The Constitution's design is not neat. Ever since 1789 Congress has shaped administrative agencies and monitored the performance of the executive branch. The Senate confirms the leading appointments in the executive branch, and Congress, by manipulating the purse strings, has been able to dictate a large share of patronage appointments. On the other side, the executive has a share of legislative power in the right to recommend measures and veto acts of Congress, and some presidents have been able to exert considerable influence on legislation by informal persuasion.

Nevertheless, for most of the nineteenth century, the Constitution worked more or less according to the doctrine of separation. Congress by its law-making powers took the initiative in policy making. If the record gave cause for dismay from the framers' standpoint, it was in the weakness and dependence of the executive during the period of presidential nomination by congressional caucus (1808–1824) and in the corruption that resulted from congressional dominance for much of the period from the end of the Civil War to the end of the century, especially from 1869 to 1892.

During the twentieth century, however, this pattern has decisively changed, and the result has been a "constitutional revolution."[5] Congress continues to play a major role. It is probably the strongest, most independent legislature in the world. When it is aroused, it can exact high tribute from other elements of the system, forcing them to take its judgment and desires into account. Nevertheless, modernity has disturbed the constitutional balances. Congress rarely takes the initiative anymore. Most of the time it lets the president define the agenda, then reacts to his proposals. Moreover, it has equipped him for leadership by giving him councils and policy-planning bureaus.

How did this shift come about?[6]

It began with the advent of total war. The first in American experience was the Civil War. For three months at the beginning of that war (the "eleven-weeks dictatorship," as Clinton Rossiter called it),[7] Lincoln governed alone, raising troops, imposing a blockade, advancing public funds for weapons and supplies to private agents without an appropriation, suspending the ancient writ of habeas corpus. Later during the war, Lincoln as commander in chief directed the Union's military effort, defined and redefined the aims of the war, and set the terms for ending it. He also took the initiative, toward the war's end, in developing policies for reunion and reconstruction. In short, he performed as modern presidents do.

When war came in the twentieth century, Lincoln's precedents were there, and first Woodrow Wilson, then Franklin D. Roosevelt, eagerly employed them. Furthermore, particularly in World War II, the boundaries of war became fuzzy. By the lend-lease deal before the war and by the extension of wartime emergency powers into the postwar period, presidents assumed power to dispose of property and direct the economy without statutory authority or with only the broadest emergency powers. By the 1950s peace had become cold war, and the president's vast emergency powers seemed to have become virtually perpetual.

It was not just war that disrupted the Constitution's balances.[8] The complexity of the national economy produced a demand for regulation that could not be satisfied by statutes. The legislative process was too slow, Congress lacked expertise, and laws could not contain the requisite detail without becoming ludicrously long and complex. Congress was unwilling, however, to delegate its rule-making powers to the executive branch. It therefore created the so-called independent regulatory commission—independent, that is, from the president, who was forbidden to superintend or discipline commissioners once their appointments were confirmed. This constitutional innovation had its precedent in the Interstate Commerce Commission in 1887. It was modified and strengthened when Congress established the Federal Reserve Board in 1913 to regulate banking and control the money supply and the Federal Trade Commission in 1914 to define and prevent "unfair" commercial practices. In the 1930s the device was further adapted to regulate trade unions, securities markets, and the communications industry. These commissions, combining quasi-legislative, quasi-executive, and quasi-judicial powers,[9] occupied a space not provided for in the Constitution.

Meanwhile, the demand for governmental services caused a proliferation of agencies in the executive branch. The National Park Service in the Interior Department, the Forest Service and the Bureau of Animal Husbandry in the Agriculture Department, the Weather Service and the Census Bureau in the Commerce Department, the Antitrust Division in the Justice Department, among many others, were given important functions and attracted public servants with high professional standing and commitment. Meanwhile, Congress, recognizing the temptation to convert this huge bureaucracy into a vast political army, established the civil service system.

Gradually, during the first quarter of the twentieth century, elected officials began to feel a need to promote efficiency by a regular accounting of the federal government's activities.[10] Congress, concerned primarily to bring discipline and order to the proliferating operations of the executive branch, passed the Budget and Accounting Act of 1921, which placed the Bureau of the Budget in the Treasury Department and required the president to prepare an annual summary of all planned expenditures of the federal government. Until that time Congress dealt with governmental activities piecemeal through its committee structure, and no one anywhere in government examined the fiscal policy of the government as a whole.

During the 1930s, as the New Deal brought an expanded sense of the government's proper role in the economy and society, administrative science began to find a better acceptance for the notion that government ought to be run on a model analogous to the business corporation, that is, with a pyramid of authority centering on the chief executive. In 1937 the President's Committee on Administrative Management, chaired by Louis Brownlow, made recommendations for strengthening the management of the executive branch. Brownlow's group called for the creation of the Executive Office of the President and urged that the Bureau of the Budget be brought into the presidential orbit. Congress accepted these recommendations and under the same impulse acceded to a modification of its traditional authority over the shape of the executive branch when, in the interests of economy and efficiency, it gave the president power to reorganize the bureaus, subject to a legislative veto.

The culminating shift in the distribution of constitutional power came with the gradual emergence of the president as chief legislator. In tracing this development, James Sundquist has noted a series of "firsts."[11] William H. Taft was the first modern president to present draft legislation to Congress. Taft's initiative aroused resentment in Congress, but his successor, Wilson, gained acceptance as legislative leader of the national Democratic party and instituted the practice of presenting bills to Congress in person. The press, for the first time, began to speak of the "administration's bills" in Congress. President Warren Harding attempted to take the matter another significant step when he addressed the Senate from the vice president's chair, urging defeat of a pending bill on soldiers' bonuses. He accomplished his immediate purpose when the bill was recommitted, but an angry debate broke out over his allegedly "unconstitutional" appearance. Senator Robert H. LaFollette insisted that the framers were "careful" to withhold from the president "any express or implied authority to oppose legislation in the making or to participate in the deliberations and debate of either House on a pending measure."[12] In 1932 President Herbert Hoover addressed the Senate on a pending revenue bill, and he too stirred up a partisan hornets' nest. Since then no president has addressed either house of Congress on an immediately pending piece of legislation.

With the coming of Franklin Roosevelt, however, the modern presidency entered its second period of major legislative influence (the first was under Wilson), and this time the pattern proved durable. Major portions of the New Deal program were drafted at the White House or in administrative agencies, sometimes with the participation of congressmen but on the executive's turf. Democratic leaders in Congress acted as the president's lieutenants. Soon the president's role was institutionalized through the assignment of a White House aide (Judge Samuel Rosenman) to draft legislative messages. Under Harry Truman came the first full-time congressional liaison specialists, a function that was upgraded by Dwight Eisenhower and tied by John Kennedy into a system of departmental legislative liaisons.

As the habit of presidential initiative in legislative policy became ingrained, Congress began to provide the presidency with institutional means to discharge the responsibility. Most fundamental was the Bureau of the Budget, which under Truman coordinated the submission of administration bills to Congress and presented the administration's position on pending legislation. The Employment Act of 1946 established the Council of Economic Advisers. This body was originally intended by congressional conservatives as a restraint on liberal presidents, who seemed oblivious of the harsh truths of the "dismal science," but the availability of economists who would tell any given president what he wanted to hear soon made it possible to convert the council into a useful tool for presidential policy making. In 1949 Congress created the National Security Council to assist the president in the formulation of defense and foreign policy. The trend continued with the legislative mandate in 1962 for a manpower report, with the establishment in 1969 of the Council on Environmental Quality, and with the creation in 1970 of the Domestic Council.

By the 1970s the expectation that presidents would take the lead in proposing national policy in virtually all fields was fixed and well implemented. In each case Congress has joined in looking to the president for leadership in fashioning national policy and in equipping him with staff to perform this role. The president has become chief legislator not by usurpation, not even by congressional neglect or passive acquiescence, but by positive congressional delegation.

Why did Congress do it? Apparently for two reasons. First, Congress lacks the capacity to act quickly and secretly, particularly in economic management and national security. Yet modern conditions often seem to demand such action. Thus a Democratic Congress gave President Richard Nixon the authority to impose wage and price controls whenever he deemed them necessary to control inflation, and it gave a succession of presidents broad latitude to use military force to protect American interests in Europe, the Middle East, Latin America, the Far East, and Southeast Asia.

The unique contribution of Congress lies in deliberation. Its bicameral structure and the careful consideration by committees ensures that Congress will not act hastily or without consulting interested parties. It came to be seen as part of the genius of the constitutional system that, when action had to be taken quickly, the president was there to do it. In a modern economy and in a world full of adversaries controlled by dictatorships, it seemed a sign of the framers' prescience that the American government was equipped with a president capable of decisive, energetic, and, if need be, secret action, thereby allowing Congress to maintain its traditional virtues of openness and deliberation.

The other perceived deficiency of Congress from the standpoint of modern leadership is that it lacked the ability to integrate the elements of policy into a national program. Again, this weakness was the other side of a peculiar strength of Congress, namely, its ability to devote attention, through its committees, to particular areas of policy. In some parliamentary regimes, bills are assigned to legislative committees randomly. This system helps to bring a general perspective to bear on proposed policies but reinforces the committees' amateur standing, so to speak, as far as the substance of policy is concerned. By contrast, an American legislative committee, as its members and staff gained seniority, became a formidable influence in a particular area of policy. As congressmen devoted themselves to a particular subject, however, they diminished their involvement in other areas, partly because of time constraints and partly in deference to their colleagues. No one in Congress devoted much time to developing a general perspective.[13]

Repeated attempts have been made to organize Congress for a more integrated approach to policy making, either by strengthening the partisan steering committees or by appointing ad hoc committees to draft legislation for a multifaceted problem such as energy or welfare reform.[14] Sundquist concludes, however, that despite these efforts, there has been "no fundamental improvement in the integrative capacity of the Congress, with the single—though major—exception of the budget process."[15] Even there the costs have been high. Places of great power have been raided and robbed of their traditional roles. In the budget process the appropriations subcommittees, as well as the standing authorizing committees, suffered diminution. Overall, little in the primary incentive system, what has been called "the electoral connection," encourages congressmen to wield personal leverage over the policy-making process. Not many voters are interested in what a congressman has done to adjust the checks and balances of the constitutional system.

Other factors besides the inability of Congress to act quickly or to aggregate policies into a program help to account for its loss of weight in the tug of war with the presidency. Congress, composed of members of various wings of both major parties, reaches its decisions through bargaining, and it is difficult for anyone to give principled reasons for its decisions. Bickering occurs in the executive branch on the way to decisions, too, but it usually takes place behind closed doors, sometimes under the protection of executive privilege. Once the decision is made, the president can announce it himself, giving the appearance of unity, decision, vigor. No wonder people look to the president, rather than Congress, for leadership.

Sundquist suggests that President Nixon's triumph in the battle of the budget in October 1972—in which Congress, virtually acknowledging its impotence and incapacity, authorized the president to impound funds to achieve fiscal responsibility—marked the nadir of congressional influence. Since then Congress has attempted to recover its influence, particularly in budgeting and fiscal management but also through the use of the legislative veto in such fields as environmental management, regulation of the marketplace, and national security. Now the Supreme Court, in the *Chadha* case, has cast these congressional tactics under a cloud. In his dissent, Justice Byron White complained that the majority, by striking down a promising adaptation of constitutional principles to modern demands, was being unrealistic. But the Court was right to decide as it did. The roles of Congress and the president are not interchangeable. The framers assigned those roles as they did because of the characters of the two branches. When a pitcher loses his stuff, it is no solution to send the catcher out to the mound. They have different equipment and different skills.

The creaking operation of the budget process shows that Congress has come about as far as it can come. It can never again assume leadership of the American government. Modern conditions forbid it. Political opposition or plain incompetence may cause the president to slip from the driver's seat, but 535 members of Congress cannot take his place. As now organized, Congress cannot proclaim national objectives and programs, and it cannot fundamentally reorganize itself without sacrificing its peculiar contribution to our constitutional

47

system. Congress represents the elements of the American Union. It cannot proclaim those interests with one voice. That is why the congressional response to a presidential address is always so weak. Who speaks for Congress? No one. A chorus cannot conduct a symphony.

The problem with the constitutional system is rooted in the separation of powers—not in its principles, but as it now functions. The framers of 1787 separated the powers of the federal government for two reasons: to promote vigorous administration and to prevent tyranny. As *The Federalist*—particularly those papers written by Alexander Hamilton—makes clear, the framers created a separate executive so that compromises, which were unavoidable in the legislative process, would not carry over into the administrative process and hobble it. Other numbers of *The Federalist* (particularly those written by James Madison) emphasize the dangers of oppression when all the powers of government are united in one place. *Federalist* No. 51, for example, reflects American fears that a party might use its powers of appointment to corrupt the legislature, as Robert Walpole and the Whigs had done in early Georgian England. This is a fundamental aspect of the rationale for the separation of powers. Madison's constitutionalism was intended partly to frustrate the control of government by a unified national party. It cannot be stressed too much that it was *not* Madison's intention to cripple the federal government, to make it incapable of formulating a policy and implementing it. His own performance as House leader during Washington's first term shows that he had no aversion to decisive legislation. What he wanted to prevent was the president's dominating the legislative process, by astute use of patronage, in service of a domineering national "faction."

To ask whether Madison and Hamilton and the other framers would have been pleased with the way their system worked—whether it ever worked as they intended—is a question of infinite complexity, as difficult and probably unanswerable as it is, fortunately, irrelevant for our purposes. What we do need to decide is whether the system now serves the fundamental constitutional values that we share with the founding generation.

These constitutional values are complex and subtle. Here I cannot do more than summarize them briefly. Two are fundamental: that governmental authority must be accountable to popular will and that power must be checked and balanced. The framers were aware that these values were sometimes in tension, but they were convinced that they were not contradictory, and they believed that the viability of the Republic—indeed, the future of republican government—required that they both be achieved. Ultimately, the people must rule, but no one—no person, no group, no class—is virtuous enough to rule alone.[16] Reinhold Niebuhr captured the faith that holds these propositions together in one of his famous aphorisms: man's capacity for goodness makes democracy possible; man's tendency to evil makes democracy necessary.

The trick in incorporating these values into a constitutional scheme is to see that the will of the people, which must ultimately prevail, does not become tyrannical. Madison, in *The Federalist*, offers two solutions to this problem. One (in No. 10) is to "expand the sphere" to include a large, varied population, so that there will be many interests but no simple majorities. The other (in No. 51) is to make the structure and processes of government complex (by the separation of powers, bicameralism, judicial review, federalism), so that foolish and wicked schemes will be exposed and popular majorities can be rallied to oppose them. Madison remarks that a reliance on the people through elections is the first line of defense for popular government but experience has taught the need for "auxiliary precautions." The ambition of public officials occupying juxtaposed positions in the constitutional structure is that additional safeguard in the Madisonian framework.

How have these safeguards worked, and what is their status today? Certainly the first, the one outlined in No. 10, still operates to protect liberty and foil tyranny. The country is far larger and more complex than it was in 1787, and it is thus even more difficult to piece together a majority coalition in support of legislation or policy. In these circumstances, to win an electoral majority for tyranny seems virtually impossible.

Certainly, too, Madison's second protection, outlined most succinctly in No. 51, stands. The American governmental process is nothing if not complex. A proposal must pass through an intricate maze before becoming law. Nor do the obstacles to policy melt away at that point. At the implementing stage, many additional opportunities arise to block or rebend the compromises that emerge from the legislative process. In short, the system operates to make it extremely difficult for the federal government to take decisive action.

Does the system still serve the constitutional values to which the framers were and we are committed? In two important respects I think not. In the first place, the framers would have been appalled at the extent to which the spirit of the legislative process now infects the administrative process. In their view responsiveness to interest groups was a virtue in the legislative process but not in the executive. Factions were the bane of administration. Administration needed to be vigorous, decisive, objective. That was the whole point of the separation of powers, as that doctrine was understood in 1787.[17] Let the representative assembly reflect the various interests, but let the executive be unified, and let him be chosen through a process that would encourage the winner to transcend the factions that compose the nation so that he could administer the law energetically and fairly.

What has happened instead is that the spirit of the legislature, operating primarily through legislative committees, has permeated the administrative branch. Through the appropriations process and through oversight hearings, links are forged between congressional committees, administrative bureaus, and groups in the private sector (suppliers of goods and services, professional associations) that are particularly concerned about a given area of policy. Typically the general public has little knowledge of the policy in question or interest in it; so the policy subgroup is left pretty much to its own devices. Sometimes a scandal or other vicissitude will bring one of these hidden corners of policy to light; sometimes they are hit by a tidal wave, such as a decision to cut domestic spending across the board. Normally, however, they are immune from such exogenous shocks.

From a constitutional standpoint, the important thing about these policy subgroups is that they operate virtually without reference to the separation of powers. The authorization, appropriation, and administrative processes are of a piece, dominated by the same considerations, if not the same people. The administrative bureau is responsive to the same forces that operate in the legislative arena. When the party that controls the White House is different from the one that dominates on Capitol Hill, the coalition that administers a program may be organized differently from the one that passed the legislation and appropriated the funds, and the difference may result in an about-face. This is no less a perversion from the standpoint of the framers' doctrine. What the framers sought was decisive, objective administration of the law once enacted and until amended or repealed. What we get is a continuous political process.

Given the shift of initiation and discretion in modern times from the legislative to the executive branch, it may be a good thing that the executive is not free to exercise this discretion without reference to political constraint. The point, however, is that the separation of powers is not operating as the framers intended.

This brings me to the second respect in which the current operation of the separation of powers violates enduring constitutional values. According to Madison's exposition in *Federalist* No. 51, the complexity of the constitutional system was intended to make innovation difficult and thus to prevent the quick adoption of unwise schemes. It was a conservative strategy, designed to block new departures until there was a broad consensus that they were needed and well conceived. The framers were leery of the tendency of governments to attempt too much, both in domestic engineering and in imperial adventures. They thought government should be lean in its structure and modest in its ambitions; so they created a government that would subject ambitious schemes to close scrutiny and offer abundant opportunity for skeptics to show that proposals were flawed or ill advised or contrary to the public interest. The structure they created was full of opportunities for vetoes.

The irony is that this structure now operates to protect a bloated government. Just as it was extremely difficult to pass a program of federal aid for health care, it is now virtually impossible to enact reforms to "contain" the cost of hospitalization. Just as it was perilously difficult to get Congress to prepare for World War II and to agree in 1950 to build military forces to back up our commitments to oppose Communist aggression, it is now almost impossible to impose rationality and efficiency on defense procurement.

The history of policy making in the twentieth century shows a pattern. A need emerges. Groups organize to promote a federal response to that need. Constitutional processes foil those groups for many years. A crisis develops. The electorate finally chooses a president and clear majorities in both houses of Congress with a mandate to meet the need. The stalemate is broken. The president proposes and Congress enacts a sweeping program to meet the need. Then the system settles back into a deadlock that lays an icy grip not only on groups that see other needs but also on those that seek to reshape or terminate existing programs.

Thus, in important respects, the constitutional system no longer operates as the framers intended. It prevents elected officials from framing coherent policy, and it hinders executives from enforcing and implementing the law vigorously and steadily. It deflects the electorate from rendering a coherent judgment on the performance of the government and the promises of the opposition. It encourages administrative and judicial confusion by dividing the will that appoints people as administrators and judges. It induces candidates, the press, and the public to give excessive and inappropriate attention to electoral politics, at the expense of attention that needs to be given to the process of governing.

Why have we survived for two hundred years with such a system? For three reasons: first, because we are a rich and patient nation, able so far to prosper despite gross inefficiency and the neglect of many problems; second, because of innovations (such as regulatory commissions and the legislative veto) of dubious constitutionality; and third, through episodes of presidential "dictatorship."[18] Can we, by these means, continue to survive as a constitutional democracy? Not much longer.

Proposed Revision of Our Constitutional System

In approaching constitutional reform, some people have concluded that, because the commitment to the existing system is so strong and the process of amendment so difficult, it is better to present a small change that would work at least some improvement than to set forth a fundamental revision that seeks to correct all the problems at once.[19]

I conclude otherwise. It is true that the amendment process is daunting, but it is not much more inviting for small changes than for large ones. The Constitution has been amended sixteen times since the Bill of Rights. Eight of the changes deal with the rights of citizens (blacks, women, eighteen-year-olds, and those who make or sell alcoholic beverages). Two of them clarify ambiguities in the powers of Congress (to enact an income tax) and of the judiciary (to entertain suits against states). The six others bear directly on the structure of the government, but four of them are of marginal significance. One provides that candidates for vice president be separately designated; one specifies a time for presidential and congressional terms to begin and provides for the death of a president-elect or vice president-elect before his term begins; one authorizes a nonvoting representative in Congress for the District of Columbia; and one establishes procedures to fill a vacancy in the vice presidency and to replace a disabled president.

These amendments correct flaws in the Constitution, but they do not affect its basic structure. Only two do that: the Seventeenth, which provides for the direct election of senators; and the Twenty-second, which limits a president to two full terms. That there have been only two such changes in almost two hundred years does not encourage the thought that changes of this kind are easy to make, however mild they may seem to their proponents.

Against even this modest record of success must be weighed the history of massive frustration for incremental reformers. Take the electoral college, for example. The need for reform is obvious. Three times the constitutional process has resulted in the election of presidents who failed to win even a plurality of the popular vote. Twelve times electors have voted for candidates other than those to whom they were pledged when voters chose them as electors. It is not hard to imagine circumstances in which such faithless electors might throw the nation into crisis. Yet the electoral process remains unreformed despite decades of strenuous effort and hundreds of proposals offered by such disinterested groups as the American Bar Association and a distinguished panel gathered by the Twentieth Century Fund.

A specific, limited proposal, such as the single, six-year term for presidents, may have a chance of enactment, just as the two-term limit for presidents and the direct election of senators did. But a narrow proposal cannot correct the derangement of our national governance. Is it realistic to expect a single, isolated politician, however long his term and whether he is looking forward to reelection or not, to be able to command support in Congress for his program? A political genius might be able to do that, but if we ever found such a person, would we be happy or wise to limit him or her to a single term? What if the president were not a genius, were in fact incompetent, though not guilty of "Treason, Bribery, or other high Crimes and Misdemeanors"? For six years we would be saddled with such a person. What tensions would build up? What suffering would occur? What dangers? Or—the likeliest case of all—what if he were competent but politically at odds with Congress? What if a stalemate developed between a president who saw the public interest one way and a Congress dominated by people who saw it another way? How would the length of the president's term or the certainty of his retirement affect such a stalemate? We cannot be sure, but it seems as likely to exacerbate the tensions as to relieve them.

Those who say that we ought not to tinker with the system are correct. A constitution is an organic whole. Its parts interact. We cannot change one part without causing other parts to act differently. When the Seventeenth Amendment brought the direct election of senators, the whole party system underwent fundamental change. If a proposed change is profound enough to correct a major problem, it is almost certain to ramify and produce effects in far-flung parts of the system. No one will be wise enough to anticipate all these effects, any more than even the wisest framers accurately predicted how their system would operate. But it behooves us to recognize that we cannot correct fundamental problems by making minor adjustments. If the problems are minor, we ought not to act at all. If they are major, we need to take the whole system into consideration.

Assuming then that the current derangement is fundamental, we need to consider basic revisions in the constitutional structure. We need to remove the obstacles to a stronger, more accountable system of political parties. We need to fortify the representative branch by simplifying its structure and tying it more closely to the executive. We need to provide a way to resolve deadlocks between the branches by referring them to the nation.

The following changes would help to accommodate the traditions of American constitutionalism to the demands of modern governance.

- Abolish the separate House of Representatives and Senate.
- Arrange representation in a unicameral Congress so that each state gets two seats plus an additional seat for each measure of population. In other words, adopt the framers' electoral college compromise for representation in Congress.
- Elect the president and all members of Congress at the same time. Set a limit of (five?) years on their terms of office, but leave them eligible for reelection.
- Provide for the calling of new federal elections by law, that is, by a majority of Congress, with the president's concurrence. In the event of disagreement, allow a two-thirds majority of Congress to call new federal elections without the president's concurrence; and allow the president to call new elections at any time on his own initiative. In any case, provide that elections be held within sixty days of being called, that the president and all members of Congress run for election concurrently, and that a new five-year limit on terms of office begin after each election.
- Allow presidents to appoint members of Congress to administrative offices and to dismiss them from those offices. Provide that appointments to all major offices, including judicial and ambassadorial, be made by the president with the consent of Congress.
- Establish a National Council (or Federal Council) consisting of about one hundred notable persons, who would elect one of their number to serve as chief of state, to issue the call for elections, and to superintend their conduct. The council might serve other useful functions, too, such as the review of certain types of legislation, including a suspensive veto. It might also be a potential source of authority in time of national crisis.

The primary purpose of this rearrangement would be to modify, though not to eliminate, the separation of powers. Vesting legislative authority in a single chamber would simplify the structure, making it easier for the people to locate responsibility. It would also strengthen the legislature in its relations with the executive. The essential purpose of the separation of powers is not to clog the machinery of government but to avoid the concentration of power in one place. It serves liberty not by blocking government but by requiring cooperation. If cooperation ends, one or the other of the participants must be able to bring government to a halt and refer the dispute to the nation.

The rearrangement outlined here preserves an independent executive and legislature. Building on the American tradition of local roots in legislative elections, it retains in Congress an independent body with the means and incentive to oppose a president who departs from the popular will or abuses his trust.

It encourages comity between the branches by the carrot of permitting the president to appoint members of Congress to his cabinet and the stick of allowing either branch to take the government to the nation in the event of an inability to agree on fundamental policies. The framers in 1787 forbade the appointment of legislators to the cabinet for fear that the president would corrupt them by dangling lucrative offices before them. As several framers anticipated, presidents have nevertheless influenced some legislators by offering administrative appointments to their cronies. By eliminating the provision (in Article I, section 6) that prevents legislators from serving in the executive branch, we would open the way for able leaders in Congress to display and develop executive talents, and we would encourage the integration of legislative and administrative approaches to policy.

Bicameralism. One important feature of this rearrangement is that it eliminates bicameralism as we know it. The convention of 1787 was committed to bicameralism, partly for reasons outlined in *Federalist* No. 51, that is, a commitment to structural complexity for its own sake. In the compromise over representation, one chamber (the House) reflected population and the other (the Senate) the states. Several leading framers, particularly Madison, did not want the Senate to represent the states; but others, particularly those from small states like Connecticut and Delaware, saw the states as reserving a measure of sovereignty, and they insisted that the state legislatures choose senators.[20] The Seventeenth Amendment broke the direct connection between state legislatures and the Senate, but a clause in Article V guarantees that no state may be deprived of equal representation in the Senate.

Bicameralism poses a difficult problem for revision. The Senate has always been, and still is, the place of service for many of the nation's ablest political leaders. Next to the presidency, a seat in the Senate is the biggest prize in American politics, and it naturally draws the highest talents. To criticize the role of an upper chamber in a bicameral system may seem to disparage the contribution that senators, and the Senate as a body, make under the current system. (By contrast, the House of Lords was relatively easy to push aside, by playing on class antagonisms and egalitarian sentiments.)

We need to ask, not whether senators and the Senate make a contribution now, but whether, in a different system, those talents and energies might be put to better use. If we eliminated the Senate, how would we preserve the values it contributes? Would there be a place for extended debate? Would foreign policy and presidential appointments be given careful scrutiny? Would the concerns of small states gain a fair hearing?

We should not be sentimental about the contributions of the Senate to our present system. Extended debate sometimes degenerates into filibuster, allowing a small minority to prevent the enactment of legislation backed by a large majority. If we want to give certain groups a veto over public policy, perhaps we could find another way to do it, without inviting contempt for legislative debate.

Senators often use their powers of confirmation of appointments not to insist on high standards but to block personal enemies or to gain places for political allies. These shenanigans, like the poor, will always be with us. They inevitably accompany any system for reviewing public appointments, and they are probably no worse under the constitutional system than under systems, such as those in many states, where a specially elected council must consent to a chief executive's nominees. If, however, we feel that appointments ought to be reviewed by a representative body, there are other ways to do it. We need not keep the Senate for that purpose.

On foreign relations, we certainly need some place where debate about the nation's policies can be forced. The Senate's responsibility in this area derives from its power to confirm ambassadorial appointments and to ratify treaties and from its participation in the congressional power to declare war, to raise military forces, and to appropriate funds. It is these latter powers, which the Senate shares with the House, that give real teeth to the Senate's traditional role in this area. Only rarely does the Senate's unique power to ratify treaties and confirm ambassadors provide the occasion to assert its special role in foreign relations. More typically, that occasion comes when the Senate is considering foreign military assistance or the Senate Foreign Relations Committee is conducting hearings on a controversial executive agreement.

The president's power in foreign relations unquestionably needs to be checked. As many senators themselves have insisted, however, the Senate has not performed this role very effectively in recent years. The "imperial" presidencies of Lyndon Johnson and Richard Nixon careened on for almost a decade, waging war without a declaration, making secret deals that entailed enormous commitments for the nation, conducting espionage and domestic surveillance in the name of national security. Much of this went on without the administration's informing the Senate or even its leaders; often the administration presented the Senate with accomplished facts. In reaction, Congress passed the War Powers Resolution in 1973, but early tests (the *Mayagüez* episode, the attempted rescue of hostages in Iran, the dispatch of marines to Lebanon) made it clear that the president still had the initiative and that the Senate's review, if there was one, often did not come in time to prevent an unwise policy from becoming established. A system that promoted closer collaboration between president and Congress could hardly fail to improve on this record, by inducing broader accountability on foreign policy.

As for the concerns of small states, they would be met in part by the incorporation of the electoral college compromise as the basis of representation in Congress. They would also be served by the deep-seated commitment to federalism, which respects the states as traditional guardians of local culture and agents of distinctive approaches to education, economic development, and personal life style. As for the guarantee in Article V, if thirteen or more states refused to ratify on this ground (or any other), the proposal would die; but if thirty-eight states were persuaded that effective, accountable government required a unicameral legislature, Article V would not prevent the change.

Concurrent Terms for President and Congress. Another major aspect of this rearrangement is the concurrent election of the president and all members of Congress. This feature stands in contrast to the Constitution of 1787. The framers provided that the president, senators, and representatives in Congress serve nonconcurrent terms so that a wind of passionate public opinion blowing at a given moment could not sweep the nation toward disaster. Such a gust might result in the election of a president and a majority in the House, but two-thirds of the Senate would presumably be immune, having been elected earlier. (The judiciary would also be isolated from such a momentary seizure—but I do not propose here to change that.)

Staggered elections have unquestionably been a centrifugal force in national politics. After midterm elections Congress often displays fresh independence of the president, even when he has been able to dominate during his first two years in office. Sometimes, though, the patterns are surprising. Reagan's strong victory in 1980 was accompanied by a Republican victory in the Senate, the chamber that is supposed to resist sudden shifts, but not in the House. Nevertheless, nonconcurrent elections and the differing lengths of terms have often contributed, as intended, to a deadlock between the president and Congress.

Staggered terms inhibit the concerting of policy. That may, at times, prevent errors, but it always frustrates a clear popular verdict on governments and their policies. The question is, If we adopted concurrent elections, would the system have sufficient resistance to the momentary delusions of popular opinion? I think it would. The resistance would come from the deep-rooted traditions of localism in legislative elections. As Willmoore Kendall once pointed out, there are "two majorities" in the system created by the framers in 1787.[21] One, the presidential, focuses on the nation's ideals and its global context, which are relatively abstract considerations in the minds of most voters. The other, the congressional, counts the costs of policy very carefully. Kendall argued that presidential electoral campaigns tend to be plebiscitary; would-be leaders and their campaign organizations manipulate gross images in an effort to attract huge categories of votes. Congressional politics is less grand, more intimate. During campaigns and between them congressmen tend to deal with their districts through the leaders of particular groups. Kendall argues that the framers established these two majorities in national politics deliberately, believing that policy resulting from an accommodation of these two outlooks would be stronger and sounder than policy issuing from either alone.

Kendall saw staggered elections as a crucial device for keeping the president and Congress separate and independent. He was less concerned than I am about the dangers of stalemate and incoherence. Would the distinctive contributions of the presidential and congressional majorities survive the passing of staggered elections? I believe they would, perhaps in a somewhat weakened form but sufficiently for the purposes of liberty and sound policy. This nation is not dominated by a single capital, as Great Britain and France are. Its regions are strongly marked by varying conditions and traditions. The same district can repeatedly give a clear majority to Democratic candidates for president but retain its liberal Republican congressman. A state can vote for a Republican candidate for president but keep its conservative Democratic senator. In a country as diverse as the United States, there is no reason to suppose that the electorate will be so seized by an ideological passion that it will sweep away its traditions of localism in a single swing. Nor will members of Congress or candidates for Congress lack incentive to establish their independence from national trends, where those trends are at variance with local opinion.

Irregular Elections. Another feature of the proposed rearrangement is the provision for calling federal elections at irregular times to break stalemates between the president and Congress. Under present arrangements we are perpetually in the midst of a presidential campaign. Everyone knows when the next presidential election will be and the one after that. In these circumstances there is no way to shorten campaigns or reduce their costs. Prudent politicians will lay their plans many years in advance, lining up advisers, technicians, and financial support, courting favorable attention in the media, focusing as much energy as possible on their campaigns, regardless of the cost to the process of governing. Meanwhile, public attention is distracted from the substance of policy, and party organizations are relegated to marginal roles in preparing electoral campaigns. Candidates, especially those in opposition to the incumbent president, have no choice but to build personal organizations. By the time nominations are made, these personal organizations are so formidable that they can operate without much help from the parties.

If elections occurred irregularly, partisan organizations would have to be ready for them at all times. They would have to develop means of selecting their candidates quickly, and they would have to have their platforms ready at all times, at least in broad outline.

National Council. Let me add a word of explanation about my last proposal, the one calling for a National Council. The American tradition lacks two related elements: a chief of state separate from acting political leaders; and a council of elders, to which politicians and other public notables might retire at the end of their active service and from which they might, on occasion, make useful contributions to the national well-being. This twin problem might be solved by the creation of a National Council, composed of former elected officials (presidents, members of Congress, perhaps governors) and possibly other persons appointed by the government for distinguished national service. Or it might be a Federal Council, with one member chosen by each of the fifty states for a specific, perhaps staggered, term of office. If the council's membership was appropriate, certain types of legislation might be referred to it for review and recommended amendments, with the proviso that the council could not delay the enactment of legislation by more than, say, sixty days (a "suspensive veto"). The council would choose one person from its own members to act as chief of state for a fixed term. This official would call and superintend federal elections when the government directed and provide continuity during the period between governments. Most constitutional governments have such a figure, whether it be a monarch or an elected or appointed president. It is normally a ceremonial office except in circumstances of extreme crisis.

A Parliamentary System? Would this rearrangement give the United States a parliamentary system? No, it would not. The essence of a parliamentary system is that the legislature chooses the chief executive and cabinet or, rather, the nation chooses party members to serve in an assembly and the prevailing party or coalition chooses the executive. In the American system, as framed in 1787 and as it would remain under these rearrangements, the legislature and the executive are both separately and popularly elected.

Parties may, of course, attempt to bridge the separation. That happened between 1808 and 1824 under the Constitution, when congressional caucuses nominated the presidential candidates. The Democrats made another feeble attempt during the 1950s when Paul Butler, the national chairman, tried to organize a council to draw legislative leaders into association with elements of the party that were preparing to draft a platform and nominate candidates for the presidency and vice presidency. Ever since the Jacksonians invented the national convention, however, such attempts at "party government" have been frustrated. The rearrangements proposed here would be more hospitable to party government than the design of 1787, but the persistence of the separation of powers in modified form would still constitute an obstacle. Everything would depend on the skill of political leaders in putting together a slate of candidates for executive and legislative office that could win a national majority.

Conclusion

My attempt here has been to build a revised system of government with American materials. These proposals contain no social engineering, no attempt to import a foreign system and graft it onto this nation. They begin with American political ideals and principles and with American forms of government. Having concluded that the design of 1787 no longer serves those ideals and principles, having determined that the Constitution as framed in 1787 is no longer "adequate to the exigencies of government and the preservation of the Union" (quoting the resolve of Congress that called the convention of 1787 into being), I have proposed a rearrangement of some of its elements. It would retain essential features of the original design: a Bill of Rights; an independent judiciary with powers of judicial review; a separation of executive and legislative branches, rooted in separate constituencies; and a federal system. It would, however, remove a key barrier to cooperation between the political branches by allowing members of Congress to serve in the cabinet. It would permit the retention of the traditional legislative committees but simplify the structure of Congress. It would retain the traditional way of allocating weight in the electoral process for the presidency (although the role of electors might well be eliminated, and we might need to devise a way to resolve situations in which no candidate for president wins a majority of the electoral votes).

Perhaps the most radical departure from the design of 1787, apart from the unicameral legislature, is the provision for calling irregular federal elections. I make this suggestion to deal with the tendency of the government to fall into stalemate, particularly during the last two years of a president's term, and to induce more harmonious, cooperative relations between the president and Congress.[22]

Under present arrangements, when the president and Congress are politically estranged, presidents are sorely tempted to govern autocratically. Until a four-year term has run its course, decisions must be made, the bureaucracy must be guided, and foreign relations must proceed whether the president and Congress are working harmoniously or not. There is no way to resolve stalemates, no matter how deeply antagonistic the political branches may be, and no way to remove a discredited administration. Even impeachment only removes one leader, and he must be proved guilty of a gross crime. Otherwise he is secure in office, no matter how incompetent he may be or how alienated from Congress or the prevailing temper of the nation.

The other advantage of irregularly timed elections is that they might greatly shorten the time devoted to electioneering. In fact, they offer the only way to control the length of campaigns, short of repealing the First Amendment. In regimes where it is possible for the government to call elections at any time within a prescribed limit (five years, six years), parties must be in a continual state of readiness, so far as possible, but they cannot gear their operations toward specific target dates. In consequence, they tend to have regular conferences for renewing their platforms and to have strong central coordinating committees and strong district committees, which can mobilize quickly for an election. The parties in such regimes are not always strong. They can be riven by factionalism and doctrinal disputes, just as parties are in America from time to time. But there is a strong incentive for political energy to flow toward getting a party ready for a short campaign, rather than grooming personal candidacies for a long campaign.

I began by citing several problems—the absence of an industrial policy, illegal immigration, the arms race, the deficit—which our constitutional system seems unable to solve. I traced this impasse to the fact that the system was designed in and for less demanding times and argued that a simpler, more integrated system would be both more effective and more accountable. Would the changes proposed produce sound policy? Not necessarily. That would depend on the wisdom and skill of our leaders and the health of our culture. What they would do is to remove the excessive obstacles to coherent policy and improve the chance that the electorate could empower a government and hold it accountable for its actions.

It is time to renew the American experiment in constitutional democracy. Its development has been fitful in recent years, as Congress and successive administrations have sought ways to adjust the existing structure and processes to the incessant demands of modernity and as the Supreme Court has groped for reasons for deciding which accommodations are sufficiently in accord with the framers' design and which are not. Despite these creative and dedicated efforts, the feeling has grown that we have lost our way, that our institutions no longer serve the principles that we share with the founding generation. The proposals set forth here are imperfect. They may be thought too timid or too radical as the nation comes to understand its situation and its needs. But if they are seen as arising out of the American tradition and as moving in the direction of a system of government that is both effective and kept accountable to the popular will, perhaps other minds or, even better, the collective mind of the American people will deem them worthy of criticism and improvement.

Notes

1. Note the exchange between Roger Sherman and James Madison early in the federal convention (June 6, 1787). Sherman would have restricted the federal government to national defense and foreign relations; Madison thought it must also protect private rights and establish justice. It is not clear exactly what Madison meant, but in *Federalist* No. 10 he argues that the primary object of modern legislation is the regulation of commerce. Thus the list of powers in Article I, sec. 8, probably reflects Madison's concept fairly closely. But see also his motion on August 18, 1787, to give Congress power to "establish an University." The motion was defeated on September 14, partly on Gouverneur Morris's argument that it was not necessary, being encompassed in the power of Congress over the seat of government.

2. Indeed, many (Hamilton, Gouverneur Morris, John Rutledge) were impatient to spur the nation into greater involvement with the cosmopolitan world. Others—Elbridge Gerry, Edmund Randolph, and George Mason, as well as Thomas Jefferson, watching from Paris—were more apprehensive

about this imperial impulse, but they were dissenters, not prime movers, in the constitutional revolution of 1787.

3. See the 1980 Republican platform, *Congressional Quarterly Almanac* (1980), pp. 58B–84B.

4. Richard Neustadt, *Presidential Power* (New York: John Wiley, 1960), p. 33.

5. I have borrowed this term from Edward S. Corwin. In an essay published in 1948, he warned that since 1917, through two world wars and a severe economic crisis, revolutionary changes had occurred in the powers of government but the effect of those changes on the structure of government had been slight. See "Our Constitutional Revolution and How to Round It Out," reprinted in *Presidential Power and the Constitution: Essays by Edward S. Corwin*, ed. Richard Loss (Ithaca, N.Y.: Cornell University Press, 1976), pp. 157–77. He concluded that "unless we are prepared to forego altogether the values of constitutionalism, we need to give some deliberate attention to that element of the Constitution which has remained relatively unresponsive to crisis; I mean the structural element."

6. The review that follows is drawn from two decades of study, and it is neither possible nor necessary to cite sources for each assertion. The best recent summary of these developments is James L. Sundquist, *The Decline and Resurgence of Congress* (Washington, D.C.: Brookings Institution, 1981). Sundquist's book is comprehensive and gracefully written, and I found it utterly convincing.

7. Clinton Rossiter, *Constitutional Dictatorship: Crisis Government in the Modern Democracies* (New York: Harcourt, Brace and World, 1948), p. 318; cf. pp. 224–30.

8. In fact, as Corwin insists, the great constitutional transformation we associate with Franklin Roosevelt's presidency began not in 1940 but in 1933.

9. Humphrey's Executor (Rathbun) vs. United States, 295 U.S. 602 (1935).

10. Curiously, the initial impulse for the preparation of a comprehensive government budget does not seem to have owed much to concern for fiscal policy as such. Public finance was still a primitive science. No one seems to have anticipated the effect that government spending was beginning to have on the economy as a whole.

11. Sundquist, *Decline and Resurgence*, pp. 130–40.

12. Robert H. LaFollette, quoted from *Congressional Record*, August 22, 1921, pp. 5415–21, in Sundquist, *Decline and Resurgence*, p. 132.

13. Some observers argue that another factor militating against broad congressional policy making is that the legislative time span is short. Members of the House serve just two years, senators six. The short House term, especially, tends to dictate a shortened horizon for Congress. Members thinking about reelection need a record that will bear fruit quickly. But, to only a slightly lesser degree, so do presidents. A minor but telling example: it was very difficult to get President Carter to think about the bicentennial of the U.S. Constitution. First elected in 1976 and hoping for reelection in 1980, he knew that he would not be president in 1987. I doubt that the differing length of terms contributes much to presidential dominance.

14. Donald Robinson, "If the Senate Democrats Want Leadership: An Analysis of the History and Prospects of the Majority Policy Committee," in *Policy-making Role of Leadership in the Senate*, papers prepared for the Commission on the Operation of the Senate, 94th Congress, 2d session, pp. 40–57.

15. Sundquist, *Decline and Resurgence*, p. 436.

16. Cf. Madison's speeches on August 7 and August 31 at the federal convention; his argument in *Federalist* No. 51 that a dependence on the people is the primary control on government; and his contention in No. 63 that the "cool and deliberate sense of the community" must ultimately prevail in all free governments over the views of its rulers. Cf. also Hamilton, on September 8 at the federal convention; and in *Federalist* No. 71, where he argues that the deliberate sense of the community must govern the conduct of officials. The best exposition of this point is Martin Diamond's classic essay "Democracy and *The Federalist*: A Reconsideration of the Framers' Intent,"*American Political Science Review*, vol. 53 (March 1959), pp. 52–68.

17. See Gordon Wood, *The Creation of the American Republic, 1776-1787* (New York: W. W. Norton, 1972), chap. 13.

18. See Rossiter's discerning analysis, in *Constitutional Dictatorship*, pt. 4.

19. U.S. Congress, Joint Economic Committee, *Hearings on Political Economy and Constitutional Reform*, 97th Congress, 2d session, November 1982, pt. 1, p. xi.

20. As late as August 7, 1787, Madison seems still to have wished that the Senate might somehow represent property rather than the states.

21. Willmoore Kendall, "The Two Majorities," *Midwest Journal of Political Science*, vol. 4, no. 4 (November 1960), pp. 317–45.

22. Two recent studies of American governance lay heavy stress on the need for cooperation between the president and Congress to make the Constitution work. The Price-Siciliano panel of the National Academy of Public Administration calls it "collaboration" (*A Presidency for the 1980s*, published in November 1980), p. 4; Arthur M. Schlesinger, Jr., in *The Imperial Presidency* (New York: Houghton Mifflin, 1973), calls for "the restoration of comity" (chap. 9).

4

The Separation of Powers and Modern Forms of Democratic Government

William B. Gwyn

To enquire, as some have done in this country in recent years, Does the separation of powers still work? is to ask one or more of three distinct but related questions. (1) Is the prescriptive doctrine of governmental organization associated with the expression, which was developed during the seventeenth and eighteenth centuries, universally valid? (2) Is the doctrine manifested in the major forms of modern representative democracy, and have its effects been beneficial or detrimental? (3) Is the doctrine reflected in the operations of actual governmental systems, and to what effect? There are difficulties in evaluating what is commonly called the separation of powers at each of these levels of analysis, and a fully adequate analysis at each level requires consideration of the other levels as well. This essay is concerned with all three. Its treatment of the third focuses on the government of the United Kingdom, which is frequently said not to incorporate the separation of powers.

The Validity of the Separation of Powers Doctrine

The separation of powers is a rather late addition to a body of organizational prescriptions articulated over the centuries by Western political writers as necessary to achieve or protect certain important values. The entire intellectual tradition, usually referred to as constitutionalism, is a broad one concerned not only with prescribing governmental arrangements but also with revealing the social, cultural, and economic prerequisites for their success. Although constitutionalists do seem to have been more concerned with protecting people against government than with the success of government in attaining societal goals, governmental efficiency has not been wholly neglected. The authors of *The Federalist*, the greatest work of American constitutionalism, were certainly equally concerned with achieving a government both safe and efficient. The constitutionalist goal, according to Alexander Hamilton, was "that happy mean, which . . . combines the energy of government with the security of private rights."[1] Similarly James Madison stressed the necessity of "combining the requisite stability and energy in Government, with the inviolable attention due to liberty, and to the Republican form."[2]

Positively, the goal of constitutionalism has historically been referred to as "liberty," "the public interest," "the common good," or "the rule of law." All these words refer to various aspects of a single objective. Government should be constituted so as to maximize the protection of members of society from one another and from other civil societies while minimizing opportunities for government itself to harm its citizens. Men should be free to live as they like as long as they do not act immorally or hurt others; their persons and property should be interfered with only when known legal rules require interference to protect a common interest in which they share. This was a time when the role of government was mostly confined to that of night watchman, but it is not difficult to see how constitutionalist ideas might be modified to take into account the much broader role of government in the twentieth century.

Negatively, the goal of constitutionalism has mainly been the avoidance of "tyranny," which in this context meant a grave abuse of governmental power by rulers pursuing their own interest at the expense of the life, liberty, and property of the governed. Tyranny is not inefficient government, for the tyrant may be very efficient in exploiting his subjects for his own benefit. It is corrupt government in the sense that tyrannical rulers attempt to maximize their own interests to the detriment of other members of the society in which they live.

All constitutionalist prescriptions are influenced by a view of human nature that may be said to range between black and gray. As noted by David Hume, "Political writers have established it as a maxim, that, in contriving any system of government, and fixing the several checks and controuls of the constitution, every man ought to be supposed to be a *knave*, and to have no other end, in all his actions, than private interest."[3] Over two centuries earlier, Machiavelli had made the same point when he wrote, "All those who have written upon civil institutions demonstrate (and history is full of examples to support them) that whosoever desires to found a state and give it laws must start by assuming that all men are bad and ever ready to display their vicious nature, whenever they may find occasion for it."[4] One should note that neither Machiavelli nor Hume says that the writers they refer to believed that all men were depraved or incapable of unselfish behavior but rather that they believed it wise to make such an assumption when designing governmental institutions. Some men may be capable of great sacrifice for the public interest, but partiality to oneself and the groups with which one identifies oneself occurs so frequently in human experience that it would be foolish to ignore it in arranging governmental institutions. In legal terms this maxim, which I shall term the partiality principle, requires the rule of "natural justice" that a man should not be allowed to be the judge in his own case.

All constitutionalists have believed that arbitrary power (that is, unlimited government) will be abused. Many drew this conclusion from an extremely dark conception of human nature and would agree with Thomas Gordon and John Trenchard that "of all the passions which belong to human Nature, Self-love is the strongest."[5] Some constitutionalists, such as Hamilton and Madison, have recognized that benevolence and altruism may often outweigh self-love in determining behavior, but they have nevertheless argued for limited government because, as Madison put it in *Federalist* No. 51, men are not angels. Abuse of unrestrained power might not occur at all times as Gordon and Trenchard were inclined to believe; but it would, given the imperfection of men, occur sometimes, and that is reason enough to place effective limits on it.

The aim of constitutionalists has been to arrange political institutions and influence the conduct of both citizens and governors by fundamental laws so as to prevent, as far as possible, self-love from frustrating the achievement of the common good. The major means has been, in Harrington's famous phrase, "the empire of laws and not of men." Both governors and the governed are subject to just legal rules providing for the common interest and civil liberty. Civil liberty (Montesquieu's "political liberty") meant being restrained only by laws that, by minimizing opportunities for the abuse of governmental authority, allow people to live with a feeling of security. Montesquieu summed up this aspect of constitutionalism when he wrote, "The political liberty of the subject is a tranquility of mind arising from the opinion each person has of his safety. In order to have his liberty, it is requisite the government be so constituted as one man need not be afraid of another."[6]

How can the likelihood of the law's incorporating the common interest be maximized? The constitutionalist tradition out of which the separation of powers doctrine developed concluded that an assembly elected by "the people"[7] must either make or consent to the laws. If the law has been made in the common interest, the problem still remains of guaranteeing that those administering the government will obey it. The solution, according to seventeenth- and eighteenth-century English constitutionalists, was to have the legislature call delinquent officials to account through the impeachment process.

The separation of powers doctrine can be understood only in light of the constitutionalist tradition described above. The doctrine was first articulated in England during the troubled middle years of the seventeenth century. Its early formulations usually spoke of only two governmental "powers," legislative and executive, the latter referring to what were later to be usually distinguished as executive and judicial powers. Only when the independence of the judiciary was seen as threatened by a monarch was it necessary to distinguish between the functions of judges and those of the chief executive. The need for the separate exercise of executive and judicial functions was recognized in England as early as the fifteenth century, but not until the middle of the eighteenth century and Montesquieu's famous restatement of the English doctrine was it joined with the seventeenth-century insistence on a separation of legislative and executive (including judicial) functions.

Assessing the validity of the separation of powers doctrine is rendered more difficult by the fact that during the century after the first appearance of the doctrine, five versions of it were articulated. Four of these were concerned with achieving liberty and the common interest, the fifth with governmental efficiency.[8]

1. *The rule-of-law version.* As a guarantee of the rule of law, those who make the law should not also judge or punish violations of it. If those who execute the laws also make them, they are in effect unbound by them, and the evils caused by human partiality will follow. This version of the doctrine is the purest in the sense that it is meaningless except in the distinction between making law and applying the law. "Law" in this context is not what students of jurisprudence call "particular laws" (commands enforced by the courts referring to a particular person, place, or thing) but general rules of behavior. The principle of the rule of law, as understood by at least some theorists of the separation of powers (such as Locke), does not require that executive officials possess no discretionary power or have no power to make legal rules or orders themselves. What is required is that discretionary actions be taken and legal rules made by the executive within limits set by more general known laws made by a legislature not subject to the will of the executive.[9]

2. *The accountability version.* Frequently accompanying the rule-of-law version was the proposition that if the legislature was to perform its function of calling delinquent governmental officials to account, those officials should not dominate the legislature. If they were allowed to do so, they would judge their own cases. Englishmen making this argument were thinking of their country's experience with legislative impeachments and failed to consider that institutions other than a legislative assembly might perform the function of punishing or removing from office officials who had abused their authority. In this sense accountability requires not the independence of the legislature from the executive but the independence of whatever institution performs the accountability function. In all modern forms of democratic government, elected legislative assemblies do indeed take a part in exercising that function; but so do the courts, in some countries ombudsmen, and, most important of all, the electorate.

3. *The common interest version.* Occasionally during the late seventeenth and early eighteenth centuries, Englishmen argued that if civil and military officers were allowed to be members of the legislative assembly, they would form a faction there that would pursue its own rather than the common interest. This proposition is part of a larger argument, usually rejected in our own century, that a legislative assembly will not achieve the common interest if it is composed of groups each pursuing its own interests. Today, decisions arising out of bargaining and compromising among groups with conflicting interests are seen by pluralists as often being in the common interest; however, even they would oppose the idea of a legislature in which a single group is able to determine decisions or have a greatly disproportionate influence to the distress of other groups in society. To this extent, the common interest version of the separation of powers seems to be universally valid.

4. *The balancing version.* The balancing version of the separation was very much influenced in its origins by the distinctly different English theory of the mixed constitution, which gave supreme legislative power jointly to the monarch, the House of Commons, and the House of Lords. In this theory checks and balances take place within a tripartite legislature. The perception of the royal veto not as participation in legislation but as an executive check on it, joined with recognition of the legislature's ability to call executive officers to account and to raise taxes and appropriate money for their support, led to a balancing version of the separation of powers in which the legislative, executive, and (later) the judicial branches of government are seen as each empowered to check the exercise of the primary function of the others. It is this version that most people in this century seem to have

in mind when they refer to the separation of powers and often criticize it for reducing governmental effectiveness and accountability. The balancing argument did not become common until the eighteenth century and was unacceptable to seventeenth-century English republican exponents of other versions of the separation of powers, who rejected the idea of an executive officer empowered to veto laws enacted by the people's representatives. Only after Americans devised the idea of electing the chief executive as well as the legislature was republican thought able to accommodate the idea of the executive checking the legislature. In judging the validity of the separation of powers, it is important to realize that one may criticize or reject the balancing version while accepting other versions as valid.

5. *The efficiency version.* Ironically, the separation of powers, which has so often been criticized during the past century for reducing governmental effectiveness, was often advocated during the seventeenth and eighteenth centuries for increasing it. The efficiency version was based on the assumption that, to preserve liberty and the public interest, a large representative assembly was required to make or consent to legislation. It was then argued that such an assembly because of its very size could not execute the laws with necessary "secrecy and dispatch" and that a much smaller organization was therefore required to perform the executive function. This version of the doctrine was initially popular in England during the mid-seventeenth century, when the Long Parliament attempted to exercise executive functions, and flourished again for the same reason in North America among such critics of government under the Articles of Confederation as John Adams, John Jay, Thomas Jefferson, James Madison, George Washington, and James Wilson.[10]

In judging the validity of the separation of powers doctrine, it is important to remember that it was never intended as a complete prescriptive theory for safe and effective government. Of the five reasons that have historically been given for requiring the legislative, executive, and judicial functions of government not to be exercised by the same people, four are compatible with and complementary to one another. The accountability and balancing versions, though not compatible, are both concerned with the need for some sort of checking mechanism within government. Four versions aim directly at providing a governmental organization that will reduce the likelihood that public officeholders will exercise their authority in their own interest to the great harm of other members of society. The separation of powers is not, however, the only organizational means for achieving this aim. Intragovernmental limitations can also be provided by dividing the functional branches of government. Those members of the Philadelphia convention who perceived the legislature as the most powerful branch of government believed bicameralism to be of great importance as an internal check on Congress. Today, in fact if not always recognized in theory, the executive branch of democratic governments is also divided between two partially independent sectors—the party political executives and senior career civil servants.[11]

The separation of powers is concerned only with prescribing certain aspects of the internal organization of government. Also of great importance are external limitations on the exercise of governmental power. In Madison's view such intragovernmental arrangements as the separation of powers and bicameralism were "auxiliary precautions," while "a dependence on the people is no doubt the primary controul on the government."[12] He was referring, of course, to republicanism, which requires that at reasonably short intervals the adult population of the political community be able directly or indirectly to choose the membership of the legislative assembly and the major officers of the executive branch. In this century, besides the electorate, organized interest groups through institutionalized quasi-corporative arrangements have come to be another significant extra-governmental check on government.

As for the effectiveness of government in attaining its proper objectives, the separation of powers in its efficiency version is concerned with only one aspect of this large and important subject. Above all we must recognize that neither the separation of powers nor any other constitutionalist doctrines can produce a government capable of consistently making and implementing policies that achieve their objectives. Policy success depends upon too many other factors besides government organization, such as knowledge of solutions to public problems, the quality of political leadership, and the reaction of mass and elite opinion to policy proposals.

Most controversy about the separation of powers has centered, not on the proposition that all government power should not be concentrated in the hands of one person or group of persons, but on the question of what governmental arrangements will or will not satisfy the requirement. From the doctrine's beginnings in the seventeenth century, people have differed strongly over this question. Republican purists of the interregnum rejected the balancing version on the ground that the executive should not be allowed to prevent the people's assembly from having its way. The executive in the proposed Leveller constitutions was elected by the legislative assembly and was clearly inferior to it. Hence the accountability version was acceptable while the balancing one was not. The authors of some of the first state

71

constitutions adopted at the time of the American Revolution held similar views. In 1787–1788 the new Constitution of the United States was attacked by its opponents for violating the separation of powers and extolled by its supporters for manifesting it so perfectly. At least one provision of the Constitution would have been a violation of the doctrine in the eyes of Montesquieu: any governmental system in which the chief executive could be accused and tried by the legislature was "une république non libre."[13] About the same time that Hamilton and others were arguing that judicial review of acts of Congress was implied in the new Constitution and consistent with the separation of powers, in France men were rejecting judicial review for violating the doctrine, which was, however, evoked in support of a system of administrative courts separate from the regular judiciary.[14]

For the past century, there has been much more agreement in the English-speaking world about the institutional arrangements satisfying the separation of powers. Scholars and publicists have come to perceive American presidential government as the fullest embodiment of the doctrine. Parliamentary government, however, which was first established in Britain, is frequently described as fusing or concentrating governmental power in contradiction of the doctrine. If this description is correct, unless we are prepared to say that the citizens of Western European countries with parliamentary systems are living under tyranny without freedom and security (which clearly is not true), then the separation of powers doctrine is not universally valid. In the next section of this essay I consider the major forms of representative government in the contemporary world to determine whether they are compatible with the separation of powers.

The Presidential, Parliamentary, and Assembly Forms of Government

For well over a century writers on government have commonly distinguished among certain major forms, or types, of representative government. Until the Russian Revolution they limited themselves to two forms—parliamentary and presidential—but since then at least some taxonomists have recognized a third, assembly government. It has long been understood that not all actual representative governments (for example, the Swiss) fit these categories, and the French Fifth Republic has alerted us to the existence of hybrids, of which there are far more, concentrated in the third world, than is commonly known. The threefold classification has been abstracted from historical experience; each form has a prototype created in one country, which then became an influence elsewhere.

What has variously been called "parliamentary," "cabinet," or "responsible" government evolved in Britain during the late eighteenth and early nineteenth centuries and was subsequently influential on the continent when the absolute monarchical form of government was abandoned. Still later European imperialists carried knowledge of parliamentary government to their colonies in other parts of the world.

The prototype of "presidential," or "congressional," government was the national government created in the United States in 1787, which has been very influential in Latin America. More recently personalist authoritarian regimes in black Africa have adopted dominant presidencies while often retaining aspects of the parliamentary systems that had been established at the moment of independence. In Europe, France is a striking example of a country that has added an elected president with considerable authority to a parliamentary system to strengthen executive leadership.

"Assembly," or "convention," government was tried briefly in England during the interregnum, but it was French experience that suggested it to the twentieth century. Ever since the Revolution the French have customarily allowed assemblies elected to provide new constitutions also to govern the country while the constitution is being prepared. The brief, revolutionary Paris Commune of 1870, however, was the immediate inspiration of constitutions providing for assembly government in this century. In *The Civil War in France*, Karl Marx put his imprimatur on assembly government as the proper form for a successful proletarian revolution, and Lenin, after seizing power in Russia, followed his ideological master's lead.[15]

The abstraction of the concepts of presidential, parliamentary, and assembly government from actual historical political systems has led to some differences of opinion about precisely what characteristics should be included in their definitions. Definition has been particularly a problem with parliamentary government; there has been a tendency to include in its definition characteristics of British government that would exclude other governments commonly considered parliamentary. It is frequently stated, for example, that in a parliamentary system members of the cabinet must be members of the legislature, which is true in Britain but forbidden by the constitutions of the Netherlands, Norway, and Luxembourg, which otherwise have parliamentary governments. Some include as a requirement of parliamentary government a dual executive: a monarch or president, who as head of state appoints the head of government, the prime minister. But would anyone seriously contend that Sweden's government is any less parliamentary since the adoption of its new constitution in

1974? That constitution, while retaining a purely ceremonial monarchy, vests the nomination of a new prime minister in the speaker of the legislature, whose nominee must be approved by the legislature.

Rather than cause ourselves taxonomic difficulties by overloading the definitions of the three forms of modern representative government, it is best to accept a classification that distinguishes them along one generally agreed upon dimension. That dimension is the relation between elected assemblies and the head or heads of the executive government. Not surprisingly, the classification has often led to discussions of the relation of the three forms of representative government to the separation of powers doctrine.

Since the classification ignores the judiciary, the degree of the latter's independence from the legislature and the executive is not relevant in applying it. Therefore, even if, as some writers contend, there is no separation of legislative and executive power in parliamentary government, there can be and indeed is throughout Western Europe an independent judiciary. In parliamentary systems with independent judiciaries the separation of powers doctrine is at least partially satisfied. Such a government, in Montesquieu's opinion, provides a moderate degree of "political liberty," though not as much as a system in which all three branches of government are independent of one another.[16]

Presidential Government. Although before the adoption of the United States Constitution there was considerable disagreement about what institutional arrangements were required by the separation of powers, after 1787 the notion became widespread that the form of government prescribed by the Constitution fulfilled the doctrine better than any other. Indeed, for some writers it appeared to be the only type of government to embody the doctrine. As Madison and Hamilton had observed, all that the separation required was (1) that the three powers of government or any two of them not be exercised by the same person or groups of persons and (2) that none of the three branches of government be able to determine the activities of the others. In Madison's words, "It goes no farther than to prohibit any one of the entire departments from exercising the powers of another department. . . . Where the *whole* power of one department is exercised by the same hands which possess the *whole* power of another department, the fundamental principles of a free constitution are subverted."[17] Both men also stressed that the separation should be only partial to allow each branch to exercise some of the powers of the others and thus to check the others from encroaching on it or otherwise gravely abusing their authority.

These principles might justify a variety of governmental forms, but what they soon came to be identified with was the particular form prescribed in the Constitution, which came to be called presidential government. In this type of government the legislature and the executive are considerably more independent of each other than in parliamentary or assembly government. Neither the president, the head of the executive branch, nor the legislature is able to determine the election of the other: both are directly or indirectly elected by popular vote for definite terms of office. Moreover, one may not be a member of both the legislative and executive branches of government at the same time.

Parliamentary Government. Although no one questions that presidential government embodies the separation of powers, it is frequently asserted that parliamentary government does not. Those governments that are called parliamentary share three characteristics: (1) The members of the political executive, often referred to as the government and sometimes (misleadingly) as the cabinet,[18] may hold office only so long as they possess the support, or confidence, of a majority of the members of the elected legislative assembly. Some writers have limited the definition of parliamentary government to this characteristic, but to do so neglects a major difference between it and the assembly form, which is shown in the following rules. (2) If the government loses the confidence of the legislative assembly, it must either resign or dissolve (bring about a new election of) the assembly to determine whether it or the assembly represents the electorate. To include dissolution in the definition is not necessarily to ascribe importance to it in the actual operations of a parliamentary government. The once popular notion that the dissolution power is important for maintaining support for the government in the legislature has been discredited for many years among scholars. Clearly it is not required to maintain a high degree of cohesion among the members of legislative political parties. The constitution of Norway, influenced at its inception in 1814 by the separation of powers doctrine, explicitly denies the executive the power to dissolve the legislature; yet Norwegian legislative parties, operating in what is otherwise a parliamentary system, have been very cohesive. (3) If the government fails to win a majority in the assembly after a dissolution, it has no choice but to resign and allow the formation of a new government that has the confidence of the assembly's majority.

This type of government is often said to reject the separation of powers in favor of a "fusion" or "concentration" of legislative and executive power. Although the concept of parliamentary government does imply that the political executive and the majority of the members of the legislature cannot long be in serious disagreement, that is not to say that they have been fused into a single entity exercising both legislative and executive power. In most but not all existing parliamentary systems, members of the government are also elected, voting members of the legislative assembly to which they are responsible, but they form a relatively small minority of the total membership. In Britain, for example, the law in 1980 limited the number of government ministers who might be members of the House of Commons to ninety-five, or 15 percent of the total membership. If the approximately thirty parliamentary secretaries, who are not ministers but nevertheless serve the government, are also considered, the government can compose 20 percent of the membership of the Commons. These percentages are not insignificant—especially since they are doubled for government members as percentages of a majority of the Commons—but they are still some considerable way from allowing the government to determine the decisions of the legislature.[19] In a parliamentary system, the legislative assembly and the government maintain separate existences, and each, through withdrawal of confidence or dissolution, is able to check the actions of the other. There is thus some separation of legislative and executive power in the parliamentary type of representative government.

Assembly Government. It is the assembly and not the parliamentary form of government that rejects the separation of powers.

> The legislative assembly, popularly elected, holds undisputed supremacy over all other state organs, subject only to the sovereign electorate renewing it at regularly recurrent intervals. In contrast to the dual structure of parliamentary government—which, at least in theory, presupposes two independent power holders, the assembly and the government, with reciprocally matching powers—in assembly government the executive is strictly subordinated, the servant or agent of the assembly and dismissed at the assembly's discretion.[20]

The existence of this type of governmental system in mid-seventeenth-century England prompted some advocates of the rule of law to articulate a version of the separation of powers doctrine. Over two centuries later Karl Marx, impressed by the experience of the Paris Commune, concluded that assembly government was the appropriate form for the dictatorship of the proletariat. "The Commune [elected by universal suffrage for short terms of office] was to be a working, not a parliamentary body, executive and legislative at the same time." In

1917 Lenin quoted Marx on this issue with approval, arguing that a change from parliamentarism to assembly government meant "the conversion of the representative institutions from mere 'talking shops' into working bodies."[21] Ironically, the soviets that the Bolsheviks proceeded to set up in Russia shortly afterward were to become far more purely "talking shops" than any of the Western European bourgeois parliaments.

Although Soviet writers continue to describe their governmental system in terms of the assembly model, since the adoption of the 1936 constitution they have frequently come close to supporting the efficiency version of the separation of powers. According to the most authoritative commentary on the Stalin constitution, the sovereignty of the Supreme Soviet was "not incompatible with limiting the jurisdiction of authority as between separate organs. Such limitation flows out of the extraordinarily complex functions of the Soviet state machinery governing both people and economy." Likewise, a recent commentary on the 1977 Soviet constitution has acknowledged both the "supremacy of Soviets in the system of state organs" and "the objective need for the establishment and implementation of the most powerful and effective division of labour in the discharge of state functions."[22] Thus simple-minded early Marxist ideas about a large elective assembly exercising legislative and executive powers have given way to the realization that no government in a large state can operate with any effectiveness under such conditions.

Whether an actual government is classified as presidential, parliamentary, or assembly tells us something about its constitutional rules but leaves us ignorant of all other aspects of the political system, such as the character of the judiciary and the civil and military bureaucracies, the relationship of territorial levels of government (unitary, federal, or confederal; centralized or decentralized), the electoral system, the political party and interest group systems, and the society's political culture. How one of the three forms of government actually operates in existing political systems is determined by these and other factors. For many years scholars have especially stressed the importance of political parties in determining how the three forms of government operate in the real world. Single, centralized party systems such as those in Communist countries can transform a government in which a single elected assembly is supposed to control or exercise all governmental power into one in which the assembly is little more than a rubber stamp for decisions taken elsewhere. Presidential government is often criticized because the independence of the legislative and executive branches prevents governmental policies from being made; yet in Latin America and Africa dominant personalist parties allow presidents to prevail easily over legislatures and judiciaries.[23]

For over a century much has been written about the effects of various kinds of pluralist party systems and of legislative party cohesion on the operations of parliamentary government. Until after World War II the view prevailed that parliamentary government was effective only when accompanied by a two-party system such as that found in Britain. Multiparty systems cause coalition governments, which were believed to be very unstable. The experience of France and Italy was often cited to illustrate the point. In recent decades awareness of the experience of parliamentary government in Scandinavia and the Low Countries has led to our understanding that moderate multiparty systems made up of internally cohesive parties can produce stable and effective coalition governments. It is a highly fragmented party system with low cohesion at least in the centrist parties—the condition that existed in France in both the Third and the Fourth republics—that causes cabinet instability and policy-making immobility.[24] The weak governments associated with that kind of party system are often contrasted with the strong governments resulting from a party system that produces a cohesive majority party in the legislative assembly. For the past century parliamentary government in Britain has been perceived as being of this latter sort, the prime minister and the cabinet often being described as so dominant over the legislature as to exercise both legislative and executive power. If that is the case, although parliamentary government does not violate the doctrine of the separation of powers, the British version, based on two highly cohesive political parties alternating in controlling the political executive through a majority in the legislature, does. It is to this question of the compatibility of the British parliamentary system with the separation of powers that I now turn.

British Parliamentary Government and the Separation of Powers

"The separation of powers is not part of our constitution," wrote an English scholar a few years ago and in doing so reflected an erroneous opinion widely held both in Britain and in the United States.[25] The error arises from a misunderstanding of the doctrine itself, from semantic problems in describing British government dating back to the nineteenth century, and from mistaken ideas concerning the authority of political party leaders in Britain.

We have seen that the doctrine aims at preventing "tyranny," a grave abuse of authority by government officials who are subject neither to legal rules nor to effective institutional means within the governmental system of making them accountable for their misdeeds.

According to the partiality principle, officials who are not subject to such legal and institutional constraints will be inclined to use their authority to promote their own interests at the expense of other members of society. The goal of the doctrine does not require that executive leaders not exert a very great influence in law making but rather that, if they attempt to use that influence to promote self-interested legislation to the great harm of others, the legislature be independent enough to reject it and bring them to account.

Comparisons of presidential government with parliamentary government in general and the British system in particular frequently assert that while the former incorporates the separation of powers, the latter does not. The major source of this assertion appears to have been Walter Bagehot's *The English Constitution*.[26] The praise for the effectiveness and responsibility of British parliamentary government and the condemnation of the defects of American presidential government found in this little book have directly or indirectly influenced the ideas of generations of British and American scholars. Bagehot's account of what he referred to as "parliamentary" or (more frequently) "cabinet" government has likewise been continually repeated down the years, especially his expression "fusion of powers."

In his opening chapter Bagehot extolled British cabinet government as working "more simply and easily, and better, than any instrument of government that has yet been tried." The cause of this effectiveness was "the close union, the nearly complete fusion of the executive and legislative powers. . . . The connecting link is *the cabinet*. By that new word [hardly!] we mean a committee of the legislative body selected to be the executive body."[27] Later in the same chapter Bagehot dropped the qualifying "nearly" when writing of the relation between legislative and executive power in Britain. "It is a fusion of the two. Either the cabinet legislates and acts, or else it can dissolve. It is a creature, but it has the power of destroying its creator."

Bagehot's use of the word "fusion," his description of the cabinet as "the committee which unites the law-making power to the law-executing power," and his explicit rejection of the separation of powers as a principle of the English constitution convey a very clear impression of British government as one in which legislative and executive authority are concentrated in a single organization, the cabinet. In a later chapter on the "supposed checks and balances" of British government, he distinguished between "simple" and "composite" types of government. In simple government "ultimate power upon all questions is in the hands of the same persons"; in composite government (for example, in the United States), "the supreme power is divided among many bodies and functionaries." Curiously, given the emphasis on the power of the cabinet in chapter 1, supreme authority in Britain's simple government is said by Bagehot to reside in "a newly-elected House of Commons," which on any legislative, administrative, or, indeed, constitutional question "can despotically and finally resolve." Here the cabinet is depicted as dependent on the House of Commons, which "can ensure that its decrees shall be executed, for it, and it alone appoints the executive; it can inflict the most severe of all penalties on neglect, for it can remove the executive."[28] Bagehot probably had in mind that, immediately after a general election, of the mutual checks between the House of Commons and the cabinet (withdrawal of confidence and dissolution), only the Commons's check would be operative. Still, except for this situation, Bagehot in his detailed analysis of British government did recognize that mutual checks existed. He referred to dissolution of the House of Commons as a "check" exercised by the prime minister on Parliament.[29] In the introduction to the second edition, he even wrote of impeachment, long unused in Britain, as a defense against "gross excesses" of the use of royal power by ministers, although he recognized that for "minor mistakes" resulting from "an error of judgement" the constitutional remedy would be the removal of the minister or the entire government through a vote of censure by the House of Commons.[30] Indeed, Bagehot believed that the most important function of the Commons was its indirectly choosing and directly dismissing the cabinet.[31]

Bagehot did, then, recognize some degree of independence between the legislature and the executive in Britain. This becomes even more evident in his perception of the function of political parties in the House of Commons. Parliamentary government was possible only if the legislative assembly was organized by political parties. "Efficiency in an assembly requires a solid mass of votes" behind the party leaders who form the cabinet. Although "the principle of Parliament is obedience to leaders" arising from deference, ideological zeal, and the threat of dissolution, such obedience was "wisely limited." Leaders could "take their followers but a little way, and that only in certain directions."[32] Bagehot opposed "a mechanical majority ready to accept anything." In his opinion parliamentary government could function properly only with a "fair and reasonable" party majority,

> predisposed to think the Government right, but not ready to find it to be so in the face of the facts and in opposition to whatever might occur. . . . The majority of the Legislature being well disposed to the Government, would not "find" against it except it had really committed some big and plain mistake.[33]

The government party in the Commons cannot become a mechanical majority, for when presented with proposals very unpopular with the electorate, "it would rather desert its own leader than ensure its own ruin."[34]

Not many years after 1872, when the second edition of *The English Constitution* was published, students of British government began to assert that the moderate party cohesion favored by Bagehot had given way to the mechanical majority he feared. In 1912, for example, William Sharp McKechnie wrote of the "sweeping changes" that had occurred in the British constitution since the appearance of Bagehot's book. The House of Commons now performed "as an automaton for registering the Cabinet's decrees." This change was explained by party discipline. "The modern House of Commons is no longer made up of free representatives, but of tied delegates, fettered by promises made before election, to which they are forced to adhere by pressure of the party whips."[35] A similar view was taken a few years earlier in a much more influential work, which was to remain in print for the next three decades. According to Sidney Low, the principal change in British politics since 1832 had been "the diminished power and importance of the House of Commons as compared to the ministry [that is, the government] on the one hand and the electorate on the other."[36] The cabinet was no longer controlled by the Commons but by the electorate.

> The House of Commons no longer controls the Executive; on the contrary, the Executive controls the House of Commons. . . . In our modern practice the Cabinet is scarcely ever turned out of office by Parliament *whatever it does.* . . . The real check upon a too gross and salient misuse of Ministerial power is, no doubt, the salutary fear of public opinion; but this is a restraint that would be pretty nearly as operative without the assistance of the House of Commons which does not respond to it except after a general election.[37]

Not only did the cabinet not have to worry about being turned out of office by the Commons, but it also totally dominated the legislative process. "The House is scarcely a legislative chamber; it is a machine for discussing the legislative projects of ministers, and only one among the various instruments by which political discussion in these days is carried on."[38]

Low and McKechnie were articulating an account of British parliamentary government that remains the standard version three quarters of a century later. It is not my intention to take issue with it except insofar as it suggests that the government in Britain literally

81

controls every action of the House of Commons. Although the conventional view does reflect important characteristics of British government, it often exaggerates the control of the cabinet over the Commons and misunderstands the basis for party discipline there. Even A. Lawrence Lowell, in the most carefully and intensively researched work on British politics of the early years of this century, could describe the government's majority in the House of Commons as "well-nigh automatic." Lowell, however, went on to explain that the maintenance of party cohesion required concessions from both the government and its party supporters in the Commons. "It would be a great mistake to suppose that the parliamentary system in England is developing into mere party tyranny. . . . The same forces that lead a member of a party to sacrifice his personal opinions to party necessity lead the cabinet to modify its policy in deference to the protests of a little band of supporters."[39]

The major studies of parliamentary party cohesion and dissension since 1945 bear out this view that the great cohesion of the parties is the result of concessions from both leaders and followers. The parliamentary parties, Robert Jackson has concluded, are vessels "for reconciling diverse interests" through "built-in compromise mechanisms" and "a process of accommodation" by both the leaders and the rank and file. "Most of the time the ideas of those in authority will predominate but at other times the critics will have to be satisfied to some degree or the necessary harmony and unity will be destroyed."[40] Backbench members of the majority party have been inhibited from actually defeating government proposals for fear of destroying their party's control of the executive. During the 1970s the willingness of the members of the government party to vote against cabinet proposals increased when they discovered they could actually defeat them without bringing about a resignation or a dissolution. The major scholarly authority on these developments has noted, "The assumption that MPs vote loyally with their party to the extent that they comprise no more than lobby fodder would appear to have been undermined if not dispelled by the experience of the 1970s." Although even during that period "cohesion remained the norm rather than the exception," a close examination of majority party voting in the Commons reveals "that reserves of party loyalty were not inexhaustible."[41]

Even during the 1970s the British parliamentary parties remained remarkably supportive of their leaders in the government. Today they continue to look to the government for legislative initiatives and for the very most part to accept them. The desire of government backbenchers not to jeopardize their party's control over the political executive as well as their awareness that the prime minister can promote or frustrate their political careers strongly encourages deference to the government. This, however, is not evidence of that total subordination of the majority parliamentary party to the government that would demonstrate the absence of an adequate separation of executive and legislative power in Britain. The evidence, on the contrary, indicates that British governments cannot take for granted the unwavering support of their party followers in Parliament and usually make considerable efforts to persuade and sometimes to compromise with them to maintain party cohesion.

As the experience of Edward Heath demonstrated, a British prime minister who persistently introduces controversial and divisive proposals in the House of Commons without prior consultation with his party's backbenchers and regardless of their anticipated reactions is very likely to suffer defeats on some occasions.[42] Twice during the past century large numbers of government members of Parliament (M.P.s) have been prepared to destroy the unity of their party rather than follow a prime minister whose policies they believed disastrous. On June 8, 1886, ninety-three Liberal M.P.s joined with the Conservatives to destroy William Gladstone's Irish Home Rule Bill along with the Liberal government. In August 1931, when Ramsay MacDonald, who had been prime minister in a minority Labour government, formed a new government in coalition with the Conservative and Liberal parties to deal with the country's economic crisis, he was deserted by all but eight of the Labour backbenchers.[43]

Conclusions

This essay has attempted to establish three conclusions about the separation of powers. First, as a prescriptive theory of certain aspects of the relation between governmental organizations and personnel, it contains elements of universal validity that no country should ignore in arranging its governmental institutions. Since there are other principles of governmental organization of equal or greater importance, however, it does not follow that the greater the degree of independence of the legislative, executive, and judicial branches, the better the governmental system. An attempt to go beyond what is necessary to realize the aims of the doctrine may frustrate the achievement of other values. When the question is raised in the United States, Does the separation of powers still work? what is being asked is not whether the institutional relations of American government continue to satisfy the requirements of the doctrine but whether in doing so they have weakened government in other respects. Second, both the presidential and the parliamentary forms of government theoretically satisfy the requirements of the doctrine, although in actual cases the mutual independence of the three branches of government can be totally subverted through the operations of other institutions such as political parties or the armed forces. Third, despite frequent statements to the contrary, the relation between the House of Commons and the government in the British parliamentary system does satisfy the separation of powers doctrine.

Although this essay has not been concerned directly with the recurring debate in the United States over the alleged deficiencies of the American version of presidential government, it contains some implications that contestants on both sides of the issue might want to bear in mind. Those who advocate a radical change in the U.S. Constitution in the direction of parliamentary government need not worry that they would sacrifice the values protected by the separation of powers in doing so. There may, however, be other good reasons for rejecting such a change. We have seen how the actual operations of governments based on the parliamentary or presidential principles can vary greatly with the character of their political environments. American proponents of parliamentary government have in mind the way they believe it functions in Britain, where governments are supposed to be able to make effective and coherent policies and to be clearly responsible to the electorate for their activities. Such a view ignores the fact that for the past quarter-century the once almost universally admired British governmental arrangements have been strongly criticized on a number of counts, including fragmented and incoherent policy making.[44]

Even if one accepts the rosy perception of British government, however, there is no assurance that a parliamentary constitution would operate in the same way under American conditions. There is, it is true, considerable evidence that a parliamentary form of government, especially when accompanied by two-party competition in the legislature, provides strong incentives for members of legislative parties to vote together. Still, as a major study of party cohesion has noted, historical evidence indicates that "the parliamentary system . . . is neither a necessary nor sufficient condition of absolute party unity."[45] If the American president were made responsible to a Congress the members of which are subject to strong constituency pressures and accustomed to a major role in policy making and relatively weak party loyalty, he could well have more difficulty in carrying through an effective and coherent program than he has now. Rather than the dominant governments of British parliamentarism, we might end up with the weak governments of the pre-1958 French variety.

Because a radical amendment of the Constitution along the lines of parliamentary government might have harmful unintended consequences, such a change should not be contemplated unless it can be demonstrated that serious deficiencies in federal government policy making are the result of the relation between the president and Congress as prescribed in the Constitution. Two other types of explanation for policy failures ought to be pursued fully and carefully before the Constitution is blamed. First, given that economic, social, and environmental policies pursued by the United States are similar in many respects to those pursued by other modern democratic states, some policy failures are probably attributable to circumstances shared by all such states and perhaps other kinds of political systems as well. Common ignorance, common value dilemmas, and common demands from sections of the electorate and organized interest groups can produce common policy defects in countries with different political institutions.

Those favoring the second type of explanation agree with the proponents of radical constitutional change that serious imperfections in American policy making are caused by the country's political institutions but disagree that the major fault lies in the institutions provided by the Constitution. According to Don K. Price, who exemplifies this position:

> The roots of the incoherence of policy which may lead many critics to wish to amend the U.S. Constitution do not come from the Constitution but rather from the unwritten constitution—the fixed political customs that have developed without formal Constitutional amendment, but that have been authorized by statute or frozen, at least temporarily, in tradition.[46]

Price believes that unless changes were made in such institutions as party conventions and primary elections, congressional committees, the structure of executive departments, and the Executive Office of the President, parliamentary government would not work properly in the United States and that if they were made it would not be necessary. It seems likely that a far better understanding of America's public policy failures will be provided by some combination of these two explanations than by an obsession with the separation of powers provisions of the Constitution.

Notes

1. *The Federalist*, ed. Jacob E. Cooke (Cleveland: Meridian Books, 1961), No. 26, p. 164.

2. Ibid., No. 37, p. 233. "Energy in Government is essential to that security against external and internal danger, and to that prompt and salutary execution of the laws, which enter into the very definition of good government." Ibid.

3. David Hume, "On the Independency of Parliament," in *Essays Moral, Political, and Literary by David Hume*, ed. T. H. Green and T. H. Grose (London: Longmans, Green, 1882), vol. 1, pp. 117–18.

4. Niccolo Machiavelli, *Discourses*, in *The Prince and the Discourses*, ed. Max Lerner (New York: Modern Library, 1940), bk. 1, chap. 3, p. 117. Midway in time between Machiavelli and Hume one finds Marchamont Nedham referring to "true Policy: which ever supposeth, that men in Power may be unrighteous; and therefore (presuming the worst) points always, in all determinations, at the Enormities and Remedies of Government, on behalf of the People." *The Excellencie of a Free-State* (London, 1656), p. 212.

5. Thomas Gordon and John Trenchard, *Cato's Letters* (London, 1724), vol. 1, p. 245.

6. Montesquieu, *The Spirit of the Laws*, trans. Thomas Nugent (New York: Hafner, 1949), bk. 11, chap. 6, p. 151.

7. A term that rarely referred even to all adult males until the nineteenth century. See Cecil S. Emden, *The People and the Constitution*, 2d ed. (London: Oxford University Press, 1956), app. 1.

8. The following analysis of the five versions of the doctrine is based on my *The Meaning of the Separation of Powers* (New Orleans: Tulane Studies in Political Science, 1965).

9. See Joseph Raz, "The Rule of Law and Its Virtue," in his *The Authority of Law* (Oxford: Clarendon Press, 1979).

10. Gwyn, *Meaning*, chap. 3; and Louis Fisher, "The Efficiency Side of the Separation of Powers," *American Studies*, vol. 5 (August 1971), pp. 113–31.

11. See Norton Long, "Bureaucracy and Constitutionalism," in his *The Polity* (Chicago: Rand McNally, 1962).

12. *Federalist* No. 51, p. 349.

13. Montesquieu, *Spirit of the Laws*, bk. 11, chap. 6, p. 158. Montesquieu would probably have been no happier with the British parliamentary system: "If . . . the executive power should be committed to a certain number of persons selected from the legislative body, there would be an end then of liberty" (p. 156).

14. For various interpretations of the separation of powers in the late eighteenth and the nineteenth and twentieth centuries, see M. J. C. Vile, *Constitutionalism and the Separation of Powers* (Oxford: Clarendon Press, 1967).

15. Karl Marx, *The Civil War in France*, in *Karl Marx and Friedrich Engels: Writings on the Paris Commune*, ed. Hal Draper (New York: Monthly Review Press, 1971).

16. Montesquieu, *Spirit of the Laws*, bk. 2, chap. 4, and bk. 11, chaps. 4, 5, 6, 7, 11.

17. *Federalist* No. 47, pp. 325–28.

18. The ministers who meet together in the cabinet may, as in Britain,

compose only a small minority of the total number of ministers in the government.

19. The situation in Britain is very different from that in some of the authoritarian governments of Africa, where government ministers have been a majority or near majority in the legislature; for example, 49 percent of the Zambian legislature in 1970 and 52 percent of the Western Nigerian legislature in 1965. B. N. Nwabueze, *Presidentialism in Commonwealth Africa* (New York: St. Martins Press, 1974), p. 276.

20. Karl Lowenstein, *Political Power and the Governmental Process* (Chicago: University of Chicago Press, 1957), p. 81. Douglas V. Verney has similarly contrasted parliamentary and assembly government: "Even the limited separation of powers customary in parliamentary systems is absent, power being concentrated in the assembly. There is no separate executive." *The Analysis of Political Systems* (Glencoe, Ill.: Free Press, 1959), p. 58.

21. Marx, *Civil War in France*, p. 73; and V. I. Lenin, *State and Revolution* (New York: International Publishers, 1932), chap. 3, secs. 2, 3. In the influential 1938 commentary on the Soviet Constitution edited by Andre Vyshinsky, it was argued, following Lenin's line of thinking, that "not 'separation of powers' but predominance of executive power characterizes the organization of the state governments of capitalist countries" and that the separation of powers was included in capitalist constitutions to hoodwink the masses. *The Law of the Soviet State* (New York: Macmillan, 1951), p. 314.

22. Vyshinsky, *Law of the Soviet State*, p. 318; and Boris Topornin, *The New Constitution of the USSR* (Moscow: Progress Publishers, 1980), pp. 40–41. Article 31 of the 1936 constitution explicitly precluded the Supreme Soviet from exercising authority that the constitution had vested in organizations "accountable" to the assembly, that is, the Presidium of the Supreme Soviet, the Council of Ministers, and the ministries. For an excellent Western account of Soviet constitutional development, see Aryeh L. Unger, *Constitutional Development in the USSR* (London: Methuen, 1981).

23. J. Lloyd Mecham, "Latin American Constitutions: Nominal and Real," *Journal of Politics*, vol. 21 (May 1959), pp. 258–75; Nwabueze, *Presidentialism in Commonwealth Africa*; and Earnest Hamburger, "Constitutional Thought and Aims in Former French Africa," *Social Research*, vol. 28 (Winter 1961), pp. 415–36.

24. Maurice Duverger, *The French Political System* (Chicago: University of Chicago Press, 1958), pp. 186–90; and Philip Williams, *Politics in Post-War France*, 2d ed. (London: Longmans, 1958), p. 190. More generally, see Michael Taylor and V. M. Herman, "Party Systems and Government Stability," *American Political Science Review*, vol. 65 (March 1971), pp. 28–37.

25. David Foulkes, *Introduction to Administrative Law*, 2d ed. (London: Butterworths, 1968), p. 196. Two important students of constitutionalist thought have recognized this error and argued that contemporary British government is compatible with the separation of powers doctrine. Vile, *Constitutionalism*, pp. 321–24; and John Plamenatz, *Man and Society* (New York: McGraw-Hill, 1963), vol. 1, pp. 289–91.

26. Walter Bagehot, *The English Constitution* (London: Oxford University Press, 1928). Published as a series of articles in *The Fortnightly Review* in 1865, the work appeared as a book in 1867, with a new edition in 1872. Bagehot's claim to originality in discovering cabinet government has been exploded by Vile, *Constitutionalism*, chap. 8.

27. The cabinet in Britain is not in any strict sense of the term a committee of the legislature. Its members are chosen by the prime minister, who is appointed by the monarch as a person having the confidence of a majority of the members of the House of Commons.

28. Bagehot, *The English Constitution*, p. 201.

29. Ibid., p. 215.

30. Ibid., pp. 285–86.

31. Ibid., p. 101. He had reason for doing so. Between 1832 and 1868 governments lost the confidence of the House of Commons on thirteen occasions. Before 1832 and after 1868 governments were rarely overthrown by the Commons.

32. Ibid., pp. 124–26.

33. Ibid., p. 287.

34. Ibid., p. 288.

35. William Sharp McKechnie, *The New Democracy and the Constitution* (London: John Murray, 1912), pp. 62, 71, 30. Talk of the House of Commons falling under the control of the cabinet and the prime minister was current in England as early as the first half of the 1880s. See James Bryce, "Flexible and Rigid Constitutions," in his *Studies in History and Jurisprudence* (New York: Oxford University Press, 1901), pp. 150–51. The essay was originally written in 1884.

36. Sidney Low, *The Governance of England*, rev. ed. (London: Ernest Benn, 1914), p. 54. First published in 1904, the book was reprinted fourteen times by 1931.

37. Ibid., p. 81.

38. Ibid., pp. 75–76.

39. A. Lawrence Lowell, *The Government of England*, rev. ed. (New York: Macmillan, 1909), vol. 1, p. 326; vol. 2, pp. 95–96.

40. Robert J. Jackson, *Rebels and Whips* (London: Macmillan, 1968), pp. 308–9.

41. Philip Norton, *Dissension in the House of Commons, 1974–79* (Oxford: Clarendon Press, 1980), p. 458. Rebellions by Conservative M.P.s resulted in the Heath government's being defeated six times by the House of Commons in 1972–1974. Norton attributes twenty-three defeats of the Labour governments of 1974–1979 to Labour backbenchers. See also John E. Swarz, "Exploring a New Role in Policy Making: The British House of Commons in the 1970s," *American Political Science Review*, vol. 74 (March 1980), pp. 23–37. Rightly cautioning against exaggerating the changes of the 1970s is Richard Rose, "Still the Era of Party Government," *Parliamentary Affairs*, vol. 36 (Summer 1983), pp. 282–99. A questionnaire given to M.P.s in 1984 asked them to respond to the statement, "I would never vote against my Party on a three line whip." A three-line whip is a communication from the party leadership to its

parliamentary rank and file informing them that a matter coming up for a vote is of the greatest importance. Of the M.P.s responding (50 percent), only 20 percent of the Labour M.P.s, 5 percent of the Conservative M.P.s, and none of the Alliance M.P.s agreed with the statement. Jorgen Rasmussen, "From the Horse's Mouth," *British Politics Group Newsletter* (Spring 1985), p. 17.

42. Heath's autocratic style of leadership and its effect on Conservative backbenchers are examined at length in Philip Norton, *Conservative Dissidents* (London: Temple Smith, 1978).

43. In May 1941 dissident government supporters helped to drive from office Neville Chamberlain, although they did not cause a government defeat in the House of Commons. At the end of the debate on the failed Norwegian campaign, forty-one government supporters (including thirty-three Conservative M.P.s) voted with the opposition, and sixty more abstained.

44. In a recent book by the members of the University of Essex Department of Government, British government is stated to be inferior to the parliamentary systems of France, West Germany, and Japan with respect to making effective and coherent policies. This defect is explained by "fragmented centres of power and lack of central coordination." What the authors have done is to look beyond the cabinet's relation to the legislature to observe its weakness when confronted by other centers of political power. Ian Budge, David McKay, et al., *The New British Political System* (London: Longman, 1983), chap. 9. For the variety of criticisms of British government since 1960, especially for not dealing adequately with the country's economic problems, see my "Jeremiahs and Pragmatists: Perceptions of the British Decline," in William B. Gwyn and Richard Rose, eds., *Britain: Progress and Decline* (London: Macmillan, 1980).

45. Julius Turner and Edward V. Schneier, Jr., *Party and Constituency: Pressures on Congress* (Baltimore: Johns Hopkins University Press, 1970), p. 29. For the relationship between parliamentary government and legislative party cohesion, see Leon D. Epstein, "Political Parties," in Fred I. Greenstein and Nelson W. Polsby, eds., *Handbook of Political Science* (Reading, Mass.: Addison-Wesley, 1975), vol. 4, pp. 263–66; Ergun Ozbudun, *Party Cohesion in Western Democracies* (Beverly Hills, Calif.: Sage, 1970); and Robert Harmel and Kenneth Janda, *Parties and Their Environments: Limits to Reform?* (New York: Longman, 1982), chap. 6.

46. Don K. Price, *America's Unwritten Constitution* (Baton Rouge: Louisiana State University Press, 1983), p. 9.

5

The Separation of Powers
Needs Major Revision

Charles M. Hardin

The subject is the separation between the legislative and executive branches of government. Article I of the Constitution creates, empowers, and limits the Congress; it also imposes reciprocal limitations on the states. Article II, modified by the Twelfth and Twenty-second amendments, creates, empowers, and provides for the election of the president (and vice president). Article I empowers the House of Representatives to impeach and the Senate to try the president. The Twenty-fifth Amendment attempts to provide for the replacement of a president who is "unable to discharge the powers and duties of his office."

The practical effects have been that the president and the Congress have somewhat different constituencies, as the "competitive struggle for the people's votes" shows in elections. Moreover, neither the president nor the Congress exercises significant influence on the nomination of the other. The last example of strong congressional leverage in nominating a president, an aberration, was exercised by certain senators in the choice of Warren G. Harding in the deadlocked Republican convention of 1920. In 1938 even President Franklin D. Roosevelt proved unable to influence key nominations to the House and the Senate.

Recently the separation has been attacked. Lloyd N. Cutler, in his essay in this volume, wrote: "The separation of powers between the executive and the legislative branches, whatever its merits in 1793, has become a structure that almost guarantees stalemate today." C. Douglas Dillon questioned "whether we can continue to afford the luxury of the separation of powers . . . between the executive and the legislative branches." J. William Fulbright urged "serious consideration to a merger of power between the executive and the legislature . . . under what we normally call a parliamentary system."[1]

The former chairman of the Joint Economic Committee, Henry Reuss, said that the advocacy of a parliamentary system for the United States is unrealistic but recommended examination of changes "of a milder nature," such as enabling Congress to remove the president by a vote of no confidence and, in the event of a "serious policy deadlock," enabling the president to dissolve the Congress and call for new elections in which the presidency would also be at risk. He would thus incorporate two vital elements of the parliamentary system.[2]

An Expanded View of the Problem

The problem of reforming the Constitution of the United States is not viewed in its proper scope and depth. Potential reformers base their arguments on the inability of our government to govern effectively, and those who answer them generally accept this ground for the debate. The effectiveness of the government is an important issue to which I shall return. But the problem goes deeper. It may involve the preservation of constitutional government itself, that is, of government that is effective but also *limited*.[3] Limits are contained in laws that the government of the day cannot change except under extraordinary circumstances (such as the threat of a clear and present danger to national survival) and then for a limited time. The laws must be interpreted by an independent judiciary.

The idea of such fundamental or natural law emerged in the Roman Republic, as did an adumbration of a judiciary. The entire populace was conceived as the true source of law. Nevertheless, the power of the emperor soon prevailed, followed later by the power of the kings by divine right;[4] and, although the idea of constitutionalism was kept alive, especially by the jurists, the only remedy for the abuse of powers remained revolution. The institutional means for making governmental power accountable to the people began to be foreshadowed by the Glorious Revolution in England in 1689 and then were slowly realized.

Only in the last half-century has full adult suffrage prevailed in a number of industrialized mass democracies to provide the theaters for testing whether constitutional democracy can thrive in "modern" conditions. How to convey the brevity of time involved? If our perspective as sentient human beings is a million years, only during the last 0.005 percent of that time have we had significant experience with modern constitutional democratic government. We remain novices.

Of primary concern is the role of the people as the source of law and of government, as the preamble of the Constitution emphasizes. Yet current political debate either ignores the role of the people or invokes it in the most unreflective stereotypes.[5] A thorough examination of the role of the people, their participation in government, and the question of majority rule should be central to considerations of constitutional reform.

Next comes the president, the single executive, chosen by the people and capable of being viewed as their embodiment. From this personification imperial characteristics may emanate, strengthened by echoes of *vox populi vox dei*. Can a power-hungry president be controlled? Can a failed or badly faltering president be legitimately and quickly replaced?

Finally, there is the egregiously bad effect on the American polity of fixed calendar elections. Constitutional democracy requires periodic elections, but their specific timing can wisely be left to the discretion of the government. This, too, is a matter of the first importance.

Implications for the Constitution

If the critique of separation of powers is persuasive, the fault can be corrected only by making a number of basic changes in the Constitution. Simpler remedies, such as the single six-year term for presidents, will not do. I suggest a change that consciously replaces the separation of powers between the president and the Congress with a separation between the government and the opposition (no less important than the government). The new Constitution might require elections of the government, that is, of the president and the Congress, at one time. The president would be elected directly or through the electoral college, compiling a majority by states, as now. The presidential loser would be given a seat in the House of Representatives, there to become the leader of the opposition. If they became disenchanted with their losing candidate, the members of the opposition party might remove him; but (as in the Bonn constitution) they would be required to replace him. With this one move the people, who in our political mythology have ordained and established the Constitution, would, in their palpable experience as the electorate, create both the government and the opposition.

The House of Representatives would be empowered to call for a vote of confidence, which, if carried against the president, would require either his resignation or his invocation of the power to dissolve both Congress and his own incumbency and call for new elections. The House would be elected from single-member districts. The mode of election of the president and the House would, as now, virtually ensure that the periodic contest for the people's vote would be essentially between two parties, unless one of the two major parties temporarily split. For the system to work, the president and a majority in the House must belong to the same party. Some device (at least two have been suggested)[6] would be needed to favor this result.

Members of the Congress would be eligible to serve in the government and would ordinarily fill most cabinet posts. Opening a track that is now closed to natural congressional ambitions, this change would sustain the interest of outstanding people in congressional careers. The Senate would be reduced in authority but—again as in the Bonn constitution—might retain power over certain cultural affairs as well as a suspensive veto over the economic and social matters on which the federal government is empowered to legislate. If such a reform took place, many able senators would compete for seats in the House, which would become the pathway to the cabinet and the presidency. The vote of confidence, a crucial part of the proposed arrangement, is borrowed from the theory of parliamentary government. History strongly suggests that the parliamentary reciprocity between government and legislature, in which the latter can employ a vote of confidence, requires one house to be paramount.

"We, the People of the United States"

From the first theories of constitutional government based on the rule of law, the people have been held to be the source of law. The framers' assertion that "We, the People of the United States . . . ordain and establish this Constitution" is both historically sound and inspired. It enunciated a necessary myth based on an essential core of fact, although the latter was more symbolic than literal. Of some 4 million people in the United States in 1790, fewer than 500,000 white adult males were eligible to vote. One calculation, based on the uncertain evidence available, estimates that fewer than 160,000 actually voted for delegates to all the state ratifying conventions. Of these, perhaps 100,000 favored the Constitution.[7]

It is essential that the people, as consciously as possible, create the government that operates the Constitution. This is what the proposed changes intend. If the election is arranged so that a majority government emerges, those who voted for it can properly feel that they share in the governance. What of the losers? Let them take consolation in the words of W. Ivor Jennings: "To find out whether a people is free it is necessary only to ask if there is an Opposition and, if there is, to ask where it is."[8] Everyone wants to be on the winning side; but, for the good of the country, both sides—the government and the opposition—are necessary. Formal education in democratic constitutional government on this point would be confirmed by experience at the polls.

The mode of election will virtually guarantee a majority government elected by a majority of voters. In theory and in the essential myth, the Constitution comes from the whole people. But governments rest on majorities. Popular governments, as Madison said in *Federalist* No. 51, must be able to control the governed. There must be a way to agree on a rule that will be generally obeyed. That does not mean that a rule will necessarily be right. Nothing guarantees that the majority will be right. It is simply the agreed democratic way of settling disputes.

Having the president elected by the people is the primary means of reducing the major parties to two and of guaranteeing a majority base for the government. This sharp departure from the parliamentary form of government seems necessary to avoid a multiparty system.[9] It will properly compel nearly all voters to choose between the government and the opposition. To repeat, voting should then be educational as well as political. The voter will share the onus of governing—or of opposing.

Suppose that the directly elected president faces a vote of confidence in a House chosen from single-member districts. How can the people's choice be unseated by mere members of Congress? It should help the people to accept this result if they are taught the necessity, in grave emergencies, of being able to replace the president quickly. It should also ease their acceptance if they come to see the president as less the choice (and the reincarnation) of the people and more the head of the majority party in Congress, from which he comes and by whom he is nominated. The radical shortening of campaigns should lessen the tendency for the president to personify the people. It will also help if the president continually faces organized opposition headed by his opponent in the last election, who has an electoral claim almost equal to his own. Finally, the government may choose to dissolve and let the results of the adverse vote of confidence be confirmed by the voters.

Implied in this argument are the following propositions. First, there is a division of labor in politics. Constitutional democracy means not that the people rule but that they select the government that rules. Second, the mandate theory, now out of hand in Britain as much as in the United States, must be rewritten so that people understand that their vote confers a mandate to govern, not a command to carry out specific promises candidates may have made. More on this later. Third, democracy does not mean that people get their hearts' desires but that they always have a second chance.

94

Replacing a Failed Leader

One of our most glaring constitutional weaknesses is the inability to replace a president who has failed politically. The prime example of the reverse is the shift from Neville Chamberlain to Winston Churchill in England in 1940 when the survival of the English nation (and perhaps of considerably more) appeared to be at stake. Later Churchill wrote: "The loyalties which center on number one are enormous. If he trips he must be sustained. If he makes mistakes they must be covered. If he sleeps he must not be wantonly disturbed. If he is no good he must be pole-axed."[10] Britain used the device also in World War I, when Prime Minister Herbert Asquith was replaced by David Lloyd George, and again in 1956, after the Suez crisis, when Prime Minister Anthony Eden was succeeded by Harold Macmillan. In 1974 both West Germany and Japan used a similar procedure to change prime ministers. Yet experience suggests that, except under seriously flawed constitutions such as those of the French Third Republic and of Weimar Germany, the device will not be abused by overuse; the leader who has climbed to the top of the greasy poll is too valuable to the governing party to be easily discarded. The ability to replace a failed or faltering leader quickly, and in a manner thoroughly acceptable to the public, is a strength of party government that also goes far to ensure that the new leader will be knowledgeable and appropriately experienced in the art of government. Under similar circumstances the United States is unable to act. Impeachment exists only for criminal actions and, applied to presidents, is virtually unworkable. The untested Twenty-fifth Amendment is extremely cumbersome and would probably be used only in the event of physical disability.

The Escape from Rigid Calendar Elections

Rigid calendar elections in the United States have patently grotesque results and threaten serious danger to the Republic. Yet the debate on constitutional reform is so focused on stalemate that it ignores this obvious flaw. Let us look initially at the domestic side.

First, fixed calendar elections cause interminable campaigns. Knowing the exact date of elections, aspirants to public posts campaign early. Incumbents feel compelled to meet them, and the race is on. Members of Congress now begin their next campaigns on the Wednesday following their November victories. Presidential aspirants begin at least two years early. The result makes for voters' ennui.

Second, endless campaigns greatly increase election costs. It is not sufficient to answer that only a small fraction of the gross national product is involved. Members of Congress are reportedly becoming obsessed with money. A member hears that a colleague has a $500,000

95

campaign fund. "A kind of fever takes over . . . soon everyone thinks he has to raise five hundred thousand dollars."[11]

Third, the hunt for funds not only consumes an unconscionable amount of time but induces a distortion of the political process. The sheer congressional obsession with money, though only a matter of degree, is a distortion. So is the inclination to rate some committees as more lucrative than others. Committees that preside over massive expenditures or taxes or that supervise either the bestowal of large benefits or the imposition of expensive regulations are obviously interesting to business and labor political action committees (PACs). By contrast, the judiciary committees and the committees dealing with foreign policy are less lucrative.[12] Then, too, the sheer multiplication of PACs constitutes a serious distortion. It might be enough to make James Madison tear up his analysis of the control of factions in *Federalist* No. 10 and throw it away. Finally, the Congress and the executive are both caught in the grip of postponement. Large issues such as tax reform, the rationalization of entitlements, controversial treaties, the reexamination of subsidies, and the modernization of such formulas as the consumer price index are all put off "until after the election," a phrase that becomes as elusive as "when the work's all done next fall" was in an earlier America. The complaint of inducing stalemate is often made against our system. Stalemate is, in part at least, a function of fixed calendar elections.

Fourth, and perhaps weightiest of all, calendar elections undermine political parties defined as organizations of voters intent on controlling the personnel and policies of government by winning elections. To achieve their aims—and, from the standpoint of the country, *to perform their proper functions*—political parties need to control nominations. How else can the parties be held accountable?[13] The quality of the candidates that a political party offers the public is the most important criterion for judging it. The ability of political parties to control their own labels is destroyed by the interminable campaigns and by the primary elections that they facilitate.

The cure calls for a shift to periodic elections with the actual dates left to the discretion of the government. Governments would be empowered to dissolve their executives and legislatures and to call for new elections. This provision would help restore the United States to the evolutionary course of constitutionalism: the royal prerogative becomes the prerogative of the citizens' government.[14] The victorious party would take over immediately. The transition would be accomplished in a matter of weeks.

Would not the people be denied a share in nominations? Who would be denied? Primary elections are notorious for poor turnouts.

They are carnivals for special interests where every conceivable group can strive to influence the choice of candidates. Primaries deprive political parties of their essential control of their own labels. Thus the primaries mask and confuse the function of the elections: the popular choice of a government and the rule of the majority. By splintering the parties, the primaries demolish the meaning of majority rule—of rule by an extended majority that, because of its size and inclusiveness, as many students of American politics since Madison have pointed out, tends to produce a moderate government.

An examination of calendar elections thus forces us back once more to the political role of the people. Once more we need to clarify and bring home the crucial popular role in making governments and oppositions. Moreover, interminable campaigns dilute and wash away in boredom the spirit of emotional commitment that a brief campaign should engender in the voters to infuse strength into our democracy.[15] One more point: we should also recognize that elections by discretion retain in the hands of the government an essential opportunity to display its sense of timing, which is often essential in politics. Proper sensitivity to timing is also something on which people can judge politicians. But we blithely give all this away by nailing our elections, willy-nilly, to the calendar.

Calendar Elections and Foreign Affairs

Now let us turn to foreign affairs. Calendar elections present potential enemies with excellent opportunities to harass us when we are most vulnerable. Because of the unique historical insulation of the United States from foreign foes, the threat is new. Even World War II was twenty-eight months old when Pearl Harbor was attacked. If a third world war comes, we will be in it from the start. Since 1812 we have had only two presidential elections during great wars, in 1864 and 1944. As late as August 1864, President Abraham Lincoln required his cabinet to sign a paper that, unknown to them, had their joint resignation on its reverse side. If General George B. McClellan had defeated him in November, Lincoln could immediately have transferred the government to him. In this century's two world wars, we were the only belligerent that could continue electoral politics as usual.

Moreover, our protracted campaigns and our disjointed and often unaccountable government invite not only foreign enemies but Americans to take ill-considered actions. On October 19, 1960, the John F. Kennedy campaign released a statement calling for support for Cubans intent on overthrowing Fidel Castro. "Thus far these fighters for freedom have had virtually no support from our government."[16] Actually, a covert effort by the Central Intelligence Agency

(CIA) to help unseat Castro was under way, repeatedly spurred on by Vice President (and candidate) Richard M. Nixon, who hoped that Castro would be toppled in time for the event to win votes for him in November. Although enraged at Kennedy, Nixon ironically felt constrained to denounce him for being "wrong and irresponsible because [his proposal] would violate our treaty commitments." Kennedy won a narrow victory. The Bay of Pigs became his, presented to him with the apparent intent to make him feel compelled to carry on. He did. It failed. He lamented, "How could I have been so stupid?"

Peter Wyden wrote: "If Kennedy had not been thoroughly defeated by Castro [at the Bay of Pigs] Nikita Khrushchev almost certainly would not have dared to precipitate the Cuban Missile Crisis of 1962," which, as former CIA Director William E. Colby has said, brought the world "as close to Armageddon" as it has come.[17]

Whether or not Colby exaggerated, the cooperation of the United States in a plot to overthrow and to assassinate the leader of a foreign government with which we are not at war should at the very least call for the most careful consideration by the government in power throughout the event. But the Bay of Pigs was planned and pushed by a very few persons in the CIA during a protracted presidential campaign in which both principals made it a political football.

Other flaws in the American Constitution are exposed by the Bay of Pigs: presidential hubris and the tendency, in spite of (or, more accurately, because of) the separation of powers, for agencies of government to get "out of control." But here I am at pains to point out that it is logical to assume that the architects of the Bay of Pigs were consciously exploiting the opportunity provided by the fixed calendar election.

One more example: When the bombing of North Vietnam was completely halted on November 1, 1968, the U.S. Military Command in South Vietnam instituted a policy of "patrolling more aggressively" and "engaging the enemy far more frequently than before." The tactics were part of what one highly placed U.S. official described as the "total war" strategy of General Creighton W. Abrams. On March 7, 1969, CBS News reported, in effect, that General Abrams had seized the opportunity between the election and the Nixon inaugural so to escalate the fighting that the incoming administration would have no alternative but to fight on.[18]

By this discussion of the role of the people in facilitating a quick and legitimate way to replace faltering presidents and of the folly of continuing our thoughtless commitment to calendar elections, I hope to have shown that consideration of our constitutional problems should go beyond questions of efficiency. I now turn to the question of our ability to form a government that can concert a policy and get it passed.

Malfunction in Policy Formation under and because of the Separation of Powers

What has rallied an impressive number of former ranking members of government—senators, congressmen, cabinet secretaries, and presidential advisers—to the cause of constitutional reform (or, at least, to careful and serious consideration of reform in a search for remedies that can be vigorously recommended to the public) is the conviction that the government is failing to enact proper policies. Its failure appears to be caused by—or to be unavoidable because of—structural problems in government.

The eminent advocates, or near advocates, of structural change have been careful not to propose specific reforms. Properly calling for an initial period of research before a formulation of recommendations can take place, they have been fairly specific on what is wrong and what, in general, must be done to make it right. Lloyd N. Cutler has deplored our government's "inability . . . to propose, legislate, and administer a balanced program" in both foreign and domestic policy. By implication, the president must be able to count "on the total or nearly total support of his own party" to achieve "a legislative majority which takes the responsibility for governing."[19]

C. Douglas Dillon found that, after 150 years of excellent service, our Constitution has recently been subject to serious strains associated with population growth, technological change, the erosion of party loyalty, and an explosion of organized interests, all accompanied paradoxically by rising voter apathy and a growing disenchantment with government. He cited the growth of insupportable deficits, the failure of rational taxing and spending programs, and the questionable ability of the country to deal with foreign crises. Our problem is not the lack of knowledge of what needs to be done. "Rather, it stems from the inability of our system to clearly place the responsibility for action in any one place." In foreign affairs, "it is essential for a nation with the economic, military and political power of the United States to be able to speak with one, clear voice."[20]

A meeting of public persons and political scientists in Washington, D.C., in January 1981 led to the tentative formation of the Committee on the Constitutional System (CCS), which aims to press the examination of possible structural faults in the system of government of the United States into formulation of a program of reform that could be recommended to the public. Other meetings followed, and in November–December 1982, under Chairman Henry Reuss, the

Joint Economic Committee of the Congress held hearings on political economy and constitutional reform. All this brought forth counterarguments.

The Criticism by Arthur M. Schlesinger, Jr.

Arthur M. Schlesinger, citing the Civil War and the Great Depression, contended, first, that our problems are no greater now than they have been in the past. We have coped in the past because we had presidents of sufficient stature. What we need is not constitutional reform but more capable politicians. Second, our problem is not that we cannot make and execute policies but that we do not know what policies to propose. Third, the real difficulty lies in the divisions in public opinion. "When the country knows and speaks its mind, Congress will not fail to act."[21]

Dillon answered Schlesinger by arguing that nuclear armaments have destroyed our insulation from world events and economic problems have been deepened and complicated by the international nature of the economy. The United States can no longer wait for its "maze of politics" to act or for a "magical consensus of the people" to show the way.[22]

Part of Schlesinger's argument was based on his criticism of the British parliamentary system, through which, members of the CCS had said or implied, a government could be formed and a program enacted. He declared that the promptness with which Parliament passes a government's program was "a function of Parliament's weakness, not of its strength," quoting Churchill to Roosevelt during World War II. Whereas Roosevelt was concerned about getting congressional approval, Churchill said that he never worried about Parliament; "but I continuously have to consult and have the support of my Cabinet."[23] When J. William Fulbright suggested that, in a proposed parliamentary system, cabinet ministers, by virtue of their own political strength, might somewhat chasten and control a president, Schlesinger asserted that Prime Minister Eden had not consulted his cabinet in the Suez adventure of 1956.[24]

Dazzled by Schlesinger's ability to cite the British prime minister-cabinet relationship simultaneously on both sides of the argument, one might still suggest that both his examples are subject to different interpretations. The heart of parliamentary government is the adversarial relation between government and opposition. But the same constitutional principle that requires an opposition in time of peace demands, in a war that virtually all are united to win, a coalition government. Opposition members join the cabinet, which then becomes not only the collegial base of the pursuit of victory but the central theater of political debate.[25] Churchill would naturally expect to consult his cabinet.

In the Suez incident, however, Britain was not at war. The parliamentary system operated in the classical manner, with strong discipline on both sides of a vigorous parliamentary debate that found the Conservatives espousing traditional imperial responsibility and Labour rejecting international power politics. Perhaps Eden did not consult his full cabinet as early as he might or try hard enough to mobilize his parliamentary support. But some cabinet consultation was accompanied by a display of parliamentary discipline that may have been a bit too exemplary.[26]

The Counterarguments of James Q. Wilson

An elaborate criticism of the conceptions and intentions of constitutional reformers has been made by James Q. Wilson, first in a televised American Enterprise Institute Public Policy Forum in November 1980 and then in a paper prepared for AEI's Public Policy Week in December 1980.[27] In the forum, appearing with Henry O. Brandon, Lloyd N. Cutler, and Laurence H. Silberman, with John Charles Daly as moderator, Wilson contrasts proposed reform to create a government manifest in a "single will," presumably of one person, with the ideal, attributed to the framers of the Constitution, of coalition government. However disparate the interests that composed it, the coalition "would emerge only on the principle of the common good." This may happen at times, as in the Civil Rights Act of 1964. But to imply that it is a dependable principle seems to proffer an "invisible hand" that invariably leads to a choice better than anyone intends.[28] This may become a version of the utopian fallacy.

Like Schlesinger, Wilson argues that the policy choices we now face are no more grave than previous governments have encountered; and Dillon's answer is equally applicable. Wilson then says that it is "intellectually . . . unlikely that we can devise a program that corresponds to a theory of governance based on the act of a single will or intelligence." This entirely different argument, a council of despair, may be right. But what else can we rely on? Wilson's own spirited defense of American foreign policy since World War II is a tribute to American will and intelligence.[29]

Then Wilson turns to a favorite theme: public opinion will not support constitutional change. The fundamental basis of the argument advanced by potential constitutional reformers is not what the American people expect.

> They do not wish to have an opportunity to vote yes or no on
> a party's cohesive performance in office, in which it takes

responsibility for the policies that have been put in place, because the American public does not exist as a public. It is a collection of separate publics that have discovered, or would readily admit if it were pointed out, that if they have to vote yes or no on a comprehensive set of policies, they cannot do so. They are torn with too many internal contradictions.[30]

Elsewhere, however, Wilson has remarked that "what the people want as a whole is different from what they want when polled one at a time."[31] Constitutional reformers can agree and say that they want political institutions that will give priority to what people want as a whole. What provides both the realization and the proof of constitutional democracy is the voters' periodic choice between contending parties to create a government. It is this choice, not the opportunity of people to vote on every issue, that validates democracy (although just here the vexing question of the mandate threatens to rise again). This argument may appeal to Wilson, who declares that considerations of the U.S. budget prove "conclusively that the public interest differs from the summation of private wants (something that my colleagues in political science like to deny, but this fact establishes it)."[32]

Yet Wilson returns to the theme that public opinion will not prove compatible with the kind of constitutional reforms envisaged: in other words, his "ultimate skepticism" about the reforms suggested by Cutler. The lack of a national consensus and some of the public's dissatisfaction with government may result from government's having "promised more than it could achieve" and its consequential inflation of the currency to provide it, thus "harming . . . a style of life that most Americans thought was their birthright." Wilson then says that some suggested "institutional reforms . . . would . . . feed this process by enlarging expectations, enlarging the role of the president as the national leader conducting not an election but a plebiscite," in which "the president's proposals would be put forward, based on assembling a coalition by offering as much as possible to as many as possible." This would "lead to enlarged, and ultimately frustrated, expectations."[33]

Wilson has exposed one of the most difficult problems faced by constitutional democracies in mass industrial societies. I differ from him in believing that periodic elections to choose a government for a reasonable amount of time to grapple with the monsters will produce a better approximation of policy in the public interest than what we have now. Our interminable electoral extravaganzas greatly stimulate the excesses of plebiscitary government; the presidential sweepstakes is supplemented by ceaseless, separate, localized congressional campaigns.

Look at England, the mother of parliaments, to which constitutional reformers and their opponents both appeal (Wilson refers to England's "dizzying reversals" of policy to suggest that parliamentary government has often failed). England saw an early flowering of the idea that government can gratify all human desires while continually creating full employment in an expanding economy—what Samuel H. Beer has called "hubristic Keynesianism." In Britain the overweening attempt to reify an economic theory into an earthly heaven had many sponsors. "It is no exaggeration to say that Göring's Blitz was the force that coalesced all the converging strands of Christian humanitarianism, utilitarian pragmatism, idealistic statism, Fabian socialism, and aristocratic paternalism into the social program pursued since the War."[34] There appears to be no question that the parliamentary system produced a convergence of the parties (Butskellism) that facilitated the excesses of the planned economy and the welfare state. Yet, with whatever wrenching of its political institutions and socioeconomic costs, the British parliamentary system under Margaret Thatcher is currently struggling to create an economically viable polity. Beer's latest examination of Britain's problems assumes that the parliamentary system that has governed "exceptionally well" in the past will continue to cope.[35] His search for remedies is in the realm of ideas, not institutions.

With ratios of people to resources much more favorable than Britain's, the United States also encounters great difficulty in its macroeconomics and its public accounts: staggering deficits; social security and Medicare verging on bankruptcy; welfare generosity; defense bonanzas. We hear much of entitlement programs, but these are built on other programs like the rivers and harbors that have historically succored groups with political influence. The result, to borrow Wilson's phrase, was to endow a considerable number of influential Americans with what they believed to be their just birthright. This selective sharing of the spoils has long been celebrated as the American way: "Deal me in!" "A little plum for everyone." "Politics: Who Gets What, When, and How?" "The burden—and the glory, too—of American democracy."[36] Periodically the generosity has been stigmatized. But what has roused the public's bile, roiled the political waters, and raised concern over whether we can govern ourselves has been the extension of the loaves and the fishes to the multitudes. Combined with inflationary surges, income tax bracket creep, and a growing anxiety about job security, costly public programs for low-income people have triggered a middle-class backlash.

Sobered by these problems, let us look further into Wilson's argument, turning to his paper "What Can Be Done?"

Wilson on the Separation of Powers

"The separation of powers, far from being a stumbling block to good government, is in fact its guarantor, for it impedes action and thus reduces the chance of precipitous policy."[37] Oddly enough, this statement is soon followed by a lament that government now undertakes "a vast array of tasks, disposes of a sizeable part of the gross national product, and has in place a bureaucracy with broad discretionary powers." Once there was a "legitimacy barrier"; now there is "virtually no subject on which the government may not—or does not—have a program."[38] Coalition politics could once be selective; the largesse extracted from government could be held to bearable proportions. (I am interpreting Wilson's argument here to be in keeping with my earlier statement that generosity is politically supportable so long as the number benefiting is limited.) Now, however, politics has become so inclusive that coalitions have to embrace virtually everyone.[39]

Meanwhile, American politics has become "disaggregated."[40] From the late nineteenth century until the end of World War II, the United States evolved strong state political parties and a degree of partisan organization within the House of Representatives that helped to contain and shape the nation's inherently chaotic and individualistic politics. But the disintegration of these disciplinary forces was not joined by a dissolution of the surfeit of governmental programs.

In this situation elites and their political ideas have assumed novel significance. Elites are not new: witness the framers of 1787. But Wilson now says, "at no previous time has there been so conspicuous a gulf between the ideas and interests of the average citizen and the ideas (and possibly the interests) of political elites."[41]

The talk of elites is perplexing. Is Wilson suggesting that the people have a collective wisdom that, if discovered, will provide specific answers to intricate and difficult public problems? Even with respect to the gap that Wilson notes, I am puzzled. The late V. O. Key, for example, concluded his *Public Opinion and American Democracy* with the statement: "The data tell us almost nothing about the dynamic relations between the upper layer of activists and mass opinion. The missing piece of our puzzle is the elite element of the opinion system."[42] Wilson may have other elites in mind. But he does refer to the disaggregated and particular interests that form around the proliferation of public programs—"the bewildering array of specific taxes, subsidies, entitlements, and regulations [that] has helped to create an equivalent array of specific factional interests that work hard to guard their politically defined stakes."[43]

104

Here the relation between the elites and the citizenry seems to be replaced by the competitive scramble of factions. Suddenly the system that Madison lauded as a frustrator of the pernicious effects of factions seems ironically to have created a plethora of factions. This observation suggests that the disaggregation Wilson noted earlier may have been replaced by a new and different kind of aggregation around the proliferating public programs. To carry on Wilson's train of thought, as I understand it, the disaggregation, coupled with the growth of government, the bewildering array of more or less ineffectual programs, and the heightened significance of elites, has given politics an unusual volatility.[44] The volatility is evanescent, however; people are briefly stirred by the ideas expressed by elites, but the established structure is too vast and complex to be changed except incrementally.

We have, then, an eternal and ubiquitous contest between elites and their ideas, on the one hand, and organizations or institutions with their established ways of acting (and the rationales therefor), on the other. Wilson suggests three consequences for policy making. First, some institutions—courts and the media, because they can spawn ideas quickly and communicate them easily—will excel legislatures, corporations, and the bureaucracy, where action requires coordination of many people with increasing convictions about their rights. Second, it will be harder to assemble power within institutions like parties, the bureaucracy, and Congress because of the spread of individualistic values. Third, individual values will be progressively stated as rights, especially by those (who are growing in number) with more formal education. The effect will be to increase and harden individualism.[45]

This brings us to Wilson's final problem concerning the improvement of governmental processes, which appears to threaten if not to destroy the prospects of fundamental constitutional reform. The problem arises from the number of line decisions, as distinguished from point decisions, that must be made. Point decisions are relatively simple. A person is appointed to, or fired from, a position. A bill is signed or vetoed or an executive agreement or order approved. By contrast, line decisions require that many people be induced to act concertedly over time to build an army, to impose a blockade, to create an infrastructure, to found a new technology. Point decisions are problems of choice, line decisions of management. Point decisions "are profoundly shaped by the prevailing *ideas* of the political elite," whereas line decisions require the assembling of *"organizational resources."*[46]

"Policies that require making and managing line decisions will probably continue to be thought unsatisfactory, for I see no means to reassemble the institutional bits and pieces that lie scattered about

us." (Scattered by the proliferation of programs and the disaggregation of institutions, I take it.) "Designing a reasonable tax or energy
policy, curbing the rapid growth in entitlement payments, increasing
dramatically the combat readiness of the armed forces, or improving
the administration of regulatory laws will continue to be exercises in
frustration." (But Wilson does hold out some hope for guillotines,
such as sunset laws, expenditure limits, and legislative vetoes—the
last named apparently now dashed by the Supreme Court in an
excellent example of the triumph of the judicial elite.)[47]

"What can be done?" There is some hope that a "determined and
clear-eyed president" will display a "willingness to use, or threaten to
use, such [military] force as we have."[48] Indeed, in the AEI forum,
Wilson conceded something to the constitutional reformers "with
respect to the conduct of foreign affairs."

Generally, for Wilson, the idea of improvement is a chimera,
whether we try to achieve it by means of fundamental constitutional
change or otherwise. I now turn to the countervailing interpretation
of Walter Dean Burnham.

Walter Dean Burnham: An Alternative View

Burnham observes the same events that Wilson does, offers some
similar interpretations, especially regarding the disaggregation of institutions, but concludes that the central problem is one of constitutional reform. Strongly criticizing separation of powers, Burnham
finds the United States "the most dynamic society and economy on
earth [coexisting] with the most antique and undeveloped constitutional structure to be found in any Western country."[49]

America came to grief in 1965–1975. Proliferation of government
proceeded along with the disaggregation or fragmentation of political
institutions.[50] Describing America's political system as feudal,[51] Burnham discerns "no small part of the American regime's crisis [as
seeming] to relate specifically to the number of discrete centers of
power within the polity."[52]

These power centers are targets of groups demanding action.
Each power center responds in its own way. "The state's response is
therefore disaggregated." Programs are authorized and financed;
agencies are created; they establish links with clientele groups and
with appropriate persons in government, including "key actors in the
ultrafragmented American legislative process."[53] What emerge are the
famous "iron triangles," semiautonomous complexes of policy formation and execution.[54]

What happens is that in the "feudalized" structure of American
government, whose complications "overwhelm the capacity of any
ordinary citizen to understand who or what is responsible for any-
106

thing that happens," "people and institutions . . . are able to go into business for themselves." This, I take it, is to be understood quite literally. Burnham is observing an intrusion of capitalism into government. "The independence of these various power centers gives a cast of private enterprise—even at times laissez-faire private enterprise—to the activities of the state." "The fundamental issue is curbing what amounts to private enterprise within the state itself."[55]

This is central to Burnham's interpretation. It is not anticapitalist, but it is intensely critical of a corruption of government that appears to grow, in part at least, out of the confusion of private enterprise with public operations. There may also be a question of degree. At some point of escalation, a "little honest graft" becomes overpowering. Some large defense industries have recently been found to have outrageously overcharged the government. At the same time, defense industries are reported to lavish favors on strategically located members of Congress whose natural interest in money has reportedly become an obsession.[56] Burnham apparently shares Wilson's concern with big spending and the easy multiplication of governmental programs, as he does his concern with excessive disaggregation.[57] But his central focus differs from Wilson's on the growth of elites, the disparity between their ideas and those of the average citizen, and the progressive metamorphosis of citizens' demands into rights.

It is not surprising, then, that where Wilson mentions sunset laws, limits on spending, and the legislative veto, Burnham argues for much more fundamental structural changes. He calls for a "steering mechanism" in the state to guide corporate capitalism. This, in turn, will require a state that is able "to take on a reasonably clear political responsibility, shared by teams of politicians elected to be in charge of the steering mechanism." What is needed is "a political structure that could offset the tendency of individual legislators, legislative committees, and agencies to run their own show, defend their own turf, and go into business for themselves with some concentration of internally sovereign power at the center of the state."[58]

Although he offers no blueprint (no "magic formula"), Burnham suggests that "ineffective as parliamentary democratic regimes may be at coping with the pressures of an adverse environment, the traditional constitutional structure of the United States may well be even more ineffective."[59]

How the Separation of Powers Works: An Appraisal Respecting Domestic Policy

With reservations respecting his "steering mechanism," I favor Burnham's view over Wilson's. The ills of overcommitment that Wilson

107

decries were nourished by the system that he lauds. Wilson's stress on the difference of opinions between the public and the elites overlooks "the changeability of public moods,"[60] as well as the role of the "heroes of the press,"[61] in informing public opinion and helping to marshal it in support of policies that might be produced in a constitutional system that has not only a strong government but also a vigorous, articulate, institutionalized opposition.

This does not denigrate "the people." Far from it. The people are the source of law; but it is "the people" in the sense used by Edmund Burke in his illumination of the social contract: "a partnership not only between those who are living, but between those who are living, those who are dead, and those who are to be born." Public opinion is "the great source of power, the master of servants who tremble before it"; but, as Lord Bryce also said, public opinion remains "impalpable as the wind," even when analysts are telling us precisely what it is saying.

I have also not forgotten that in England just this kind of government-opposition system produced the dizzying changes in policy Wilson decries (the "stop-go" policies, as they are frequently denigrated as). Such oscillations flourish in mass democracies trying to survive the political-economic uncertainties of a universe exploding in murderous technology and cutthroat competition.

I turn now to the disaggregation of government that Wilson laments. Much of it, at least, grows straight out of separation of powers, which encourages the formation of quasi-independent programs, typically composed of strategically placed members of Congress, federal bureaucracies, and clientele groups, triumvirates that seek to dispose of government power and money for their specific ends. These are the iron triangles. Government—Congress, the bureaucracy, and the parties—disaggregates into such triangles; but the triangles, in another sense, are themselves aggregations: prototypes of pluralism. Old systems disaggregate, but new conglomerates form.

An example was provided in the debate on the federal tobacco program in the House of Representatives in July 1945. The chairman of the House Committee on Agriculture, Representative John Flannagan (Democrat, Virginia) said, "The tobacco program has been the most successful agricultural program ever inaugurated in this country. It works. If this House will continue to leave the tobacco program to the tobacco growers and their representatives in Congress, it will continue to work." The ranking Republican on the committee, Representative Clifford Hope (Kansas), retorted that the tobacco program "was not only a closed shop proposition but a closed union with a closed shop."[62]

Elsewhere I have used the military to exemplify the growth and influence of the iron triangles (I called it "bureaucracy") in the United States. The military remains influential. As a Democratic House member remarked to Elizabeth Drew, respecting Representative Les Aspin's chairmanship of an Armed Services subcommittee:

> Being chairman of a defense subcommittee means you are now dealing with a constituency out there—the Pentagon. It means being able to deliver favors to your colleagues, but in order to do that you have to have the support of the Pentagon. The same thing is true in other areas, like agriculture: they need you and you need them, and you help each other.[63]

How lucrative a position in certain triangles can be is suggested by a *Wall Street Journal* article, "Legislative Lucre: Fees for Congressmen from Interest Groups Doubled in Past Year: Defense Industry Forks Out Money to MX Adherents."[64] I agree with Burnham that our system of separated powers tends to corrupt both government and capitalists. The hidden hand is encouraged to pick the taxpayer's pocket.

I have some reservations about Burnham's "steering mechanism," as well as about government's engaging in comprehensive "industrial planning," as one current vogue urges. The development and execution of an industrial plan seem to call for a much more centralized government than ours.[65] Advocates of industrial planning may have an incentive to support the kind of constitutional reform that members of the Committee on the Constitutional System seem inclined to favor. At the same time, a vigorous debate has been joined by antagonists of industrial planning.[66] But the question of constitutional reform need not be defined as an issue between liberal Democrats and economic conservatives. The tax and spending reforms that our system needs are frustrated because of the system's "inability to place the responsibility for action in any one place," as C. Douglas Dillon put it.[67] Compare a recent statement by William E. Brock III, the president's trade representative, on the immense debts currently owed by certain third world countries:

> Let's look at the debt in the quantifiable sense. Not only do you have to pay principal, you have to pay interest. These interest rates have been unreal in part because the United States has been unable to get its deficits under control. You cannot separate these problems anymore. You can't separate protectionism, debt, exchange rates, monetary policy, and fiscal policy.[68]

Alan Greenspan has expressed similar sentiments. Hence the spectrum of potential support for reexamination of our constitutional system on economic grounds is broad.

In short, in coping with fiscal and monetary policy, as well as with general economic policy, whether one embraces industrial planning or rejects it but still acknowledges the need for a stable, united government capable of mounting and pressing on with a comprehensive approach, one can join in the search for a better governmental structure. The policies that will need to be formulated and implemented will, no doubt, be replete with the line decisions on which Wilson thinks that comprehensive government will founder. The answer to Wilson is that the government will be more able to make and carry out the difficult decisions with a system shorn of the rigidities and fragmentations that now repeatedly frustrate, compromise, and defeat comprehensive, long-range policies.[69]

An Appraisal of the Separation of Powers in Foreign Policy

A historical argument can be made that the separation of powers has not served the United States well in foreign and military policy (the conduct of war), but I shall deal only with the period since World War II. The constant jarring of our "separated institutions sharing powers" has resulted in an enormous growth of power delegated to the president. Congress has ("temporarily") handed over immense powers to the only institution capable of acting with vigor, secrecy (sometimes, anyway), unity (on occasion), and dispatch. Then Congress found a way to control the president, who would be allowed to act subject to a congressional veto. But this imaginative experiment in legislative transvestitism was censored in 1983 by a puritanical Supreme Court.

Meanwhile, the United States has become exceedingly overcommitted throughout the world. After World War II the earlier American rhythm seemed to prevail: to demobilize and disarm at breakneck speed (though never to disarm as much as after the previous conflict). But only briefly. The cold war began, followed by the Korean "police action." What ensued was labeled "pactomania."

In 1958 the United States was giving military assistance to sixty-three nations. Under the North Atlantic Treaty of 1949 we had a collective defensive alliance with eleven European nations plus Canada, Iceland, and Turkey. We had similar defensive arrangements with twenty-one nations in Central and South America. We had given an implied promise of unlimited support to the Southeast Asia Treaty Organization. The Baghdad Pact had all the marks of our handiwork except our signature. We had bilateral defensive agreements with the

Philippines, Japan, Formosa, Korea, and Spain. Walter Lippmann wrote that Secretary of State John Foster Dulles

> has gone around the world promising every nation that would accept . . . an American military guarantee. In this Dulles has shown himself to be not a prudent and calculating diplomat but a gambler who is more lavish than any other secretary of state has ever dreamed of being with the promissory notes guaranteeing the blood, the treasure, and the honor of this country.[70]

All this coincided with a national relaxation. Americans were reported to be happy with the world and pleased with themselves. Despite warnings from various sources about the disregard of prudence, lulled by a feeling of security that President Dwight Eisenhower seemed to exude, there was very little critical political analysis. But a particular problem was building as presidents, from Harry Truman through John Kennedy, increased American commitments in Southeast Asia.

Here it is appropriate to refer to a thoughtful evaluation of the American and British systems made in 1964 by Leon D. Epstein, based on British politics in the Suez crisis of 1956. At least in the 1950s, the British parliamentary system generated impressively cohesive majority support for the government. At the same time the prime minister had been gaining strength to become "a genuine chief executive and not just the first among equals." Because of these two developments, Epstein suggested that the American system might require its president, more than the British required its prime minister, to seek political support and to be "responsible" to public opinion. Similarly, he thought that Parliament had perhaps been less able to get the necessary facts to inform its debate properly, even in the vaunted question periods. The American legislative committees, by contrast, might arm Congress with "an independent opportunity to press the executive both before and after policy commitments are made."[71]

These expectations of how the American system would work were tested by the Vietnam War. Between 1966 and 1972 Congress voted 145 times on measures designed to restrict American military involvement in the war but succeeded in enacting only some restrictions on military involvement in Laos, Cambodia, and Thailand—all without effect. In 1971 Congress twice passed resolutions urging President Nixon to set a deadline for ending military activities in Vietnam. On both occasions the president said that he did not consider the resolutions binding. Only in 1973, with the Ervin committee's disclosures on Watergate and related events and with President

111

Nixon's Gallup poll ratings plummeting, was Congress able to set a deadline of August 15 for the cessation of military action by the United States in Vietnam. In October 1973 Congress passed the bill that became the War Powers Act; the president vetoed it, but the veto was overridden by the Congress the following November.

The Vietnam War can be regarded as the culmination of a trend, lasting perhaps six decades, of the expansion of the president's war power as commander in chief. In 1969 a Senate study that prefigured the War Powers Act declared: "The fact that Congress has acquiesced in . . . the transfer of the War Power to the Executive is probably the most important single fact accounting for the speed and virtual completeness of the transfer."[72] The report attributed the transfer to the novelty of the new situation and a sense of urgency, real or contrived; the cult of executive expertise; and historical memory (shame at having rejected membership in the League of Nations).

Memorable statements marked the march of presidential authority. On committing the United States to defend South Korea, President Truman, noting his full control of the armed forces as commander in chief and "in the broad interests of American foreign policy," asserted a "traditional power of the President to use the Armed Forces . . . without consulting Congress." This, the Senate Report of 1969 declared, was the first presidential assertion of inherent powers, and it added: "Scarcely a voice of dissent was raised in Congress." In 1951 the Senate Foreign Relations and Armed Services committees held joint hearings on the proposal to send six divisions to Europe. Invoking the plentiful sweep of presidential authority, Secretary of State Dean Acheson found it "clear that this authority may not be interfered with by Congress in exercise of its powers under the Constitution." The situation was so serious, he said, that there should not even be debate. When Congress acted during this period, it was usually to acknowledge, in effect, the inherent discretionary use of presidential authority. Thus the Middle Eastern Resolution of 1957 stated that "the President could determine to use Armed Forces to defend Middle East Nations against communist aggression." In 1966 Secretary of State Dean Rusk declared: "No would-be aggressor should suppose that the absence of a defense treaty, congressional declaration, or U.S. military presence grants immunity to aggression." In 1970 an assistant attorney general said: "The President's authority to invade Cambodia must be conceded even by those who read executive authority narrowly."

Despite the War Powers Act, the United States had even more worldwide military commitments in 1983 than in 1958, when Walter Lippmann excoriated John Foster Dulles for his imprudence. Referring to President Ronald Reagan's military exercises in and around Honduras in 1983, Richard Halloran reported American military officers' private statements that the exercises "would underline the world-wide commitments that overextend the armed forces instead of demonstrating American military power to potential adversaries." In 1973, when the War Powers Act was passed, the global American military involvement was manifest in "323 sizable installations outside the continental United States. . . . In 1983, the total is 359, not including foreign military bases to which Americans have access but do not control." The annual financial costs of American military commitments in Europe, Asia, and the Persian Gulf region were estimated at $212 billion.[73]

Something there is that does not love a debate. Our system is not structured to fix responsibility on a government to govern and on an opposition to debate the government by offering alternatives. Congress can impose specific limits on the executive, such as tying approval of a Soviet-American trade agreement to a Soviet concession to liberalize the migration of its citizens, barring arms sales to Turkey pending a settlement on Cyprus, denying most-favored-nation status to members of OPEC in retaliation for the 1973 oil embargo, or forbidding clandestine aid to antigovernment forces in Angola. When it comes to sharing actively in the formulation and administration of a complex foreign policy, however, the War Powers Act may simply help the president in sending a resounding message to foreigners that the country is behind him.

The debacle in Iran illuminates the kind of issue that the American separation of powers simply does not acknowledge. The issue involves the ability to nourish, defend, and improve "fragile client states," as Stanley Hoffmann calls them. We have unquestioningly accepted the responsibilities of John Foster Dulles's extravagant commitments in the Persian Gulf, in much of Asia and the South Pacific, and in Central America. "In all such cases . . . the dilemma is the same: responsibility without actual control, or control at a prohibitive cost and with inconclusive or horrifying results."[74]

Conclusion

In his historical analysis of constitutionalism, Charles H. McIlwain dwelt on the government and the rights of citizens established in law, using the terms *gubernaculum* and *jurisdictio* to designate them because the theory of constitutionalism and an adumbration of its practice were first achieved in Rome.[75] The history of constitutionalism was manifest in the continuous struggle between *gubernaculum* and *jurisdictio*, that is, between governmental order and private rights. "Constitutional history is usually the record of a series of oscillations." The sixteenth century witnessed the ascendancy of order. In England the seventeenth century saw a swing back toward private rights, the eighteenth a return to strong government, "but now, as never before, a power vested in the national assembly instead of a king."[76]

McIlwain thought that in the twentieth century the reconciliation of *gubernaculum* and *jurisdictio* remained "probably our most serious practical problem." Indeed, he stressed "the same necessity now, as in past ages, to preserve these two sides of political institutions intact, to maintain every institution instrumental in strengthening them both, and to guard against the overwhelming of one . . . by the other." "Never in recorded history, I believe, has the individual been in greater danger from government than now."[77]

McIlwain staunchly opposed enfeebling government. "Among all the modern fallacies that have obscured the true teachings of constitutional history, few are worse than the extreme doctrine of the separation of powers and the indiscriminate use of the phrase 'checks and balances.'" He could find little historical background for the theory of the separation of powers "except the fancies of eighteenth-century doctrinaires and their followers. Political balances have no institutional background whatever except in the imagination of closet philosophers like Montesquieu."[78]

Power must be concentrated to be held accountable. McIlwain lamented our inability to fix responsibility. He could find no "good precedents" in history "for this dissipation of government," which has "worked disaster ever since it was adopted." If this tendency went much further, it would precipitate a reaction that might sweep away "every protection of any sort, legal as well as political, to leave the individual naked and unprotected against the ever-present danger of arbitrary government."[79]

It is appropriate to end this paper with McIlwain's summation. We badly need a united government that can act steadily and comprehensively on the macroeconomic problems inherent in a modern industrial giant like the United States. In foreign and military policy the need is even more imperative. That government should be a constitutional democracy, not through the retention of the same system that has proved inept in economic policy and persistently imprudent in foreign policy, but through a change to vest control in periodic elections animated by a continuing, vigilant opposition.

Notes

1. Lloyd N. Cutler was counsel to President Jimmy Carter. C. Douglas Dillon was secretary of the Treasury in the John F. Kennedy administration

and had earlier served as ambassador to France and as under secretary of state for economic affairs. J. William Fulbright, U.S. senator from Arkansas 1944–1975, was chairman of the Committee on Foreign Relations. Henry R. Reuss, representative from Wisconsin 1954–1983, was chairman, Joint Economic Committee. See Joint Economic Committee, U.S. House of Repesentatives, *Hearings on Political Economy and Constitutional Reform*, 97th Congress, 2d session, pt. 1, p. 16 (Cutler); p. 191 (Dillon); p. 221 (Fulbright). Hereafter cited as Reuss 1982.

2. Ibid., p. ix.

3. Charles H. McIlwain, *Constitutionalism: Ancient and Modern* (Ithaca, N.Y.: Cornell University Press, 1940, 1947).

4. Dangerous neighboring states were a strong argument for absolute monarchies. Martin Malia, "Poland's Eternal Return," *New York Review of Books*, September 29, 1983, p. 20.

5. James Q. Wilson is an exception. See below.

6. See Cutler, in Reuss 1982, pp. 28–29; and Charles M. Hardin, *Presidential Power and Accountability* (Chicago: University of Chicago Press, 1974), chap. 10.

7. Walter Lippmann, *The Public Philosophy* (Boston: Little, Brown, 1955), p. 33, citing Allan Nevins.

8. W. Ivor Jennings, *The British Constitution* (Cambridge: Cambridge University Press, 1942), p. 78.

9. In one respect it would be superior to recent results in England, where governments have often been elected by less than a majority. The Labour government of 1974–1979 was elected by less than 40 percent.

10. Winston Churchill, *The Second World War*, vol. 2, *Their Finest Hour* (Boston: Houghton Mifflin, 1949), p. 15.

11. Richard Gephardt (Democrat, Missouri), quoted in Elizabeth Drew, "A Reporter at Large: Politics and Money," *New Yorker*, December 6, 1982, p. 96.

12. Ibid., p. 122.

13. Pendleton Herring, *The Politics of Democracy* (New York: Rinehart, 1940), chap. 7.

14. This is a central argument in McIlwain, *Constitutionalism*.

15. Walter Lippmann, *Public Opinion* (New York: Macmillan, 1922).

16. Quoted in Peter Wyden, *Bay of Pigs* (New York: Simon and Schuster, 1979), p. 65.

17. Ibid., p. 7.

18. Hardin, *Presidential Power and Accountability*, pp. 106, 219.

19. Lloyd N. Cutler, "To Form a Government," *Foreign Affairs* (Fall 1980); reprinted as chapter 1 of this volume.

20. C. Douglas Dillon, "Remarks," Fletcher School of Diplomacy, Tufts University, May 1982.

21. Reuss 1982, p. 223.

22. Ibid., pp. 247–48.

23. Ibid., p. 224.

24. Ibid., p. 257.

25. Jennings, *The British Constitution*, pp. 190–91.

26. Leon D. Epstein, *British Politics in the Suez Crisis* (Urbana: University of Illinois Press, 1964), esp. chaps. 5, 9.

27. Henry O. Brandon et al., *President vs. Congress: Does the Separation of Powers Still Work?* (Washington, D.C.: American Enterprise Institute, 1981); and James Q. Wilson, "What Can Be Done?" in *AEI Public Policy Papers* (Washington, D.C.: American Enterprise Institute, 1981), pp. 15–31. (Page references to the latter are to the manuscript version.)

28. Compare Edward C. Banfield, *Political Influence* (Glencoe, Ill.: Free Press, 1961), p. 328.

29. Brandon et al., *President vs. Congress*, pp. 6, 13–14.

30. Ibid., p. 10.

31. Wilson, "What Can Be Done?" p. 27; Wilson cites Aaron Wildavsky.

32. Brandon et al., *President vs. Congress*, p. 14.

33. Ibid., p. 22.

34. Samuel H. Beer, in Beer and Adam B. Ulam, *Patterns of Government* (New York: Random House, 1962), p. 208.

35. Samuel H. Beer, *Britain against Itself* (New York: Norton, 1982), p. 209.

36. References are to David M. Potter, *People of Plenty* (Chicago: University of Chicago Press, 1954); Herbert Agar, *The Price of Union* (Cambridge, Mass.: Riverside Press, 1950); and Harold Lasswell and Robert J. Samuelson, "The Campaign Reform Failure," a review of Elizabeth Drew, "Politics and Money," *New Republic*, September 8, 1983, p. 35.

37. Wilson, "What Can Be Done?" p. 2.

38. Ibid., p. 8.

39. Ibid., p. 10.

40. Ibid., pp. 4, 10, 14, 18, 22.

41. Ibid., p. 10.

42. V. O. Key, *Public Opinion and American Democracy* (New York: Knopf, 1961), p. 536.

43. Wilson, "What Can Be Done?" p. 13.

44. Ibid., pp. 14, 18.

45. Ibid., p. 21.

46. Ibid., pp. 24, 25.

47. Ibid., pp. 28–29.

48. Ibid., pp. 31, 27.

49. Walter Dean Burnham, "The Constitution, Capitalism, and the Need for Rationalized Regulation," in Robert A. Goldwin and William A. Schambra, eds., *How Capitalistic Is the Constitution?* (Washington, D.C.: American Enterprise Institute, 1982), pp. 77, 83.

50. Ibid., pp. 92, 101.

51. That is, "any arrangement which creates linkages of autonomous power only weakly connected to some central, nominally sovereign, authority." James Madison is Burnham's authority, along with his own observation of events, for this observation.

52. Burnham, "The Constitution," p. 103.

53. Ibid., p. 101.

54. See my *Presidential Power and Accountability*, chaps. 4–6, for a discussion of iron triangles, which I call "bureaucracy."

55. Burnham, "The Constitution," pp. 103, 105.

56. See Brooks Jackson, "Indefensible Costs: Moves to Close Bases, Reduce Other Waste in Military Often Fail," *Wall Street Journal*, July 16, 1982; and idem, "Leaky Defense: Pentagon's Big Empire Is Rife with Rip-Offs and Policy Is Spotty," *Wall Street Journal*, January 17, 1983. See also articles cited in note 64.

57. Burnham, "The Constitution," pp. 102–3.

58. Ibid., pp. 93, 104, 105.

59. Ibid., pp. 105, 103.

60. Richard E. Neustadt, *Presidential Power* (New York: Wiley, 1960), p. 4.

61. Kurt Riezler, "Political Decisions in Modern Society," *Ethics*, pt. 2 (January 1954).

62. Charles M. Hardin, "The Tobacco Program: Exception or Portent?" *Journal of Farm Economics* (Spring 1946).

63. Elizabeth Drew, "A Political Journal," *New Yorker*, June 20, 1983, pp. 48–49.

64. Brooks Jackson and Edward F. Pound, *Wall Street Journal*, July 28, 1983; cf. Jackson's article in *Wall Street Journal*, August 17, 1983.

65. Sidney Blumenthal, "Drafting a Democratic Industrial Plan," *New York Times Magazine*, August 28, 1983.

66. Kenneth H. Bacon, "The Outlook," *Wall Street Journal*, September 12, 1983; and Art Pine, "The Outlook," *Wall Street Journal*, September 19, 1983.

67. Reuss 1982, p. 189.

68. *New York Times*, section E, July 10, 1983.

69. An apt illustration, although it deals with defense rather than with economic policy, is supplied by Representative Les Aspin's projection of what would be necessary to implement a policy based on the Scowcroft Commission's report on the MX missile. The policy would have to be maintained over at least ten years. Elizabeth Drew, "A Political Journal," *New Yorker*, June 20, 1983, p. 74.

70. Walter Lippmann, *Chicago Sun Times*, August 14, 1958.

71. Epstein, *British Politics*, pp. 202–4.

72. Report No. 91-129, *National Commitments*, to accompany S. Res. 85, 91st Congress, 1st session, April 16, 1969.

73. Richard Halloran, *New York Times*, July 24 and 31, 1983.

74. Stanley Hoffmann, "In Search of a Foreign Policy," *New York Review of Books*, September 29, 1983, pp. 53–54.

75. McIlwain, *Constitutionalism*.

76. Ibid., p. 136.

77. Ibid., pp. 139, 140.

78. Ibid., pp. 141–42.

79. Ibid., p. 143.

6

The Separation of Powers and Foreign Affairs

L. Peter Schultz

The question to be addressed is, Does the separation of powers still work? Although it is refreshing to have the Constitution and one of its most prominent characteristics taken seriously, one must ask what is meant by the question. For in an immediate sense, it seems beyond question that the separation of powers still works. That is, the federal government functions, by and large, according to the design of the Constitution, proposed legislation being dealt with first by Congress, then by the president, and sometimes by the Supreme Court. Moreover, it is also beyond question that each of the three departments has sufficient power to affect public policy and that, in disagreements between departments, the ensuing struggle is closely contested precisely because the separation of powers still works. Despite contentions that the president or the Supreme Court has become "imperialistic," none of the departments can simply override the wishes of the others or work its will in disdain for those other departments.[1] That each department is, in an important sense, independent is evidence of the continued vitality of the separation of governmental powers into three departments.

The question, therefore, is not so much whether the separation of powers still works in this immediate sense as whether, by working, it serves the public or national interest. That is, is a defense of the separation of powers as persuasive today as it was in 1787, when the Constitution was drafted? Or has the separation of powers become obsolete, a political device that despite or because of its venerable age should be consigned to the dustbin of history? Stated more fully, the question is, Does the separation of powers serve the ends of government as they are conceived today as well as it served the ends of government as conceived in 1787? And the answer given by very many commentators today is a decisive no.

The separation of powers is said to have outlived its usefulness because today a premium should be placed on governmental action—planning as well as implementation—whereas in 1787 a premium was put on governmental inaction. In 1787 it was thought that that government was best that governed least, whereas today it is thought that that government is best that does the most to advance, by positive measures, the general good. Because "positive government" requires planning and coordination between the departments of the government, the separation of powers, which is conceived as turning the departments into rivals or opponents, does not serve the needs of contemporary society and should be, at the very least, modified.[2]

It is my contention that, when properly conceived, the separation of powers does serve the ends of government, even as those ends are understood today. Common perceptions notwithstanding, the separation of powers is consistent with positive government, although the separation does affect in important ways the character of such government. As evident in the constitutional provisions dealing with foreign affairs, the subject of this essay, the separation of powers serves not only the cause of "deliberate" government but also the cause of "efficient" or "vigorous" government. By dividing the power to deal with foreign affairs, the framers of the Constitution sought to establish a government of comprehensive yet differentiated powers, a government that provides ample opportunity for "secrecy and dispatch" as well as for deliberation.[3] In sum, the separation of powers constitutes an attempt to solve one of the major problems of government, that of providing for both reasonable government and forceful government without sacrificing either. Insofar as the separation of powers looks to achieve such a comprehensive end, it is to be hoped that the separation of powers still works.

Prevailing Views of the Separation of Powers in Foreign Affairs

The two popular or prevalent understandings of the separation of powers in foreign affairs both fail to assess correctly the separation as found in the Constitution. The most prevalent interpretation is that the Constitution issued an invitation for Congress and the president to struggle for control of foreign affairs. The two departments possess parallel powers relating to foreign affairs, such as Congress's power to regulate commerce with foreign nations and the president's power to recognize foreign nations by accepting their ambassadors. According to this interpretation, the Constitution does not answer the question, Which of these two departments controls foreign policy? because under the Constitution both departments can legitimately claim and can act upon their claims to make foreign policy. Hence Congress and the president are rivals, each contesting for the prerogative of deciding the nation's foreign policy.[4]

The other popular view, espoused more forcefully in recent years, holds that Congress was intended to be the primary formulator of the nation's foreign policy but that over the years its prerogatives have eroded, with the result that the president has become, for all practical purposes, the chief formulator of foreign policy. The argument is thus that the presidency has become (or did become) "imperialistic," usurping the powers that constitutionally belong to Congress. By virtue of the march of history, what was intended to be settled by the Constitution, congressional supremacy, is no longer settled, and Congress must struggle against the president to maintain whatever prerogatives it may still possess in the area of foreign affairs.[5]

The view that the Constitution issues an invitation to the president and Congress to struggle for supremacy in foreign affairs implies that the Constitution does not settle that struggle but leaves open one of the most important constitutional questions: Who controls, or who should control, foreign policy? In this view control of foreign policy is to be decided by the rivals themselves through political combat, so that at one time Congress may be supreme and at another time the president may predominate. Put most generally, the Constitution and the political order founded on it are incomplete and therewith imperfect. The practical implication of this imperfection is great difficulty in "forming a government," as one recent influential commentator has argued.[6]

The other understanding of the Constitution, that is, intended but subverted congressional supremacy, is also based on the concept of rivalry, although it views the rivalry between the departments as settled in the Constitution—in favor of Congress. Insofar as the rivalry continues, it does so against the intentions of the framers, which suggests that those intentions may no longer be relevant in the twentieth century. Perhaps in earlier and simpler times congressional supremacy made sense, but according to this view it no longer does so with virtual national annihilation only minutes away. The best that can be hoped for is some form of controlled executive predominance, with Congress understood as a check on the exercise of executive power. As in the former argument, Congress and the president should be viewed as rivals even if the balance of power today necessarily, rather than constitutionally, favors the executive. One of the most important implications of this understanding of the Constitution is that in contemporary times the unilateral exercise of executive

120

power is constitutionally suspect. Therefore, in times of political crisis and controversy, this perspective on the relation between the president and Congress undermines the legitimacy of executive action, however necessary that action may appear to be. When exercised unilaterally, executive power is always in the shadow of constitutional suspicion.[7]

Each of these views has theoretical and practical problems. Taken together, they fail to understand the Constitution in a way that stabilizes the relation between Congress and the president. In the first view, the relation is intentionally or constitutionally unstable, while in the second it is necessarily unstable insofar as there is a conflict between the intended and the actual relations. Both views fail, therefore, to define congressional-presidential relations in a way that allows a definite and stable relation to emerge. Insofar as this is true, both views leave the impression that the meaning of the Constitution is uncertain at best and irrelevant at worst.

In fact, however, the meaning of the Constitution is far more definite than can be accounted for by either of the two popular and prevailing views. Each view fails to understand the extent to which the relation between Congress and the president was intended to be a partnership and, moreover, a partnership for the sake of energetic or "positive" government. When properly understood, the separation of powers between Congress and the president in foreign affairs constitutes a division of labor through which Congress provides the materials, both legal and fiscal, with which the president conducts the nation's foreign affairs. It is my contention that congressional power in foreign affairs primarily facilitates executive or presidential activity and only secondarily checks such activity. In sum, congressional and presidential power supplement and complement each other in a way too little appreciated. To appreciate this fact fully, let us first consider the Constitution itself.

Constitutional Powers in Foreign Affairs

When the Constitution is read with a view to foreign affairs, the first significant fact to notice is that most of the constitutional powers relating to foreign and military affairs are granted to Congress. Article I, section 8, lists two sets of powers: powers concerning economic matters and powers concerning national defense. (These two sets of powers are separated in the document by the power to establish "tribunals inferior to the Supreme Court.") Eight powers concerning foreign and military affairs are enumerated in Article I:

- to regulate commerce with foreign nations and the Indian tribes

121

- to define and punish piracies and felonies on the high seas and offenses against the law of nations
- to declare war, to grant letters of marque and reprisal, and to make rules concerning captures on land and water
- to raise and support armies
- to provide and maintain a navy
- to make rules for the regulation of land and naval forces
- to provide for calling forth the militia to execute the laws, suppress insurrections, and repel invasions
- to provide for organizing, arming, and disciplining the militia and for governing those in service to the United States[8]

Article II grants relatively few powers to the president regarding the same matters:

- to serve as commander in chief of the armed forces and of the militia when in service to the United States
- to make treaties with the advice and consent of the Senate
- to appoint ambassadors, other public ministers, and consuls
- to receive ambassadors and other public ministers
- to commission all officers of the United States[9]

It would thus appear that the Constitution intended Congress to control foreign affairs since it grants to Congress the bulk of those powers relating to foreign policy, commercial as well as military. Various commentators on the Constitution have used this distribution of powers to prove congressional supremacy.[10] Upon closer examination, however, the Constitution's distribution of powers can be seen to serve different purposes.

First, congressional responsibilities have a particular character, which might be called literary. Congress is given the power, for example, "to define and punish Piracies and Felonies committed on the high Seas," by which must be meant the power to establish by law, in writing, the definition and punishment of such crimes, since the courts would do the actual punishing. Congress itself does not punish anyone but simply establishes the terms upon which others will do so. Note also that Congress is to "grant Letters of Marque and Reprisal," that is, to confer written authorization on private vessels that will engage in conflict for the United States. Again, Congress establishes or writes the terms by which others are to act, a pattern followed in the grant that authorizes Congress to "make [that is, write] rules concerning Captures on Land and Water." From the Constitution, then, Congress is to define, to write letters, and to make or write rules. When read in this light, the Constitution's grant to

Congress of the power to "declare War" is more precise—and more limited—than is often acknowledged. Declaring is akin to writing and distinct from making. In sum, Congress's responsibility concerning foreign affairs has a distinct tone or character that we can call literary because it can be fulfilled by writing letters, rules, and regulations as well as by defining actions and declaring the nation's condition with regard to war and peace.

Second, congressional responsibility and power extend to "providing" for various institutions and activities that are indispensable for the successful conduct of foreign policy, especially a military establishment. Congress is granted the power to raise and support armies and to provide and maintain a navy, responsibilities that may be said to be limited in that they leave Congress outside the military establishment, strictly speaking. Congress "provides for" a military establishment, both legally and fiscally, but control and use of that establishment rest elsewhere, most plausibly with the commander in chief. This interpretation is supported by the grant to Congress of the power "to provide for calling forth the Militia to execute the Laws . . . suppress Insurrections, and repel Invasions," a grant that implies that neither the actual calling forth nor the use of the militia for such purposes is a congressional responsibility. Congressional action may be said to be limited to establishing the military and providing for its use while the actual calling forth and use are left to the president as commander in chief.

From this consideration of Article I it is clear that however broad Congress's power may appear to be regarding foreign affairs, it is limited and incomplete. Congress declares, but does not make, war, either private or public. Similarly, Congress provides for the engines of war, armies and navies, but the control of those engines is entrusted to the president. In both instances, it may be argued, Congress exercises its powers to facilitate the president in the exercise of his powers or the fulfillment of his responsibilities. Declaring war facilitates making war, as does providing for armies and navies, even if declaring war is not indispensable to making war in the same way that providing for armies and navies is. In other words, congressional power is competent to create and regulate a military establishment, but it is not competent to the actual use of that establishment. Use, in the form of command, is entrusted to the president. Although a significant part of the war powers is vested in Congress, it cannot be said that Congress was intended to be supreme in the sense of commanding as well as providing for, acting as well as regulating, or making war as well as declaring it. Congressional power, though

123

broad, is incomplete; it needs executive or presidential power to complete it.

Moreover, the same division of labor is evident with regard to foreign affairs more broadly conceived. Article I does vest in Congress the power "to regulate Commerce with foreign Nations," but Article II empowers the president to make treaties by and with the advice and consent of the Senate, thereby entrusting to the president and his constitutional ally, the Senate, the responsibility for solidifying the nation's commercial relations with other nations. Insofar as enduring commercial relations depend on treaties, much of the nation's foreign policy rests in the hands of the president and his appointees. Wisely, the Constitution supplements the president's power as chief negotiator with foreign nations with his power as commander in chief; often foreign negotiations require the real possibility of more forceful persuasion to be concluded successfully. Again, through Article II the president is given the power, subject to the approval of the Senate, to appoint those officials who are to conduct the day-to-day affairs with foreign nations. This power necessarily involves the president intimately in the conduct of foreign affairs and, therewith, in the making of foreign policy.

This examination of Articles I and II reveals a division of labor according to which Congress facilitates the exercise of executive power in the realm of foreign affairs. Put most broadly, Congress may be said "to provide for" the possibility of executive action or activity. Just as Congress facilitates "private war" by granting letters of marque and reprisal, so too it can facilitate "public war" by establishing military forces and, if necessary in particular circumstances, by declaring war. Thus Congress and the president need not be understood as rivals, each existing solely for the purpose of checking the other; they should more appropriately be viewed as partners, the legislature using its powers to legitimate action taken by the executive. Congress legislates so that the executive can act, either diplomatically or militarily, to secure and advance the nation's interests. This division of labor is a reflection of the conviction, shared by several of the leading framers, that although Congress can legislate competently, it cannot act, at least not with sufficient "energy" or "secrecy and dispatch" to serve the national interest.[11] Because the Congress cannot act decisively, energetically, and with dispatch, it can and should provide the means for those who can and must act. To an extent that is not often sufficiently appreciated, the legislative power serves the executive power and, therewith, also serves energetic or positive government.

Facilitating the Use of Executive Power

To argue that the legislative power should be understood as facilitating the use of executive power conflicts with much of what is commonly accepted about the Constitution and the American political order. Most especially, perhaps, it conflicts with the equation of law making and policy making. Very often, if not invariably, it is thought that because Congress makes law it was intended to be the policy maker and therefore the supreme or predominant department of the government. Insofar as the legislative power was actually intended to serve the executive power, however, as I have argued, the mistaken equation of law making and policy making stands the Constitution on its head. Such an equation virtually reverses the intended relation between the president and Congress.

The Constitution was constructed to expand greatly the realm of executive discretion and activity, especially the executive's capacity to make policy. Consider Alexander Hamilton's discussion of the nature of administration at the outset of *Federalist* No. 72:

> The administration of government, in its largest sense comprehends all the operations of the body politic, whether legislative, executive, or judicial; but in its most usual and perhaps its most precise signification, it is limited to executive details and falls peculiarly within the province of the executive department. The active conduct of foreign negotiations, the preparatory plans of finance, the application and disbursement of the public moneys in conformity to the general appropriations of the legislature, the arrangement of the army and navy, the direction of the operations of war—these and other matters of a like nature, constitute what seems to be most properly understood by the administration of government.[12]

Note that even though in "its most precise signification . . . limited to executive details," administration comprehends very significant governmental functions and therewith policy making. "The active conduct of foreign negotiations" involves those in charge of such negotiations in the making of policy, as does "the direction of the operations of war."

Moreover, preparing financial plans—submitting a budget, as we might say today—also allows the president to influence policy making, if not simply or directly to make it. Under the Constitution, administration or executive power rises well above the ministerial, requiring many more administrators than technical experts.

Since executive power under the Constitution comprehends and

125

was intended to comprehend policy making, we can make much more sense of that document than is usually done. We also can more easily defend certain practices of government that often take on an air of illegitimacy because they are perceived as conflicting with the more common interpretations of the separation of powers. With regard to comprehending the Constitution in its wholeness, consider the president's power to give Congress information on the state of the Union and to recommend measures he thinks necessary and proper for the well-being of the nation. On the view that Congress is the primary policy maker and is therefore supreme, it is difficult to make sense of those provisions that give the president opportunities to affect policy making crucially by establishing the political agenda of the nation. Under the congressional supremacy view, these provisions must be either ignored or interpreted so as to bear little resemblance to the original intentions or meaning. (Some scholars argue, for example, that the state of the Union provision requires the president to disclose information, an interpretation distinguished more by its ingenuity than by its persuasiveness.)[13]

If one drops the assumption of legislative supremacy, however, one sees that under the Constitution the president is a central figure in the legislative process because that process was intended by the framers to facilitate the exercise of his executive powers. Therefore, the Constitution establishes the president as the overseer, it might be said, of the legislative process, ensuring as far as he is able that the laws serve executive power. Of course, the president's power to veto legislation serves as his primary means of directly affecting that process.

Not only does the partnership model allow us to make more sense of the Constitution in its totality, it also allows us to reassess the constitutional merits of certain practices that, under the more common interpretations of the separation of powers, seem justified only by their necessity. Consider the delegation of legislative powers. The most common argument asserts that Congress is constitutionally obligated to legislate on any subject as completely as possible, leaving as little as possible to the discretion of the executive and certainly leaving no major policy issues unresolved.[14] By this understanding law making is the equivalent of policy making, and Congress should not delegate power to the president or other executive officials and thereby leave them the power to make policy. Hence it is common for commentators to argue that Congress abdicates its constitutional responsibilities in many instances when it makes such broad delegations of power that the executive branch determines policy.

Under the partnership model of congressional-presidential relations, however, legislation should not simply be identified with policy making, and legislation that delegates power to the executive department is not contrary to and does not violate the Constitution. Under this model law serves more to legitimate executive action, and broad delegations of power to the executive department should not be deemed to violate the Constitution simply because they entrust policy questions to the executive. While the Constitution establishes Congress as the law-making department, it leaves ample room for executive policy making, especially in the realm of foreign affairs. Although Congress is the only law-making institution recognized by the Constitution, it is not the only policy maker. When Congress deems it necessary and proper, it may confer on the executive sufficient power to make policy; it does not by so doing delegate the law-making power. If this constitutional fact were more generally recognized, the air of illegitimacy surrounding significant delegations of power by Congress would be dissipated. More important, one of the valuable tools of energetic or positive government would be firmly grounded in the Constitution rather than left to justification by history or necessity.[15]

The understanding of congressional power as facilitating the use of executive power in foreign affairs has far-reaching implications, for example, in understanding "law." According to the partnership model, law should not be identified with policy making or understood as a check on executive power. The framers were aware that in the realm of foreign affairs executive policy making is necessary and even beneficial. Since the Constitution entrusts great responsibilities to the president in the realm of foreign affairs, the law should not be seen merely as a means of checking executive power, although it might be used in this fashion. The view that the legislature and the executive are necessarily rivals seems more at home in a monarchical political order, where the monarch—the executive—represents a different class from the legislature. The distance that exists between the one, the monarch, and the many, the people, justifies a check, even a rather substantial check, on the executive power. A republican system such as ours, where the chief executive does not belong to a distinct social class and can even claim to represent the people as a whole, has less need for a legislature that sees itself simply as the executive's rival, competing with the executive for the right to make policy. In a republican system policy making can be distributed among the three departments of government to ensure that it is capable of meeting all exigencies; law may be understood as friendly to executive power and

127

in the service of energetic government.

In this view of law the function of the legislator changes dramatically; instead of adopting the stance of a rival to the president, obligated to oversee and even regulate minutely the activities of the executive branch, the legislator adopts the stance of a partner, of one who is willing to listen to the chief executive with regard to the state of the Union and with regard to measures the chief executive thinks will improve the Union. Such a legislator might well oversee the activities of the executive department, but not primarily to scrutinize or check the propriety, legal or political, of those actions.

Legislative Encroachment on Executive Power

I have argued that the relation between Congress and the president was intended to be more a partnership than a rivalry. According to this interpretation, Congress should use its power to facilitate the exercise of executive power, especially in those circumstances that require the government to act with "secrecy and dispatch," in the language of *The Federalist*. In the realm of foreign affairs, where both secrecy and dispatch are often required, the role of the legislator and the law is much different from what it is generally conceived to be. In this realm, it might be said, the law is, by and large, irrelevant, and the legislature is, by and large, incompetent. The realm of foreign affairs is decidedly the realm of executive, as distinguished from legislative, power, and this fact is recognized by the Constitution in its distribution of powers.

Typically, however, both the law and the legislature are deemed competent to any task, to any situation, foreign as well as domestic: to commanding the military as well as to establishing it, to making war as well as to declaring it. From the formulation or ratification of administrative regulations to the removal of executive officials, from the initiation of hostilities to the initiation of nuclear force, all executive actions, it is often thought, should be subject to the scrutiny, even to the control, of the legislature. By virtue of comprehensiveness the law and the legislature are supreme and should be involved in, even should approve, every significant exercise of governmental power.

In the realm of foreign affairs, the argument for legislative supremacy has had considerable effect, both in the debate over the proper scope of executive power and in recent legislative efforts to enforce the Constitution. Recently, for example, the question has been raised whether, under the Constitution, the president may unilaterally order the first use of nuclear weapons, either before or after hostilities have begun. The argument against the president's right to act in this capacity is that such use constitutes a policy question of the first order and, therefore, cannot be decided by the president alone. The assumption is, of course, that all policy questions of the first order, whether in the realm of foreign or of domestic affairs, are either constitutionally entrusted to Congress or cannot be decided without congressional approval.[16]

The problem with this argument is, on its face, a practical one. How is the legislature to make such a decision without rendering the question itself moot? For Congress to debate such a question—and debate seems implicit in all legislative proceedings—is both useless and dangerous. The practical difficulty here illustrates the very real limits of legislative power. Quite simply, in some situations the exercise of legislative power is irrelevant, and to some purposes that power is incompetent. As recognized during the Constitutional Convention of 1787, making war is one of those situations.[17] The very best to be hoped for in such situations is that the legislature would meet in executive session, that is, would pretend to be an executive body. But the suggestion of executive sessions, because of their shortcomings, only serves to illustrate the incompetence of the legislature in such situations, not the remedy.

The framers of the Constitution were aware of the problems of legislative incompetence and irrelevance, both from theory and from practice.[18] The Constitution reflects their awareness in the way it addresses the issues of war and peace, even domestic peace. The Constitutional Convention changed its original grant to Congress of the power to "make war" to the power to "declare war." This change, in keeping with the spirit of the constitutional grants of power to Congress, was made in recognition that sudden attacks require quick and decisive action, necessarily precluding consulting or obtaining the approval of the legislature. Of course, the framers recognized that sudden attacks are sometimes necessary after a war has started or even just before a war is about to commence. Most generally, the framers recognized that the making of war was beyond the competence of the legislature and that war making should therefore be entrusted to a commander in chief of considerable authority.[19]

It is not so frequently noticed that the Constitution grants the president considerable power over peace making as well. On the one hand, the Constitution entrusts the treaty-making power to the president, to be exercised by and with the advice and consent of the Senate. On the other hand, the president is granted the pardoning power, which Hamilton defends in *The Federalist* as a very useful means of restoring domestic peace:

But the principal argument for reposing the power of pardoning in this case in the Chief Magistrate is this; in seasons of insurrection and rebellion, there are often critical moments when a well-timed offer of pardon to the insurgents or rebels may restore the tranquillity of the commonwealth; and which, if suffered to pass unimproved, it may never be possible afterwards to recall. The *dilatory* process of convening the legislature, or one of its branches, for the purpose of obtaining its sanction to the measure, would frequently be the occasion of letting slip the golden opportunity. The loss of a week, a day, an hour, may sometimes be fatal.[20]

Making peace, here domestic peace, is a responsibility entrusted to the president because he can act with dispatch and in a timely fashion whereas the legislature cannot. Indeed, as Hamilton reminds us, the legislature is not always in session. That the power of making peace sometimes requires secrecy as well as dispatch again helps explain why this responsibility is entrusted to the president. In sum, the constitutional distribution of powers reflects the framers' recognition that certain situations require a kind of power different from the legislative, that certain situations, often those most critical to the life of the nation, are beyond the competence of the legislature. Once again the conclusion appears that the executive power is a necessary and beneficial supplement to the legislative.

The assumption of legislative supremacy, however, has affected the constitutional order, perhaps beyond the realm of debate. Several legislative acts reflect this assumption, the most relevant being the War Powers Resolution of 1973.[21] That resolution requires that

the President in every possible instance shall consult with Congress before introducing United States Armed Forces into hostilities or into situations where imminent involvement in hostilities is clearly indicated by the circumstances, and after each such introduction shall consult regularly with the Congress until the . . . Forces are no longer engaged in hostilities or have been removed from the situation.

The resolution also limits to three those situations into which the president may introduce troops: "(1) a declaration of war, (2) specific statutory authorization, or (3) a national emergency created by an attack on the United States, its territories or possessions, or its armed forces." Both the consulting requirements and the limits on the president's power to introduce troops into hostile situations are justified as an attempt "to fulfill the intent of the framers of the Constitution," the consulting provisions being intended to ensure "that the collective judgment of both the Congress and the President will apply to the introduction of United States' Armed Forces into hostilities . . . and to the continued use of such forces in hostilities."[22]

It would be inconsistent with the argument I have made to deny that the framers intended Congress and the president to exercise "collective judgment." It is not at all clear, however, that the framers perceived that judgment as the proponents of the War Powers Resolution do. To be sure, it is within Congress's power to try to define those circumstances under which the president would use the nation's armed forces, and such an exercise in definition is consistent with the Constitution; it facilitates the use of executive power. Indeed, it was just this implication of the resolution that led Senator Thomas Eagleton, one of its original proponents, to vote against its final version.[23] Moreover, Congress might even forbid the use of military force in certain specific situations or for certain specific purposes. Such a power seems implicit in the larger, more comprehensive legislative power. Although all this should be granted, it does not follow that Congress is constitutionally entitled to veto, or even to be involved in, the actual decision to employ the force of the nation. That decision is entrusted by the Constitution to the commander in chief, as the officer who exercises "the supreme command and direction of the military and naval forces, as first general and admiral of the Confederacy."[24] That Congress exercises some power over the military does not mean that it may exercise every kind of power, and it especially does not mean that Congress exercises the power of command over the military.

The War Powers Resolution, therefore, oversteps the appropriate bounds of the separation of powers by entrusting to Congress a responsibility that the Constitution entrusts to the president and him alone. Section 2(c) of the resolution, which defines those situations into which the president may introduce troops, may be within the power of Congress even though it is overnarrow and legalistic. Section 3, however, which requires the president to consult Congress in "every possible instance," must be read in conjunction with two other passages: section 5(b), which states that the president shall withdraw the armed forces from any hostile situation or potentially hostile situation within sixty days unless Congress (1) has declared war or specifically authorized the use of force, (2) has extended the sixty-day period, or (3) cannot meet because of an attack upon the United States; and section 5(c), which allows Congress by concurrent resolution to direct the president to remove any armed forces he has introduced. These sections make it clear that the War Powers Resolution deems Congress to be supreme vis-à-vis the president in employing the force of the nation. That is, although in certain very narrowly

131

defined circumstances the president may use the force of the nation, his decision in every conceivable instance must be legitimated by Congress and may be overridden by Congress at any time. In fact, the only time Congress need not legitimate the president's actions as commander in chief is when it cannot act because it cannot meet. Only policy made or condoned by the legislature is legitimate, and Congress is supreme in that all governmental action must have its approval.

The assumptions underlying the War Powers Resolution have a certain currency today, as reflected in the popularity of the legislative veto. Although the legislative veto takes several forms, it is derived directly from the idea that congressional approval, whether explicit or implicit, is the necessary and even the sufficient condition of constitutional legitimacy. The law or the legislature is the fountain of all authority under the Constitution, and any executive action taken outside the law, even action taken where the law is silent, is constitutionally suspect in all instances (and constitutionally infirm in most). Consistently with this interpretation, under the War Powers Resolution the president must consult Congress—that is, seek congressional approval for his actions or proposed actions—in all instances except when it is, strictly speaking, impossible. Thus, even in the exercise of his constitutional powers, in all but the most dire circumstances the president must have the approval of Congress.

This interpretation is, of course, at odds with the interpretation of the Constitution argued here. The partnership between the branches implicit in the separation of powers under the Constitution rests on the assumption that the legislative power is not competent to every governmental function. The Constitution rejects legislative supremacy because it rejects legislative omnipotence. Following a well-established line of thought, the framers of the Constitution realized that there are limits to the competence of legislatures and therefore limits to the rule of law. Not every governmental action is best judged by its legality, by its adherence to some law or to the will of the legislature; some governmental actions are best judged by their success. As Chief Justice Charles Evans Hughes said, the Constitution grants power to the federal government to wage war successfully.[25] Indeed, one can argue today that even with the War Powers Resolution in place, legal propriety has little to do with assessments of the president's decision to use military force in dangerous or hostile situations. As one commentator has noted, the "War Powers Resolution . . . has made no difference in the pattern of congressional reaction to the President's uses of the armed forces." If a military operation is "swift and successful, Congress does not object; if it fails, Congress objects vehemently that the President has not complied with the War Powers Resolution."[26] In other words, only in the face of failure does Congress seem to be concerned with the legal propriety of the president's decision to use military force. Even today success quite appropriately means more than legality in the realm of foreign affairs.

Conclusion

In conclusion I return to the question with which I began: Does the separation of powers still work? As at the outset, my answer is yes. Although the answer has remained the same, however, it should now be clear that the answer is not based on the more commonplace understanding of the separation of powers as serving the cause of inefficent but safe government. Unlike the more commonplace understanding, which judges the success of the separation of powers by the degree to which it stifles governmental activity, my conclusion about the efficacy of the separation of powers is based on the fact that the president still possesses sufficient authority to act, specifically to employ the force of the nation unilaterally if he deems such action to be in the national interest, without a reliance on the Congress. The invasion of Grenada and the subsequent response to that invasion by Congress and the people prove that the separation still works, allowing the government to meet foreign exigencies as they arise by establishing a chief executive capable of acting independently of Congress and, if need be, even independently of the law. In sum, the separation still works despite the War Powers Resolution and the attempts to undermine the separation for the sake of legislative supremacy.

As we have seen, the question of the relevance of the separation of powers, of whether it still serves the public interest, often reflects a fundamental misunderstanding of that doctrine and its purposes. All too often the separation of powers is identified with inefficient government while legislative supremacy is identified with efficient government. Inefficiency is, however, not concomitant with separation per se but only with a particular understanding of that doctrine, an understanding informed by the idea of legislative supremacy. Justice Louis Brandeis's dissenting opinion in *Myers* v. *United States* is often cited as capturing the essence of the separation doctrine: "The doctrine of the separation of powers was adopted by the convention of 1787 not to promote efficiency but to preclude the exercise of arbitrary power. The purpose was not to avoid friction but . . . to save the people from autocracy."[27] But Brandeis and his admirers fail to appreciate that the link between the separation doctrine and inefficient government depends on the principle of legislative supremacy. As

Chief Justice William Howard Taft's opinion for the Court in *Myers* illustrates, it is only after accepting the principle of legislative supremacy as the controlling principle of the Constitution that one must argue, as Brandeis does, that an "uncontrollable power of removal in the Chief Executive 'is a doctrine not to be learned in American government.' "[28] Without the assumption that legislative supremacy is the controlling constitutional principle, one might well argue, as James Madison did when the first tenure-of-office act was passed, that Congress has virtually no power over the tenure of executive officials, even that virtually all executive officers should hold their offices at the pleasure of the president.[29] It is indicative of his distance from Madison that Brandeis adopts a position held by only two members of Congress during the removal debate in the First Congress in arguing that the removal power could be controlled as Congress saw fit, even exercised by Congress itself.[30] Essentially the disagreement between Brandeis, on the one hand, and Madison and Taft, on the other, turns upon the issue of legislative supremacy and whether that principle is central to the constitutional order. Whereas Madison and Taft interpreted the principle of legislative supremacy in the light of the separation of powers, Brandeis interpreted the separation in the light of legislative supremacy. Practically as well as constitutionally, the Madison-Taft interpretation is to be preferred.

There is, then, neither a necessary nor a constitutional connection between the separation of powers and inefficient government. Every time the government acts with "secrecy and dispatch," as it did in the invasion of Grenada, such action proves that the separation of powers still works, proves that the executive is able to act independently of Congress, relying solely on his constitutional authority to legitimate his actions whether or not they prove successful. Such action demonstrates that the departments of government remain equal and coordinate, as they were intended to be by the framers. Such action also proves that the separation of powers, by serving the cause of energetic or positive government, serves the ends of government even as those ends are understood today. Despite the predominant opinion, the separation of powers does indeed work today by allowing the government to defend the cause of liberal democracy in a generally hostile world.

Notes

1. Arthur M. Schlesinger, Jr., *The Imperial Presidency* (New York: Houghton Mifflin, 1974); Raoul Berger, *Government by Judiciary* (Cambridge, Mass.: Harvard University Press, 1977).

2. "The Constitution . . . institutionalized conflict in the very heart of the American polity. The question has always remained—and has provided a central theme of American political history—how a government based on the separation of powers could be made to work." Schlesinger, *The Imperial Presidency*, p. 9. Schlesinger goes on to suggest that the separation of powers not only does not work but was intended to prevent government from working: "The Founding Fathers were good Newtonians, and the system of checks and balances . . . contained an inherent tendency toward inertia. This was all right for awhile . . . [but not] in a rapidly changing society and even more especially [not] in times of danger." Ibid.

3. Alexander Hamilton, James Madison, and John Jay, *The Federalist Papers* (New York: Mentor, 1961), No. 71, p. 424.

4. In these areas [of foreign affairs] the two branches had interwoven responsibilities and competing opportunities. Moreover, each had an undefined residuum of authority on which to draw. . . . In addition, the Constitution itself was silent on certain issues . . . among them, the recognition of foreign governments, the authority to proclaim neutrality, the role of executive agreements, the control of information essential to intelligent decision. The result, as Edward S. Corwin remarked . . . was to make the Constitution "an invitation to struggle for the privilege of directing American foreign policy."

Schlesinger, *The Imperial Presidency*, p. 19.

5. Cf. Louis Henkin, for example:

The foreign relations powers appear not so "separated" as fissured. . . . [But] in the end and overall, Congress clearly came first in the longest article, expressly conferring many, important powers; the Executive came second, principally as executive-agent of Congressional policy. . . . Surely, though building magnificently, the Framers could not foresee what the United States would become, what the world would become. . . . Realities . . . modified the theoretical divisions, for in the competition of the political branches the President has had most of the advantages and Congress has not always been able to maintain its prerogatives.

Louis Henkin, *Foreign Affairs and the Constitution* (New York: Foundation Press, 1972), pp. 32–35.

6. Lloyd N. Cutler, "To Form a Government," *Foreign Affairs* (Fall 1980), reprinted as chapter 1 of this volume.

7. By way of example, consider the opinions of Justice Black and Justice Jackson in Youngstown Sheet and Tube Co. v. United States, 343 U.S. 579 (1952). Justice Jackson puts unilateral presidential power in the "twilight zone":

When the President acts in absence of either a congressional grant or denial of authority he can only rely upon his own independent powers, but there is *a zone of twilight* in which he and Congress may have concurrent authority, or in which its distribution is uncertain. Therefore, congressional inertia, indifference or quiescence may sometimes, at least as a practical matter, enable if not invite, measures of independent presidential responsibility [emphasis added].

Jackson remained doubtful that such exercises of presidential power could be justified under the Constitution: "In this area, any actual test of power is likely to depend on the imperatives of events and contemporary imponderables rather than on abstract theories of law."

8. *The Constitution of the United States*, Art. I, sec. 8.

9. Ibid., Art. II, secs. 2, 3.

10. Cf. Henkin, *Foreign Affairs and the Constitution*, and Schlesinger, *The Imperial Presidency*.

11. Mr. Pinckney opposed the vesting of this power [to make war] in the Legislature. Its proceedings were too slow. It wd. meet but once a year. The Hs. of Reps. would be too numerous for such deliberations.

Mr. Butler. The Objections agst the Legislative lie in a great degree agst the Senate. He was for vesting this power in the President, who will have all the requisite qualities, and will not make war but when the Nation will support it.

Mr. Madison and Mr. Gerry moved to insert "declare," striking out "make," leaving to the Executive the power to repel sudden attacks.

Max Farrand, ed., *The Records of the Federal Convention* (New Haven, Conn.: Yale University Press, 1966), vol. 2, p. 318.

The President is to be "commander-in-chief." . . . The propriety of this provision is so evident . . . that little need be said to explain or enforce it. Even those of them which have in other respects coupled the Chief Magistrate with a council have for the most part concentrated the military authority *in him alone*. Of all the cares and concerns of government, the direction of war most peculiarly demands those qualities which distinguish the exercise of power by a single hand. The direction of war implies the direction of the common strength; and the power of directing and employing the common strength forms a usual and essential part in the definition of the executive authority.

Federalist, No. 74, p. 447 (emphasis added).

12. *Federalist* No. 72, pp. 435–36.

13. Schlesinger, *The Imperial Presidency*, p. 27.

14. Sotirious Barber, *The Constitution and the Delegation of Congressional Power* (Chicago: University of Chicago Press, 1975).

15. National Cable Television Assn. v. United States, 415 U.S. 336 (1974); and Kent v. Dulles, 357 U.S. 116 (1958).

16. Jeremy Stone, "Presidential First Use Is Unlawful," *Foreign Policy* (Fall 1984), pp. 94ff.

17. Farrand, *Records*, vol. 2, p. 318.

18. Charles Thach, *The Creation of the Presidency, 1776–1787* (Baltimore: Johns Hopkins University Press, 1933).

19. Cf. note 11.

20. *Federalist* No. 75, p. 449.

21. War Powers Resolution of 1973, 87 Stat. 555.

22. Ibid., secs. 3, 2(c), 2(a).

23. Thomas Eagleton, *War and Presidential Power* (St. Louis: Washington University Press, 1974).

24. *Federalist* No. 69, p. 418.

25. Cited in Hirabayashi v. United States, 320 U.S. at 93.

26. Kenneth Holland, "The War Powers Resolution: An Infringement on the President's Constitutional and Prerogative Powers," in *The Presidency and National Security Policy* (Proceedings, Center for the Study of the Presidency) vol. 5, no. 1 (1984).

27. Myers v. United States, 272 U.S. 52 (1926).

28. Ibid.

29. Madison to Monroe, December 28, 1829, *The Writings of James Madison*, ed. Gaillard Hunt (New York: G.P. Putnam Sons, 1910), vol. 9, p. 43.

30. L. Peter Schultz, "William Howard Taft: A Constitutionalist's View of the Presidency" (Ph.D. dissertation, Northern Illinois University, 1979), pp. 72–73.

7

A 1787 Perspective on Separation of Powers

Ann Stuart Anderson

Everyone knows how seldom men think exactly alike on ordinary subjects; and a government constructed on the principle of assent by all its parts, would be inadequate to the most simple operations. The notion of a complication of counterchecks has been carried to an extent in theory, of which the framers of the constitution never dreamt.[1]

The fundamental problem, in trying to make the government of the United States work effectively, is not to preserve the separation of powers but to overcome it. For anything of consequence to be accomplished, the executive and legislative branches must be brought from confrontation into a reasonable degree of harmony. . . . Insofar as this device [legislative veto] of accommodation is now rendered unavailable, the two branches are condemned that much more often to the confrontation, stalemate and deadlock that so frequently leave the government of the United States impotent to cope with complex problems.[2]

Preliminaries

Separation of powers has come in for more than its share of criticism in recent years. It is variously accused of producing deadlock or stalemate (consult the second quotation above), of dividing power from responsibility, of preventing leadership, and of simply being an out-of-date, eighteenth-century device utterly unsuited to the needs of modern government. My view is that many of these criticisms rest on a misunderstanding of separation of powers as it is embodied in the U.S. Constitution.

The device is mistakenly thought of as an arrangement of three branches of government of equal power, locked in perpetual tension and balance; hence "checks and balances." Yet, when we examine separation of powers through the eyes and words of the framers and in the Constitution itself, we find that the only example of balance is bicameralism, dividing the legislative body into two to check its excesses. When we examine checks, we find that they do not create tension but provide a constitutionally legitimate method to resolve it. The three branches are not at all equal in power, because in our representative democracy the legislative predominates. Today the weakest of the three branches, the judiciary, is the greatest violator of the separation of powers.

I propose to defend these conclusions by recovering the framers' perspective on separation of powers and correcting our understanding of the reasons why they employed it as a structural device. Those reasons—liberty and the safe use of potentially dangerous governmental powers—are more compelling today than ever.

The Supreme Court's 1983 *Chadha* decision invalidating the legislative veto on separation of powers grounds serves as a basis for considering separation of powers as it is understood today and requires us to return to fundamentals: what separation of powers meant to the framers and how that meaning was applied to the creation of the United States Constitution.[3] In spite of the salutary recognition by the Court of the vitality of separation of powers, there is much in the Court's application of the concept to be discouraged about. Most of this is not new, and much of it dates to the beginning of the Republic. Separation of powers may well be the most misunderstood part of the Constitution; certainly misunderstandings of it date from the moment it was brought into being in the document. Thomas Jefferson and John Adams were among the first to be confused.[4]

There is much irony in the Supreme Court's self-appointed guardianship of separation of powers because the Court itself has been the branch most guilty of abusing the theory as it is realized in our founding charter. This emerges clearly in the *Chadha* decision, exists to a certain extent already in *Marbury* v. *Madison* (1803), and is full-blown in *McCulloch* v. *Maryland* (1819). The facts of the *Chadha* case are briefly these. Before the Alien Registration Act of 1940, Congress had to deal with deportation of aliens through individual bills, but that act authorized the attorney general of the United States to suspend deportation of qualified aliens if the House and the Senate did not disapprove by concurrent resolution. The act was modified, and the Immigration and Nationality Act of 1952 permitted suspension of the attorney general's decision not to deport by action of either house. The attorney general's decision to suspend the deportation of Chadha, an East Indian, was disapproved by the House of Representatives, acting under section 244(c)(2) of the act. Chadha challenged this section on the grounds of unconstitutionality, and the U.S. Court of Appeals for the Ninth Circuit struck it down as "violative of the constitutional principle of separation of powers."[5] By a vote of 7–2 the U.S. Supreme Court upheld the court of appeals.[6]

The Supreme Court's understanding of separation of powers, as it is found in the majority opinion by Chief Justice Warren Burger, rests initially on the premise that the Court itself is exempt from the requirements of the concept. Second, the Court claims the exclusive right or power to define what constitutes separation of powers or its violation. Third, the Court appears to believe that the separation of powers constraints in our Constitution are intended only as a limit on legislative power. This point is nicely made in Justice Byron White's dissent when he says: "Under the Court's analysis, the Executive Branch and the independent agencies may make rules with the effect of law while Congress, in whom the Framers confided the legislative power, Art. I, (Section) 1, may not exercise a veto which precludes such rules from having operative force."[7]

In *Federalist* No. 48 James Madison, explaining how to achieve, in practice, the "degree of separation . . . essential to a free government," writes:

> It is agreed on all sides that the powers properly belonging to one of the departments ought not to be directly and completely administered by either of the other departments. It is equally evident that none of them ought to possess, directly or indirectly, an overruling influence over the others in the administration of their respective powers.[8]

What is the Court doing but exercising "an overruling influence over the others in the administration of their respective powers"? In my opinion, this is the most fundamental violation of separation of powers we find in modern American government. We ought to feel obligated to understand separation of powers as the framers understood it and as it appears in our Constitution, to assess both the Court's decision in *Chadha* and the contemporary attacks on the principle's continuing validity in our governmental structure.

Before we look at the separation of powers in the U.S. Constitution, we must consider its necessary preconditions. This understanding is found most satisfactorily in an essay by Martin Diamond.[9] Diamond makes a compelling case for the radical modernity of the device in that it depends first on political and social democracy and second on post-Lockean objectives for government. Diamond argues that the device will not work in other circumstances and, by way of cementing this argument, shows that its purpose is the amelioration of the faults of democratic government. The implication of this view is that separation of powers is utterly different from the mixed regime or from balanced government. Let us examine these claims.

Separation of powers is a modern structural device designed to remedy the defects of modern democratic government. Accordingly, it must be disentangled from the concept of the mixed regime, because the differences are so great that it is entirely misleading to believe that the two are related. By definition, a mixed regime requires a political society organized by means of different political-social classes. A mixed regime combines those classes in a governmental structure so that one part of society will not be sacrificed to the interests of another. There is no functional division of governing power, nor does there need to be. Each part has the whole of the governing power and a veto over the actions of the other parts. "This sharing or mixing of various classes in governing the regime did not at all involve the division of power, as seems to be assumed by those who lump together the separation of powers and the mixed regime. . . . The governing power was twinned, so to speak, rather than divided."[10]

In contrast, separation of powers will not work in a polity that has real and enduring social classes. In the theory, governing powers are functionally divided among three branches: legislative, executive, and judicial. This is an essential part of separation of powers theory, although there could be great disagreement about which powers belonged in which category. The three branches are expected to form a whole coherent governing power, each performing its particular function. If, however, one branch abuses its power or utterly fails to function, the structure is supposed to conduce corrective actions on the part of the other branches. The correction could take the form of positive actions or of resistance, depending on the need. We have here a mechanical device designed to "produce conflict to stay evil, but to produce unity in effectuating decent measures."[11] Why the framers believed that the device would do these things becomes clear only when we examine the meaning of checks and balance, as I will do. For the moment, let us assume that the device will work as they expected it to. Why does it require democracy to do so?

Diamond answers this question by showing what conditions would prevent it. They are not conditions found in genuinely democratic countries.

> For example, if a single ideological and disciplined political party came to prevail, what good would separation of

powers be? The disciplined ideologues would not act as the separation of powers requires, namely, as creatures of Congress, the White House and the courts, that is, behaving above all with regard to the peculiar interests of their respec-. tive offices and duties; rather, despite formal separation of powers, these disciplined ideologues would function as a unified force thereby rendering the separation nugatory. Thus we can say with certainty that the separation of powers requires that we avoid the emergence and triumph of such a party system.[12]

The same problem arises in polities with dominant family interests that would override separation of powers constraints. Diamond mentions deep religious divisions and oligarchical classes as further examples of elements of society that would make separation of powers impossible. Loyalty to ideological party, powerful family, religion, or oligarchy would nullify the separation of powers structure. But in an actual democracy, particularly of the heterogeneous and representative kind described by Madison in *Federalist* No. 10, these competing claims are nonexistent or so moderated that they ought not to threaten the division of powers structure.

Another important precondition concerns the self-limiting claim of democracy itself. The argument for self-government could be taken seriously only when the legitimate objects of government seemed to come within the capacity of ordinary citizens. The legitimate scope of government, and consequently the competence necessary to govern, were radically limited in the seventeenth century, notably in the political philosophy of John Locke but also in other very influential thinkers like Montesquieu. The acceptable purposes of government became "life, liberty, and the pursuit of happiness" as in the Declaration of Independence, or "life, liberty and estate" as in Locke.

> The task of this now limited government was to protect the private pursuit of happiness—which, it could well be hoped, would include not only a concern for self-preservation but also for nobler private interests in philosophy, science, religion, art, friendship, and the like. But still these matters were now removed as far as possible from the purview of the political.[13]

The chief drawbacks to democracy had historically been incompetence and the destruction of liberty. With the dramatic lowering of the aims of government in the seventeenth and eighteenth centuries, democracy became possible, and the structural device of separation of powers could be employed to address its classical defects.

142

From the disorders that disfigure the annals of those republics the advocates of despotism have drawn arguments, not only against the forms of republican government, but against the very principles of civil liberty. They have decried all free government as inconsistent with the order of society. . . . If it had been found impracticable to have devised models of a more perfect structure, the enlightened friends to liberty would have been obliged to abandon the cause of that species of government as indefensible. The science of politics, however, like most other sciences, has received great improvement. The efficacy of various principles is now well understood, which were either not known at all, or imperfectly known to the ancients. The regular distribution of power into distinct departments . . .[14]

Separation of powers ameliorates the defects only of democratic government, because liberty and the competence essential to liberty are not the chief ends of other forms of government.

This is an oversimplified account of Diamond's argument establishing the radical distinction between separation of powers and the mixed regime. Separation of powers will not work except in a democracy; the modern limitation of the legitimate objects of government makes democracy possible; and separation of powers mitigates the defects of democratic government. Its institution in the American Constitution is powerful testimony to the democratic *bona fides* of the framers.

Substance

We can now proceed with our investigation of what the framers meant by separation of powers and how the device was expected to work. The Federal Convention of 1787 was the first occasion in history on which political man deliberately set out to create a government based on its principles. Nevertheless, separation of powers has been misunderstood by Americans, the children of the Founding Fathers, almost from the beginning. In the common view it is equated with the fragmentation of governing power, the sacrifice of the capacity to govern in favor of protection of liberty (understood as property rights), or deadlock or viewed as synonymous with checks and balances. Even for the most careful observers, separation of powers is elusive, for many reasons. One of them is the error of seeing the framers as hostile to democracy; another is a refusal to recognize that they were committed to legislative supremacy or at least to legislative predominance. Efforts by the framers so to structure the legislative power that it would not tyrannize have been misinterpreted as creating either a government of three balanced powers with none preeminent or a government where the executive or the judicial constitutionally predominates.

The view I present here is that separation of powers was designed both to secure the liberty of the individual person and to ensure competent government. The government was given plenary powers to achieve its legitimate objects, and the exercise of those powers was rendered safe by dividing them among three branches according to function. Because the framers understood that liberty was endangered as much by too little as by too much government and because they were free of utopian perspectives, they were sensibly aware of how difficult it is to find that correct amount. Powers were divided to make possible their effective use. To this end, constitutional means (checks) were provided for each political (legislative and executive) branch. The purpose of a check, as we shall see, was to *prevent* deadlock, not to create it. The three branches were quite unequal in powers, with the legislative branch predominant by design. Balance was confined to the legislative branch; we know it as bicameralism.

The best place to learn about separation of powers in the American Constitution is at the Federal Convention. The Virginia Plan was introduced in the opening days and became, with many modifications, the framework for the new government. Written by James Madison (though introduced by Edmund Randolph), the plan proposed a national legislature "impowered to enjoy the Legislative rights vested in [the Confederal] Congress," a national executive, and a national judiciary.[15] Like the legislature, the executive was to have the executive rights vested in Congress. For the framers, what was wrong with the Confederal Congress was not that it was a mere "diplomatic body," as John Adams had written, but that it was a government afflicted with impotence because of unseparated powers. Language in the Virginia Plan refers to "rights" that were commonly understood to be legislative or executive *by their nature*, not governing powers that can be defined as legislative or executive according to convenience or utility.

A statement by Pierce Butler on May 30 points toward the significance of the proposed change in structure:

> (After some general observations) he concluded by saying that he had opposed the grant of powers to Congress heretofore, because the whole power was vested in one body. The proposed distribution of the powers into different bodies changed the case and would induce him to go great lengths.[16]

The problem with the Confederal Congress was not that it lacked power, but that it could not use the power it had. Madison argues in *Federalist* No. 38 that the states had trusted the Confederal Congress with power that was dangerous because it resided in a single body.[17] Or consider Charles Pinckney's draft of a plan for a new government, probably presented to the convention on May 29:

> In a gov't where the liberties of the people are to be preserved and the laws well administered, the executive, legislative and judicial should ever be separate and distinct. . . . The Confederation seems to have lost sight of this wise distribution of powers of government and to have concentred the whole in a single body, where none of them can be used with advantage or effect.[18]

Thus we can see that the preference for the separation of powers structure was not only to preserve liberty but also to design a government for effective legislation and "well-administered" laws. Nothing in the debates at the Federal Convention supports the view that powers were to be separated for the purpose of frustrating government and rendering it impotent in order to protect liberty.[19] Both Butler and Pinckney contrasted separation of powers with the unseparated powers of the Confederal Congress; they saw a separation of powers structure as having greater possibilities for the use of governmental powers, not, as the common understanding goes, as a means of thwarting and checking the exercise of the powers of government.

To clarify these concepts and distinguish them one from another, I propose to consider separation of powers first, then checks, and then balance. The outcome, I believe, will be true to the framers' own understanding.

What was the meaning of separation of powers as understood and applied at the Federal Convention? An essential part of separation of powers theory at the convention was the conviction that government could be divided into three functional powers: legislative, executive, and judicial. No one questioned this assumption; by 1787 it was a given—part of every delegate's intellectual baggage. Certain powers were, by their nature, legislative, executive, or judicial, although not everyone agreed on just which powers were which. This view was so deeply held by the framers that it sometimes handicapped working out separation of powers in practice, when exceptions were proposed. Departures from a strict allocation principle had to be explained and justified, and they were occasionally defeated. It is essential to understand that the delegates passed judgment according to a pure separation theory, an ideal type by which proposals were judged.[20]

Among the numerous attempts to define powers by their nature was this interesting statement by James Wilson on June 1:

> He did not consider the Prerogatives of the British Monarch as a proper guide in defining the Executive powers. Some of these prerogatives were of a Legislative nature. Among others that of war & peace etc. The only powers he conceived strictly Executive were those of executing the laws, and appointing officers, not (appertaining to and) appointed by the Legislature.[21]

Madison also attempted to define executive powers and proposed that the Virginia Plan read, "with power to carry into effect the national laws, to appoint to offices in cases not otherwise provided for, and to execute such other powers (not Legislative nor Judiciary in their nature) as may from time to time be delegated by the national Legislature."[22] The section from "and to execute" was rejected as superfluous, leaving the Wilson definition in substance. Wilson's opinion—that the powers of war and peace were legislative powers, in addition to the general power of making laws and, later, also the power of making treaties that were to be the law of the land—was not disagreed with.

The nature of judicial power is, perhaps surprisingly, more subtle and cannot be divorced from the question of a judiciary's appropriate role in a separation of powers structure. At the convention the question of what constituted powers of a judicial nature was submerged in the issue of the utility and propriety of involving the judicial branch in legislation before such legislation came to it in the form of a case or controversy. This was the recurring issue of a council of revision. The members of the convention failed to agree on the council, thus adopting a narrower definition of judicial power in their scheme. They did agree that judicial power meant expounding the laws, explaining or interpreting them.

In rejecting a council of revision, the convention refused to involve the judicial power in legislation prior to cases that would arise under general laws. Later, when President Washington asked the Supreme Court for an advisory opinion, it refused, quite consistently with the convention's understanding. It was never proposed, or even suggested, at the convention that the Court have a general power of judicial review of national legislation or of the acts of the executive. Paradoxically, the rejection of a council of revision, on the grounds that it involved the judiciary in policy, opened the way for John

Marshall's and the Federalist party's doctrine. In *Marbury* v. *Madison* (1803), Chief Justice Marshall claimed for the Court the authority to pronounce on the constitutionality of the acts of the other two branches. This would never have been possible if the convention had adopted a council of revision.[23]

Instead of associating part of the judiciary in the drafting of sober and constitutionally sound legislation, we have a doctrine (judicial review) that, in its operation, makes the judiciary, instead of the legislature, paramount in our system of separation of powers. Yet legislative supremacy was clearly the intention of the framers. I use this language—legislative supremacy—in the sense that it is used by Justice Gibson in *Eakin* v. *Raub*, in the hope of symbolizing all the complexity and subtlety of legislative preeminence in the American constitutional order:

> Legislation is essentially an act of sovereign power; but the execution of laws by instruments that are governed by pre-scribed rules, and exercise no power of volition, is essentially otherwise. The very definition of law, which is said to be "a rule of civil conduct, prescribed by the *supreme* power in the state" shows the intrinsic superiority of the legislature. It may be said, the power of the legislature, also, is limited by the prescribed rules; it is so. But it is, nevertheless, the power of the people, and sovereign so far as it extends. . . . In-equality of rank arises not from the manner in which the organ has been constituted, but from its essence and the nature of its functions; and the legislative organ is superior to every other, inasmuch as the power to will and to command, is essentially superior to the power to act and to obey.[24]

The independence of the branches is crucial for separation of powers in the American Constitution. Madison explains that "if it be essential to the preservation of liberty that the legisl; Execut; & Judi-ciary powers be separate, it is essential to a maintenance of the separation that they should be independent of each other."[25] There was much disagreement about what constituted independence and how to achieve it. Many of these issues were not resolved at the convention. The delegates agreed generally that an executive chosen by the legislature was not independent.[26] John Dickinson suggested that although the departments ought to be made as independent as possible, a "firm Executive could only exist in a limited Monarchy."[27] The final decision to provide for the choice of the executive indirectly by popular vote, using the device of electors, secured independence both from the national legislature and from the states.[28] The motive of independence was as important as that of having an executive popularly elected to represent the whole populace.[29] Actually, the convention believed that the people were to be directly represented in the House of Representatives; the initial opinions on this point by men such as Madison and Wilson amounted to saying that only the House should be directly chosen by popular election.[30] Later Wilson included the executive in the principle, primarily to serve the requirements of independence.

Once the executive was chosen, the problem of how to maintain executive independence arose. Proposals varied from giving the president an absolute veto over legislation to associating the executive with the judiciary in a qualified veto or revisionary power.[31] The veto was conceived as a self-defensive power, to enable the executive to protect itself against the possibility that the "legislature can at any moment sink it into non-existence."[32] The council of revision proposed in the Virginia Plan was to prevent immoderate or unconstitutional legislation. The two objects of the veto, self-defense and decent legislation, are not identical, but various members of the convention supported them simultaneously in the discussions.

It is instructive to remember that the council of revision, which would have associated the executive and some members of the judiciary in a veto over *proposed* legislation, was rejected primarily because the majority of delegates judged that it violated the canons of separation of powers. This doctrinaire conception of the theory led many members to regard the final arrangement of a qualified veto for the executive, with the two-thirds legislative override, as basically self-defensive. Understood as such and not as a quasi-legislative device to produce decent legislation, it is less violative of separation of powers theory. Thus reasoned many of the delegates, with the exceptions of James Wilson, James Madison, Gouverneur Morris, and Alexander Hamilton.

Those who resisted an absolute executive veto did so for two reasons: they feared too much executive power and the resulting possibility of abuse, and they disliked the appearance of setting the executive power so blatantly over the legislative.[33] Yet the proposal that the veto be simply suspensory was also rejected, unanimously.[34] Elbridge Gerry of Massachusetts came forward with the final version of the veto. But Madison and Wilson would not let the issue die, and they proposed again and again that the judiciary be associated with the executive in a revision of proposed laws. Each time, and with much debate, the proposal was rejected.[35] Each time the opposing argument was that such an arrangement violated separation of powers and that judges ought not to be involved in policy or in legislating. It was thought that the power of expounding the laws when they came before the judges in the form of a case or controversy was a considerable and appropriate judicial power. My view is that the convention's failure to adopt a council of revision, because of doctrinaire separation of powers theory, made possible the development of a kind of judiciary that is problematic in a representative democracy. Acting in the name of legislative supremacy and separation of powers, the convention's dogmatism may have made possible the severe undermining of the former and the prevention of a more subtle and profound form of the latter.

Failure to establish a council of revision was a serious defeat for Madison and Wilson. An exchange that illuminates these principles occurred on July 21. Again Wilson proposed to add the judiciary to the executive in the exercise of a revisionary power. The judiciary ought to have an opportunity for protesting "encroachments on the people as well as on themselves" explicitly, for throwing its weight along with the executive against "unjust," "unwise," "dangerous," or "destructive" laws. Madison added his reasons: to enable the judiciary to defend itself against legislative encroachment, to bolster the executive in its exercise of the veto, and to be useful to the legislature in securing a "consistency, conciseness, perspicuity and technical propriety, in the laws, qualities peculiarly necessary; and yet shamefully wanting in our republican codes."

This arrangement would benefit the community as a check against "unwise and unjust" laws.[36] In answer, those who opposed this arrangement argued that it was improper to associate judges in policy making, a legislative power, and it was dangerous to make the executive or the judiciary too strong vis-à-vis the legislature. In desperation Madison fell back almost totally on the self-defense argument: the necessity of this means to maintain separation and independence in practice. He tried to explain that if combining the executive and the judiciary violated the maxims of separation of powers, then giving the veto to the executive alone violated them also. The view that prevailed relied on the illusion that a suspensory executive veto did not violate separation of powers by improperly involving the executive in the legislative function; it merely defended against encroachments on the executive power.[37]

Independence of the branches was again at issue in the discussion of what became Article I, section 6, paragraph 2, of the Constitution.[38] Madison had proposed that members of the legislature be prevented from holding offices created by that body during and for one year after their service in it. Some argued that this provision would still allow too much executive influence.[39] The final decision represents the liberal view and the acceptance of Madison's (and Wilson's) argument that liberality is necessary to attract men of the first rank into public office. Independence is also involved in considering permanent tenure for the judiciary, impeachment provisions, appointment of the judiciary, and whether or not the vice president ought to preside over the Senate.[40]

Independence for the executive is secured by his qualified veto over legislation and his selection by popular vote, using the device of an electoral college, rather than his being a creature of the legislature, state or national. Providing for the impeachment of the executive by the House of Representatives did not violate that independence as long as he was eligible for reelection. The framers believed that if they limited him to a specific number of terms, impeachment by the legislature (impeachment by the judiciary having been rejected because the judiciary was appointed by the executive) would have compromised his independence.[41]

Independence of the judiciary is satisfied by permanent tenure. That it is not independently appointed, has no control over its own salary, and was given no power in the Constitution analogous to the executive veto or to the powers that keep the legislature independent of the executive shows its nonpolitical character.[42] The judiciary's mode of appointment—nomination by the executive, confirmation by the Senate—avoided legislative or executive control of the membership of the Supreme Court. For this reason, Madison tells us in *Federalist* No. 39, the Court was the ultimate arbiter of federal questions.

Legislative independence is maintained by giving both houses control over their internal organization and officers, as well as over the credentials of their members; providing immunity for speeches in Congress and from certain kinds of arrest; prohibiting legislators from holding other offices during their term in the legislature; and arranging for liberal compensation ultimately free from executive control.

The framers began from a theory of separation of powers. At the convention they created institutional arrangements based on this theory, and separation of powers emerged from the process enriched and enlarged as follows: certain kinds of power are best exercised by particular kinds of bodies; decent laws are most likely to come from a representative body whose members must live under the laws they have passed;[43] administration is best performed by a single executive who is responsible for those whom he appoints and for the quality of administration performed; and application of law to particular cases is best entrusted to a body of judges who are professionally knowledgeable and able to apply their knowledge free from coercion or political influence.

The framers understood the necessary conditions for liberty to be more than the absence of governmental restraint. Admittedly, to some it did mean simply no government interference with religion, speech, press, or property. Yet many of the same men believed—or understood—that government that was too weak could easily lead to the anarchy and tyranny that were characteristic of previous democracies.[44] The division of function based on the nature of the power aims to achieve another kind of protection for liberty, by increasing the possibility of decent and effective government. The view that government is the only threat to liberty betrays a serious misunderstanding of modern democracy and its dangerous potential. Decent and effective government may not always be wise, but at least it is unlikely to deteriorate into anarchy and thence into tyranny.

To maintain separation the branches had to be independent, but they were not equally powerful; they were not three branches locked into perpetual tension because the same amount of power had been given to each. The American Constitution creates three *coordinate* branches, which means three branches of the same rank, equally national, not three of the same weight or power. The legislature is preeminent; the executive and judiciary are genuinely independent of it and were given sufficient strength to prevent being overwhelmed by it.

Independence, Madison explained in *Federalist* No. 48, meant being drawn from different sources and having as little agency in the execution of the powers of the other branches as possible.[45] As we shall now see, independence included the principle of checking, which was not intended to be, and does not amount to, deadlock.

A Theory of Checks

Separation of powers is not synonymous with "checks and balances" or, as James MacGregor Burns has put it, "a balance of checks."[46] To understand the constitutional arrangement properly, it helps to separate checks from balance, but even so it is surprisingly difficult to define checks.

In the prevailing view a check is anything that impedes the expression of the popular will (as the particular observer perceives it). This theory is as follows. The framers established what was at one and the same time a government in which the three branches were approximately equal in power (check and balance = deadlock) and one in which it was eventually possible for the executive to predominate. Others observe that the Supreme Court was eventually able to pre-

151

dominate. So we must first deal with a conception based on the belief that the three branches of the national government were designed with equal governing powers.

> But *suppose* all to be of equal capacity, in every respect, why should one exercise a controlling power over all the rest? That the judiciary is of superior rank, has never been pretended, although it has been said to be co-ordinate. It is not easy, however, to comprehend how the power which gives law to all the rest, can be of no more than equal rank with one which receives it.[47]

Quite so. If the three branches are of equal power, why does one or another (except the legislature) predominate? Conceptually, deadlock can only be a problem if the three branches are equal in power or if the legislature and the executive are equal in power.

Three independent and coordinate branches were created with the ratification of the Constitution in 1789. The confusion arises because of theories of balanced government, or because of failures to recognize that devices to prevent legislative tyranny are not devices to prevent democracy, or, finally, because of inability to understand the eighteenth-century meanings of words or concepts. Either error— supposing three equally powerful branches or supposing a dominant executive or judiciary—is based on the same inability to recognize or to acknowledge legislative supremacy, both as established by the Constitution and as necessary in a representative democracy. In the words of James Wilson (June 1):

> According to (Mr. Gerry) it [the council of revision] will unite the Executive & Judiciary in an offensive & defensive alliance agst. the Legislature. . . . To the first gentleman the answer was obvious; that the joint weight of the two departments was necessary to balance the single weight of the Legislature.[48]

Aside from the debates at the Federal Convention, the *Federalist*, and the Constitution—all of which might be called empirical evidence —the theoretical and historical evidence is that popular sovereignty and self-government have always been coincident with legislative supremacy or with a legislative body. The form of government established by the Constitution was one of legislative predominance because it was a representative democracy.[49]

Yet we are taught that the framers arranged a government with three equal branches that produces deadlock in order to institutionalize an antidemocratic preference: a fear of popular majorities and a desire to protect property. Nevertheless, continues the theory, the Constitution permits, allows, or invites democratization by means of the triumph of the executive or the judicial over the other two branches. In fact, the theory continues, this is just what happened. The antidemocratic Constitution was democratized by means of one or the other of two antidemocratic devices: a powerful presidency or the supremacy of the Supreme Court. What can one say about an interpretation that relies on an "imperial" executive or an "imperial" judiciary as its radically democratic feature?[50] Recognition of legislative supremacy not only allows us to correct the mistake about three equally powerful branches and about executive and judicial supremacy but reveals the true intent of the framers in regard to democracy: their commitment to self-government embodied in their Constitution.[51]

With this understanding in hand, we can define checks and understand their purpose. They are intended first to maintain the separation of the elected branches of the government and second to enable the executive, by means of his constitutional powers, to moderate the law-making process to produce more sound and decent legislation. Ultimately, checks are to *prevent* deadlock. The political branches—legislative and executive—are given the constitutional means to resist encroachments so that, once these means are exhausted, governing will and can go on.[52] If there were no constitutionally legitimate means of self-defense, the elected branches would be likely to resort to nonconstitutional means at such times, which would destroy the Constitution and with it our form of government. To believe that the Congress was given powers to frustrate the executive and prevent the government from acting is to understand the constitutional system backward.

Because of the framers' understanding that governmental powers are by nature legislative, executive, or judicial, a check given to one branch to defend itself cannot be a power that department already legitimately possesses by nature. That would not increase its ability to defend itself. Instead, the likelihood of a dangerous confrontation between the branches would increase and produce—in actuality—deadlock. Imagine a situation without the constitutional checks, in which the legislature enacts laws and the executive, in disagreement, refuses to execute them. Government would stop while the two branches angrily confronted each other. But when the executive has a veto over legislation and the legislature has a carefully defined impeachment power, the following is what takes place. The legislature passes a law about whose soundness or constitutionality the executive has serious reservations.[53] The president vetoes the bill; the legislature passes it again, this time by the necessary extraordinary majority. The executive has had his say and is now faced with the fact that the law has sufficient—and widespread—popular support and has passed over his veto. He is prevented from seeking to resort to nonconstitutional means of resistance because of vast popular opinion against him (making it unlikely that resistance would succeed) and by the impeachment power that the legislature can use if he resorts to illegal means of resistance. So he bows to the will of the extraordinary majority of the legislature.

If the legislature had failed to pass the bill over his veto, it would have had to accept defeat, lacking the necessary extra popular support. It would have to redraft the bill to meet the executive's objections or simply go on with other concerns. In neither case would the government be stalemated or deadlocked.[54] The framers wisely avoided such an outcome. Where checks are instituted, they mix or blend other kinds of powers, with the double consequences of checking or moderating and thus avoiding the collapse of government due to an inability to act.[55]

Checks were given only to the two elected, political branches; the judiciary does not have a check provided in the Constitution. When legislative sovereignty is recognized, along with the nature of checks and balance, and analytical errors are removed, it becomes clear why the Constitution does not give the Supreme Court the general power of judicial review of the acts of the coordinate branches; the reason is that judicial power was intended to be impartial and not involved in policy. The framers created a national judiciary instead of using the state judicial systems for two reasons: to achieve uniformity of the laws—one national law for all instead of thirteen different meanings —and to institute the Supreme Court as the court of last resort in questions of the federal relationship.[56]

Some framers thought that the Court, in cases where a law was clearly in conflict with express prohibitions in the Constitution, might set aside that law. Examples of these kinds of restrictions are ex post facto laws, bills of attainder, protection of the right of *habeas corpus*— traditionally legal questions.[57] Others thought that the Court would be able to defend itself in cases involving the judicial power itself, for example, if the Court's original jurisdiction were tampered with. Madison was among this group.[58] If the Court declared that a law was a bill of attainder and that it would therefore not apply the law to the case before it, the legislature was not thereby prevented from legislating on a matter within its constitutional competence. The legislature would have had to redraft the legislation so that it did not violate the prohibition. This process would be far removed from the modern exercise of judicial review and would not set the Court over the legislature and the executive in the making of public policy.

We have powerful evidence for this interpretation of the Court's authority from the fact that an extraordinary majority at the convention refused to allow the Court to be associated with the executive in the council of revision or to be brought into the legislating process at any point before judicial questions are raised in the form of cases or controversies. We may not assume, without express evidence, that a majority that rejected this role for the Court would have intended that the Court have, instead, a general power of judicial review of the acts of the national branches.

> In the state constitutions and indeed in the federal one also, no provision is made for the case of a disagreement in expounding them; and as the courts are generally the last in making the decision, it results to them, by refusing or not refusing to execute a law, to stamp it with its final character. This makes the Judiciary Department paramount in fact to the legislature, which was never intended and can never be proper.[59]

What checks did the framers rely on? And how were they related to balance and separation of powers? In our Constitution the executive veto, shared Senate powers in foreign policy and appointments, and the impeachment power are checks. They illustrate the condition that a device must meet to be a check: it must be a power that a department would not normally possess according to its function. The executive veto is an excellent example of a check. It enables the executive branch to defend itself, it is conducive to sensible legislation, and it prevents deadlock. The shared Senate powers also have a multiple purpose, because they are designed for the same reasons and also to strengthen the executive as a counterweight to an obstreperous legislature. Advice and consent in appointments is more of an executive power than involvement in treaty making because, as framers like James Wilson argued, the powers of war and peace are legislative powers.[60] The impeachment power—to bring charges of betraying the public trust and to conduct a trial—is a judicial power given to the legislature as a check on both the executive and the judiciary. It is a check in the primitive sense, designed not to influence the quality of governing but to remove from public office persons who have abused their trust. The commitment of an impeachment power to the legislature is further evidence that the system is one of legislative preeminence, inasmuch as no member of Congress can be impeached or removed from office by the other two departments.

What is the appropriate relationship between checks and separation of powers? The two are not synonymous. Separation of powers is

155

quite possible without checks—without checks it probably would work exactly as many critics charge it does now. It would almost certainly be a completely frustrating arrangement—each department or branch possessing all the available powers appropriate to its function and refusing to cooperate with the other branches in case of disagreement—with no constitutional means of resolving an impasse. In such times the executive might follow a historic practice and raise an army, take to the field, and solve his political problems *ultra vires*. Checks were incorporated in the structure of the separation of powers to maintain the separation by keeping the branches independent, to work against hastily passed, badly considered laws, and, ultimately, to remove from office those who abused their public trust—all the while preventing governmental deadlock. Separation of powers theory does not require any of these arrangements, but one may well question how long a republican government would have lasted without them.

What of Balance?

To appreciate what balance really means in the American constitutional structure, we must turn to the following texts:

> The science of politics, however, like most other sciences, has received great improvement. . . . The regular distribution of power into distinct departments; the introduction of legislative balances and checks . . .[61]

> Mr. Randf. observed . . . that the general object was to provide a cure for the evils under which the U.S. laboured; that in tracing these evils to their origin every man had found it in the turbulence and follies of democracy; that some check therefore was to be sought against this tendency of our Governments: and that a good Senate seemed most likely to answer the purpose.[62]

> Mr. Randolph said he could not then point out the exact number of Members for the Senate, but he would observe that they ought to be less than the House of Commons. He was for offering such a check as to keep up the *balance*, and to restrain, if possible the fury of democracy. He thought it would be impossible for the State legislatures to appoint the Senators, because it would not produce the check intended. The first branch should have the appointment of the Senators, and then the check would be compleat.[63]

The balance into which I inquire here is not the equation used by Wilson (see June 1 quotation above), that the joint weight of the executive and judicial branches is necessary to balance the weight of the legislature. Neither is it the balance referred to by Madison (in the consideration of the council of revision on July 21) when he said, "But experience has taught us a distrust of that security [a constitutional discrimination of the departments on paper]; and that it is necessary to introduce such a balance of powers and interests, as will guarantee the provisions on paper."[64]

In both cases the rejected council of revision was at issue; with the exception of the remarks at the beginning of this section, I can find no other sense in which balance is mentioned at the Federal Convention in connection with the proposed government. Balance used in discussing the council of revision in no way supports the contemporary understanding of a balance of checks, since it is a case of two departments balancing one department—and both checking, thereby, the legislature—rather than the other way around.

The only way to approach the concept of balance is by means of the remarks of Hamilton and Randolph as quoted. They point to the Senate, which, I argue, is the only true balancing device to be found in the American constitutional system. The framers understood that in a representative democracy the legislature would be the branch most likely to overwhelm the other two, especially the executive, and colonial experience had taught them the likelihood of hasty and immoderate legislation. Accordingly, the leading framers, most particularly Madison, created the Senate as a balance weight against the more directly popular House of Representatives. The legislative power was thus divided and distributed between two very different kinds of bodies, with differing powers and terms of office and different means of selection. Although today both houses are popularly elected, the constituency of each is unlike the other, and this fact significantly influences the character of the two bodies. When Randolph speaks of "the democracy," he is referring to the directly elected popular House, believed by all to be *the* radically democratic element in the new government.[65]

The science of politics, however, like most other sciences, has received great improvement. The efficacy of various principles is now well understood, which were either not known at all, or imperfectly known to the ancients. The regular distribution of power into distinct departments; the introduction of legislative balances and checks; the institution of courts composed of judges holding their offices during good behavior; the representation of the people in the legislature by deputies of their own election . . .[66]

In *Federalist* No. 9 Hamilton is distinguishing separation of powers from "legislative balances and checks," or bicameralism, and also from the independent tenure of the judiciary. These are all individual devices that ought not to be mistaken for one another. Balance is not separation of powers or vice versa. Balance was introduced into the structure of the government by the creation of the Senate, with some share in executive powers. The Senate was *the* device relied on by the framers to prevent the abuse of legislative power.[67] In the language, once again, of Justice Gibson:

> The notion of a complication of counterchecks has been carried to such an extent in theory, of which the framers of the constitution never dreamt. When the entire sovereignty was separated into its elementary parts, and distributed to the appropriate branches, all things incident to the exercise of its powers were committed to each branch exclusively. The negative which each part of the legislature may exercise, in regard to the acts of the other, was thought sufficient to prevent material infractions of the restraints which were put on the power of the whole.[68]

The Senate was intended to participate fully in the appointive power and in treaty making. Where it shared in executive powers, it was to be much more of a partner than most presidents have since believed or accepted. The Senate was to check and balance the House —merely passing legislation through two different bodies serves as a significant impediment to hasty legislation and often to poor legislation as well. If the two bodies are differently constituted and one of them has a share in the executive powers, the checking and balancing are even more effective.

There is no other attempt at balance in the American system. But we discover this truth only by isolating the different elements: separation of powers, checks, balance.

Speculations

Modern critics of our separation of powers structure make a number of charges: that separation of powers causes confrontation or "stalemate and deadlock"; that separation of powers, by dividing the executive from the legislature, divides power from responsibility and reduces executive accountability; that separation of powers is archaic and generally unsuited to modern complexities and great crises; and that separation of powers is to blame for the absence or failure of leadership, defined as the inability of government to formulate, execute, and sustain coherent policies. If my preceding arguments are sound, separation of powers is being blamed excessively and erroneously. If it is not guilty as charged, we may have to look elsewhere for the source of our many troubles, and it may turn out, unfortunately, to be ourselves.

The fault, in my judgment, lies in grave mistakes in our understanding of the proper role of democratic government. Rejecting separation of powers will not make democratic man or bureaucratic man any more capable of rule than he ever was. Our problem is that we want the blessings of a free democracy without any of its difficulties or inefficiencies. The framers wanted democracy in actuality but were profoundly aware of its dangerous propensities, and they created a structure designed to minimize them.[69] We have lost their sober perspective on human affairs and human capacities and have come to believe that altering institutions can not only change the course of events but even alter the nature of man.[70] Keeping in mind the framers' healthy skepticism about democracy—that democracy is a problem always to be solved or, paraphrasing Holmes, that democracy is a system always approaching but never reaching realization— let us attempt to evaluate some of these criticisms.

Does the system produce deadlock? Well, no, it doesn't really. But it does fail to produce the *outcome* desired by liberals. The real criticism is not that government is unable to act, for it acts constantly, too much in the view of most. But its actions do not guarantee liberal policies. That is why liberals have turned to the Supreme Court, transforming it into a superlegislature, because this is a much surer thing, now that the Court has come to see itself as all-powerful. It has not always been thus. Earlier in the twentieth century progressives, notably Charles Beard and Charles Grove Haines, sought to discredit the Constitution by showing that the framers were antidemocratic. Their proof was that the framers intended the Court to have the power of judicial review of the acts of coordinate branches.[71]

In other words, the charge that the separation of powers structure produces deadlock really means that the democratic process is unpredictable and you take your chances; liberals are no longer willing to accept that price. It was their inspiration to characterize separation of powers as undemocratic and as thwarting the majority will, all actually in the cause of preventing a nonliberal majority from prevailing in policy making.

To the extent that the political branches do fail to address certain necessary questions of public policy, they are no doubt reflecting one of these realities: (1) no national consensus exists on the issue, and therefore neither political branch can take the lead; (2) many issues ought not to be touched by government in a democracy; or (3) ordinary people like ourselves are utterly incompetent to legislate or establish rules on so many issues. I enter as empirical evidence of (3) most of what the Congress and the administrative agencies do. The charge of deadlock is a bum rap; it conceals impatience or distaste with the democratic process and an unwillingness to accept its outcome.

The modern view that we can "restore" executive accountability by merging the executive with the legislature in some fashion is ironic, for the framers made the executive accountable by *separating* him from the legislature. We would do well to restore our familiarity with their reasoning. For one thing, they believed that linking him with the legislature would make him its creature. For another, they believed that responsibility could not be pinpointed if he were not separate from the legislature. If he were separate, he could not hide behind numbers. Underscoring all these reasons was their concern for the tyrannical possibilities if the executive and legislature were not separated. History teaches us the merits of this view. Has the situation changed? Do we no longer need to fear the power of government? Surely the twentieth century teaches that we need to fear it more than ever, whether in the United States, the Soviet Union, China, Germany, Spain, or Zimbabwe. What reasons do we have to believe that if we linked the executive with the legislature we would get only good results instead of all the bad ones?

If the executive can no longer be held accountable, perhaps separation of powers is not the reason. Perhaps the two-term presidential limitation—another good example of what happens when we amend the Constitution without having any real grasp of its basic principles—contributes. Accountability was, of course, exactly the reason the framers did not put a limit on the president's term: to keep him honest, using the prospect of reelection. What we got by instituting the limitation is the worst possible solution—a president may, and has, resorted to anything to win that second term, knowing that nothing in the voting booth can be done thereafter to penalize him (Nixon, after all, was punished for covering up and could easily never have been caught); and a president has carte blanche in his second term, because he cannot face the electorate again. A single six-year term would combine these monstrosities.

Probably the more basic reason why the president cannot be held accountable is that we do not want him to be. We do not want to exercise our citizenly responsibilities; we want to be led and have our decisions made for us—if not by the president, "our leader," then by the Supreme Court. By "we" I mean we citizens who elected him, not the media, whose criticism is relentless. The average citizen does not want to hold the president responsible for those he appoints or for the conduct of administration. Democracy is a lot of trouble, and it is so much easier to blame institutions for what goes wrong rather than our own irresponsibility.

To the charge that separation of powers is archaic and prevents effective dealing with modern problems, the answer is a question: What free government today deals effectively with modern problems? It is in the nature of freedom that there is a cost. Madison explains that with unparalleled brilliance in *Federalist* No. 10. Let me amend the question. What *un*free government today deals effectively with modern problems? Our own problem is that we do not accept the limitations on human capacity and we believe, as Marxism teaches (and acknowledging the widespread success of this world view is essential to understanding our age), that by manipulating the material environment we can solve all problems (or that there is a solution to every problem; we just have to find it), and we are not willing to pay the necessary price to preserve our liberty. Tocqueville warns:

> Man cannot enjoy political liberty unpurchased by some sacrifices, and they never obtain it without great exertions. . . .
> I think that democratic communities have a natural taste for freedom; left to themselves, they will seek it, cherish it, and view any privation of it with regret. But for equality their passion is ardent, insatiable, incessant, invincible; they call for equality in freedom; and if they cannot obtain that, they still call for equality in slavery.[72]

We probably need separation of powers now more than ever.[73] The danger to the populace, here and all over the world, from government itself is greater, and our own proclivities threaten us. As the framers so wisely understood, we need to be protected from ourselves:

> It may be a reflection on human nature that such devices [separation of powers] should be necessary to control the abuses of government. But what is government itself but the greatest of all reflections on human nature? If men were angels, no government would be necessary. If angels were to govern men, neither external nor internal controls on government would be necessary. In framing a government which is to be administered by men over men, the great difficulty lies in this: you must first enable the government to control the governed; and in the next place oblige it to control itself. A dependence on the people is, no doubt, the primary

161

control on the government; but experience has taught mankind the necessity of auxiliary precautions.[74]

There is no way to improve on this observation or to improve on separation of powers as a precaution against anarchy or tyranny and as an auxiliary (that is, a support) to sustain free democratic government.

Notes

1. Justice Gibson, Eakin v. Raub, 12 Sergeant and Rawle (Pennsylvania Supreme Court) 330 (1825), p. 351.

2. James Sundquist, "More Confrontation, Stalemate, Deadlock," *Washington Post*, June 26, 1983, sec. D.

3. Immigration and Naturalization Service v. Chadha, 462 U.S. 919 (1983).

4. John Adams confused separation of powers with balanced government, probably because England was undergoing a transformation from balanced government to separation of powers. The theory of balanced government is that liberty and stability are safest where the powers of government are divided among the three orders, or estates: royalty, nobility, and commons. Powers are not divided according to function, for each order has the whole with a veto on the others. This error has been picked up and passed along and occurs in the work of (among others) Richard Hofstadter, Vernon Parrington, Thomas M. Cooley, and Hannah Arendt.

Thomas Jefferson's misunderstanding is summarized in his words:

> Our country has thought it proper to distribute the powers of its government among three *equal* and independent authorities constituting each a check upon one or both of the others in all attempts to impair its constitution. . . . The Constitution "meant that its co-ordinate branches should be checks upon each other." (Emphasis added.)

Quoted in Henry S. Commager, *Majority Rule and Minority Rights* (Gloucester, Mass.: Peter Smith, 1958), pp. 31, 32. Part of the burden of this essay is to show how wrong this view is. Fortunately, neither John Adams nor Thomas Jefferson was at the Federal Convention, although many think that they were.

5. Justice White Dissent, *U.S. Law Week*, 51 LW 4929 (1983).

6. Justice Powell concurred but on different grounds and sought to narrow the scope of the decision; Justices White and Rehnquist dissented in separate opinions.

7. *U.S. Law Week*, 51 LW 4926.

8. *The Federalist*, ed. Clinton Rossiter (New York: New American Library, 1961), No. 48, p. 308.

9. Martin Diamond, "The Separation of Powers and the Mixed Regime," *Publius*, vol. 8, no. 3 (Summer 1978), pp. 33–43.

10. Ibid., p. 35.

11. Ibid., p. 40.

12. Ibid., p. 41.

13. Ibid., p. 38.

14. Alexander Hamilton, *Federalist* No. 9, p. 72.

15. Max Farrand, *The Records of the Federal Convention of 1787* (New Haven, Conn.: Yale University Press, 1966), vol. 1, p. 21.

16. Ibid., p. 34.

17. *Federalist* No. 38, pp. 238–40; see also Randolph's speech in Farrand, *Records*, vol. 1, p. 256.

18. Farrand, *Records*, vol. 3, p. 108.

19. Those who hold this view often equate the framers' concept of liberty with the protection of property rights only. It is more difficult to attack the concept if it is really designed to frustrate government in the name of what we now call civil liberties.

20. The most important example of this is the rejection of Madison's council of revision. He regarded it as a major defeat, almost as serious as the federal issue. The council is discussed at length here.

21. Farrand, *Records*, vol. 1, pp. 65–66.

22. Ibid., p. 67.

23. According to the Virginia Plan, a council of revision would have taken this form:

> The Executive and a convenient number of the National Judiciary, ought to compose a council of revision with authority to examine every act of the National Legislature before it shall operate, and every act of a particular Legislature before a Negative thereon shall be final; and that the dissent of said Council shall amount to a rejection, unless the Act of the National Legislature be again passed, or that of a particular Legislature be again negatived by members of each branch.

Before legislation was passed by the Congress, it was to be reviewed by the president and part of the Supreme Court, sitting as a council. The council was also to have authority to examine state legislation that was subject to a veto by the national legislature (another provision of the Virginia Plan) before the federal veto could become final. If the council disagreed with the national legislation or the national legislature's veto of state legislation, its dissent would stand unless the national legislature could muster an extraordinary majority.

For our purposes the significance of the proposal lies in the fact that it would have operated before legislation became the law of the land, the legislature having the opportunity to override a council decision if it had the votes. At first glance it sounds very cumbersome, but it hardly equals the Rube Goldberg arrangement that has developed in its stead (judicial review), and it does not raise the same problems for democratic government that judicial review does.

24. Eakin v. Raub, p. 351.

25. Farrand, *Records*, vol. 2, p. 34.

26. Ibid., vol. 1, p. 86; vol. 2, p. 31.

27. Ibid., vol. 1, p. 86.

28. Ibid., p. 69.

29. An additional and exceptionally important reason for electors, which is outside the scope of this paper, was to prevent corruption. The framers did not believe that honest direct popular election was technically feasible.

30. Farrand, *Records*, vol. 1, pp. 49–50. The notion of "directly chosen" leads to some confusion and may contribute to the impression that the framers are talking about balanced government. In the American system there are three ways of collecting a majority, all equally legitimate: directly by population (but in districts), as with the House of Representatives; indirectly by states, as with the Senate; and directly-indirectly, as in the case of the presidency, where the national majority is collected federally, that is, state by state. See Martin Diamond, *The Electoral College and the American Idea of Democracy* (Washington, D.C.: American Enterprise Institute, 1977), pp. 6–13.

31. Farrand, *Records*, vol. 1, p. 110, pp. 138–39; vol. 2, pp. 77, 78. See also the original Virginia Plan.

32. Farrand, *Records*, vol. 1, p. 98; James Wilson speaking.

33. For an example, see the discussion ibid., pp. 97–104.

34. Ibid., p. 103.

35. Ibid., pp. 108, 144; vol. 2, pp. 75–77, 138–39.

36. See Madison's June 6 speech ibid., vol. 1, pp. 138–39.

37. Arguments against the council of revision contradict many other actions taken at the convention, beginning with the executive veto itself, which clearly gives to the executive legislative powers, as does his shared treaty power; and many important powers given to the Senate are executive. Madison's failure to persuade his colleagues about the council may have convinced him of the need to make the strongest possible case for blending and mixing in order actually to achieve and to maintain separation. The key to the rejection of the council by the convention lies in its conception of judicial power. In no respect can the council be considered the forerunner of, or an argument for, judicial review of the acts of coordinate branches. Adoption of the council would have preserved legislative supremacy.

38. No senator or Representative shall, during the Time for which he was elected, be appointed to any civil Office under the Authority of the United States, which shall have been created, or the Emoluments whereof shall have been increased during such time; and no Person holding any Office under the United States, shall be a Member of either House during his Continuance in Office.

39. Farrand, *Records*, vol. 1, pp. 391–94.

40. Ibid., vol. 2, pp. 43, 66, 82–83, 537.

41. Ibid., pp. 63–69, 499, 511–16.

42. These criteria follow from Madison's discussion of independence in *Federalist* No. 51. See pp. 321–22.

43. This [that the supreme power of the commonwealth will arbitrarily dispose of the estates of subjects] is not much to be fear'd in Governments where the Legislative consists, wholly or in part, in Assemblies which are variable, whose Members upon the Dissolution of the Assembly, are Subjects under the common Laws of their Country, equally with the rest.

John Locke, *The Second Treatise of Government*, ed. Peter Laslett (London: Cambridge University Press, 1963), p. 379. Surely it gives one pause to consider how the American Congress no longer fulfills any of these salutary conditions.

44. See Madison's remarkable letter to Thomas Jefferson of October 17, 1788.

45. The president's source is the people through the medium of electors, the House's source is the people in their states according to population, the Senate's source was the state legislatures (regarded as excessively democratic in 1787), and the Court's source is joint executive and senatorial appointment. In every case the choice is out of the body of the people, and there is no connection in the Constitution between wealth, position, or hereditary privilege and any branch of the government.

46. Farrand, who has a remarkably complete index to the federal convention—103 pages—has no reference to "checks and balances" or to checks alone. He has approximately forty-three references to separation of powers and five cross references. The Rossiter edition of *The Federalist* refers the reader to "checks and balances" under the entry "separation of powers." Burns has one reference to separation of powers of virtually no content and many to "checks and balances," ending with the admonition, "see also Madisonian system," in his attack on the structure of American government: James MacGregor Burns, *The Deadlock of Democracy* (Englewood Cliffs, N.J.: Prentice-Hall, 1964). A quick check of many American government texts reveals very few references to separation of powers as such, in some cases none, and more frequent references to checks and balances.

47. Justice Gibson, Eakin v. Raub, p. 350.

48. Farrand, *Records*, vol. 2, p. 79.

49. Locke, who was not a democrat, writes:

> In all cases, whilst the Government subsists, the Legislative *is the Supreme Power*. For what can give laws to another, must needs be superiour to him: and since the Legislative is not otherwise Legislative of Society, but by the right it has to make Laws for all the parts and for every Member of Society, prescribing Rules to their actions . . . the Legislative must needs be the Supreme, and all other Powers in any Members or parts of Society, derived from and subordinate to it.

Second Treatise, pp. 185–86.

50. How are we to take seriously an analysis that, refusing to recognize legislative supremacy, attacks the framers for not being democrats and for creating an undemocratic government and then seizes eagerly on an "imperial" executive or an "imperial" judiciary as its democratizing device?

51. This is now easy to say because we have available to us the work of Martin Diamond, especially his seminal article "Democracy and the *Federalist*: A Reconsideration of the Framers' Intent," *American Political Science Review*, vol. 53, no. 1 (March 1959), pp. 52–69.

52. Madison writes in *Federalist* No. 51: "But the great security against a gradual concentration of the several powers in the same department consists in giving to those who administer each department the *necessary constitutional*

means and personal motives to resist the encroachments of the others" (pp. 321–22; emphasis added).

53. There is evidence that our earliest presidents, including Thomas Jefferson, believed that they could veto a law only on the grounds of unconstitutionality.

54. I will suggest some hypotheses for why this is so commonly believed in the latter part of the paper.

55. See Farrand, *Records*, vol. 2, p. 77.

56. In spite of John Marshall's reasoning in Marbury v. Madison, Alexander Hamilton writes in *Federalist* No. 81:

> In the first place, there is not a syllable in the plan [proposed constitution] which *directly* empowers the national courts to construe the laws according to the spirit of the Constitution, or which gives them any greater latitude in this respect than may be claimed by the courts of every state. I admit however, that the Constitution ought to be the standard of construction for the laws, and that wherever there is an evident opposition, the laws ought to give place to the Constitution. But this doctrine is not deducible from any circumstance peculiar to the plan of convention [p. 482].

I include the entire passage so as to avoid any question of tailoring the quotation to fit my purposes. The power of judicial review of the acts of coordinate branches has been derived by implication, unlike the executive veto and the other checks I discuss. As Justice Gibson wrote, it seems inconceivable that this massive judicial power over the other two branches would have been left to implication, thus subjecting the helpless judiciary to very dangerous political fortunes. Justice John Marshall saw the problem when he wrote to Justice Chase after Marbury that he would be quite content to trade the right to an opinion on constitutionality for being left unmolested by the national legislature.

57. Note that Alexander Hamilton in *Federalist* No. 78 and John Marshall in Marbury v. Madison use these very examples of the kinds of constitutional provisions warranting judicial review.

58. Farrand, *Records*, vol. 2, p. 430.

59. Letter from James Madison to John Brown of October 1788, in *The Writings of James Madison*, ed. Gaillard Hunt (New York: G. P. Putnam's Sons, 1900), vol. 5, p. 294.

60. Farrand, *Records*, vol. 1, pp. 65, 66.

61. Alexander Hamilton, *Federalist* No. 9, p. 72.

62. Edmund Randolph, speaking on May 31, the version of his speech in Madison's "Notes," Farrand, *Records*, vol. 1, p. 51.

63. Pierce's version of Randolph's speech; emphasis added.

64. Farrand, *Records*, vol. 2, p. 77.

65. The Senate was James Madison's solution to the problem of immoderate democratic government. He designed it and introduced it in the Virginia Plan. When the Senate was lost to the states in the Connecticut Compromise and became the vehicle of direct state influence on the new government rather than the "great anchor" Madison had supported, he switched his immense

influence from the Senate and began to build up the executive. He was, however, keenly aware of the incompatibility of a powerful executive with democratic government and said so at the convention.

> Mr. Madison thought it indispensible that some provision should be made for defending the Community agst the incapacity, negligence or perfidy of the chief Magistrate. The limitation of his service, was not a sufficient security. He might lose his capacity after his appointment. He might pervert his administration into a scheme of peculation or oppression. He might betray his trust to foreign powers. The case of the Executive Magistracy was very distinguishable, from that of the Legislative or of any other public body, holding offices of limited duration. . . . In the case of the Executive Magistracy which was to be administered by a single man, loss of capacity or corruption was more within the compass of probable events, and either of them might be fatal to the Republic.

Farrand, *Records*, vol. 1, pp. 65–66.

Like so many other moves that were made at the time, the creation of a strong executive can only be understood in relation to the status of other institutions at that time in the convention proceedings, in this case, to the federal Senate. The executive was as much a brake on direct state influence in national councils as it was a brake on the legislature. I suggest that if the Senate had not become federal, we would have seen a very different and less powerful executive; for Madison was certainly not alone in his understanding, and he could be very persuasive.

66. Hamilton, *Federalist* No. 9, p. 72.

67. Farrand, *Records*, vol. 2, p. 52.

68. Eakin v. Raub, p. 351.

69. I do not want to give the impression that I am ignoring the necessary preconditions that lie in size and diversity and social and economic freedom, so aptly described by James Madison in *Federalist* No. 10.

70. Irving Kristol has an excellent essay on modern utopian thinking, pointing out that, for the first time, utopians believe that their utopias are really possible. See "Utopianism, Ancient and Modern," in *Two Cheers for Capitalism* (New York: Basic Books, 1978), pp. 143–59.

71. Charles Beard, *The Supreme Court and the Constitution*, intro. Alan Westin (Englewood Cliffs, N.J.: Prentice-Hall, 1962); and Charles Grove Haines, *The American Doctrine of Judicial Supremacy* (New York: Russell and Russell, 1959); Beard was originally published in 1912, Haines in 1932.

72. Alexis de Tocqueville, *Democracy in America* (New York: Alfred A. Knopf, 1951), vol. 2, pp. 96–97: "Why Democratic Nations Show a More Ardent and Enduring Love of Equality Than Liberty."

73. I propose that we examine the following in our search for why our government does not work as we think it should: (1) the two-term presidential limitation, (2) the effect of permanent careers as legislators, and (3) the effect of legislators' exempting themselves from the laws that they pass.

74. Madison, *Federalist* No. 51, p.322.

8

In Defense of Separation of Powers

James W. Ceaser

> *It is with infinite caution that any man ought to venture upon
> pulling down an edifice which has answered in any tolerable degree
> for ages the common purposes of society.*
>
> EDMUND BURKE

Only once in recent history has a major democratic regime changed its
basic institutional structure with the clear aim of remaining a democracy. That change occurred in France in 1958, when Parliament could
not form an effective government in the face of the Algerian crisis and
the imminent threat of a military coup. While Parliament fiddled,
Paris nearly burned. France had lost the sine qua non of any functioning government: the power—let us call it, with John Locke, the
"executive power"—to act with energy and discretion to save the
nation from conquest or disintegration. To remedy this fatal flaw, the
founders of the Fifth French Republic, drawing heavily on the American presidential model of government, instituted a unitary and independent executive elected outside Parliament and endowed by the
constitution with a broad grant of power. The new office was designed to ensure that there would always be a force to act for the state,
even in the event of a stalemate among the political parties on the
normal policies of governing. The nation's heart would never cease to
beat.[1]

Today in the United States several prominent persons are urging
the American people to undertake a similar act of constitution making. Oddly enough, however, while many in this group proclaim their
desire to strengthen the executive office, they are recommending the
opposite course from that taken in France in 1958; they are calling for a
change from a presidential (or separation of powers) system to something akin to a parliamentary system. They propose this change not
because the United States faces an immediate crisis but because the
government does not function as well as it might—because, in Lloyd
Cutler's words, we are unable to "'form a Government' [that can]

propose, legislate, and administer a balanced program for governing."[2]

Although members of this group acknowledge possible risks in changing institutions, they can scarcely be accused of operating with a sense of the fragility or precariousness of constitutional forms. Self-proclaimed "children of the Enlightenment," they judge political life not from the somber perspective of what can go wrong but from the sunny perspective of what can be improved.[3] They urge the formation of an official commission to initiate an "act of constitutional surgery at least as severe as that of 1787."[4] In their plan for a surgical strike on the Constitution to wipe the slate clean and begin again, the proponents of change seem intent on applying the most recent theories of policy science to constitutional forms; they are advocates of zero-based constitution making.

No doubt these zero-based constitution makers possess certain advantages over defenders of the existing system. Writing about politics entails, even at its best, an abstraction from reality and a simplification of its complexity. Inevitably, therefore, those who build neat, logical systems on paper will appear more persuasive than those who rest their case on circumstance and prudence. Zero-based constitution makers are also likely to find a receptive audience for their proposals among commentators and intellectuals, many of whom delight in dismissing tradition and celebrate any "new and bold" idea that challenges fundamental beliefs. Nor is financial support for such an enterprise likely to be wanting; it is not difficult today to find well-intentioned philanthropic foundations in search of "neutral" plans by blue-ribbon commissions that promise to resolve our most pressing problems.

What is most extraordinary, however, about the current "new and bold" proposals for constitutional change is that they rely on a method of study that political scientists have for some time recognized as outmoded. Under this method zero-based constitution makers take the formal mechanisms of a regime to define its essence and then proceed to compare alternative mechanisms on the assumption that a best form can be discovered and implanted in any system. If there is one thing that the modern study of comparative politics has taught us, however, it is that the formal mechanisms of government constitute only part of what defines a regime and explains how it works. Modern political science has extended the study of regimes beyond their formal mechanisms to such other factors as informal structures (for example, parties and interest groups), social structure (for example, class and ethnic composition), and political culture (for example, animating principles and attitudes about the political world). It is to these other factors, no less than to the formal mechanisms, that we must look to understand how any system works.[5]

Within the industrialized world today are some twenty-three liberal democracies, so classified because they share certain characteristics, such as governments that reflect the preferences of broad segments of the citizenry, the protection of individual rights, and the protection of the right to associate and compete for political power. Although these regimes also possess certain institutional similarities —all of them, for example, have independent judiciaries and checks of some kind on the remaining political power—one of the most striking facts about liberal democracies is the diversity of their institutional forms.[6] This diversity should make it clear that in discussing the differences among the mechanical systems of liberal democracies, we are not dealing with a first-order question. Different kinds of institutional systems "work" to promote liberal democracy in different regimes. There is, accordingly, no practical necessity of resolving which institutional form of liberal democracy is best but, on the contrary, every reason to make such choices on prudential grounds in light of the particular circumstances in each case. American statesmen have therefore tended to act wisely in emphasizing the general form of liberal democracy while avoiding any effort to proselytize on behalf of Articles I, II, and III of the Constitution.

Of course, no one would deny that if a regime ceased to function or lost its legitimacy, legislators should weigh the respective merits of different systems, as they did in America in 1787 or in France in 1958. No one, moreover, would deny that, within a functioning regime, legislators should consider aspects of other systems to find possible ideas for improving their own. (Some in Great Britain, for example, worried that the regime has been sliding gradually into an "elective dictatorship," have looked to the performance of the committee system of Congress with the aim of adopting certain of its features to strengthen Parliament.)[7] Yet a reliance on the study of comparative institutions in these instances offers no support for its scientific character or general applicability. It is used in the first case (where the regime has ceased to function) because of the necessity of relying on theory where practice cannot provide a guide and in the second case (to improve a functioning system) only to the extent of supplying possible suggestions for change, which must then be fitted to the character of the system in place. No reasonable interpretation of what political science can teach us would suggest that the study of comparative institutions warrants any broader claim.

Constitutions in the broadest sense grow and assume their particular character from a combination of formal mechanism, informal structure, and political culture. The weight that each of these possesses in any regime is something that political scientists can only roughly gauge. The notion, therefore, that one should tear down and rebuild constitutions on the basis solely of a study of different formal mechanisms is not only radical in the worst sense but lacking in any scientific foundation. The impulse for remodeling is all the more ill advised when one considers that the bonds that tie a people to a government rest in large part on a belief in its legitimacy. Where this belief is strong, its protection may be—as it assuredly is in the United States—worth more to the well-being of a regime than any marginal gains that might be realized by instituting a better mechanical system.

The search for a best formal model for a liberal democracy is thus an abstract exercise having only a very limited practical application. If one must, however, engage in such an exercise, it is arguable that the theoretical foundation of the American presidential system is the soundest. The presidential system is the only one that, by virtue of its formal mechanism alone, provides a workable solution to the great problem of modern government: ensuring the existence of a unitary force needed to act for the nation in extraordinary circumstances while providing the means for taming and even humbling that force under normal conditions. Stating this same solution in more familiar language, we can say that the American system provides for the establishment of the executive power—in its primary or essential sense—while reducing to a minimum the threat of despotism.

In making this claim about the possible superiority of the American system, I am referring for the moment to formal mechanical properties, not to the operation of any actual regime as modified by informal factors. The formal properties of the presidential and parliamentary systems are fairly clear. Under a presidential system the essential executive force is never extinguished or in doubt; under a parliamentary system the executive force cannot be guaranteed (and in practice has not been). As one moves from the level of the essential executive power to what is commonly called "policy making" or sometimes "leadership," that is, the force that proposes, legislates, and administers a general program for governing, the comparison between the two systems yields a different result. Under the American system a policy-making structure must be created in a context that divides power and thus precludes the establishment of a unitary and extremely energetic force. The parliamentary form admits of more variation: it can allow for stalemate (from which, incidentally, derives the term *immobilisme*, which critics now apply to the American system) or for a formidable concentration of power in an executive (usually collective) that far exceeds anything possible under the American system.

What this analysis suggests is that the parliamentary system
171

leaves much more to chance or circumstance than the American system. Informal properties play a much greater role in a parliamentary system than in the American system in defining the actual character of a regime. Given a certain set of circumstances (such as two stable and disciplined parties), a parliamentary system may produce an executive force nearly as strong as that in the American system on the level of the primary executive power and a policy-making force in the executive more powerful than that in the American presidency (or in any other American institution). Given another set of circumstances (such as a large number of small and undisciplined parties), it may produce an executive force that is stalemated on the level of the primary executive power and weaker as a policy-making instrument than the American presidency. The American system, it seems, purchases the security of ensuring the existence of the essential executive power at the cost—if it is a cost—of having the possibility of a highly energetic and unitary policy-making system.

Up to this point I have indicated the properties of the American and parliamentary systems chiefly from a mechanical perspective. Suppose, however, one goes beyond mechanical forms to real constitutions as they are molded by their informal as well as their formal properties. This, it seems, is what most of America's zero-based constitution makers unconsciously have in mind; for when they speak of adopting a parliamentary model, they conceive of how that system operates (or, actually, how they imagine it to operate) in Great Britain but not, let us say, in Italy. The system that operates in Britain, however, functions as it does less because it is parliamentary than because it is British. And this is precisely the point: how can one expect, through a formal mechanical change, to replicate in America the particular, informal properties that make (today) for a strong executive in Britain? For Britain, which has had (but no longer has) a predominantly two-party system consisting of disciplined parties, it is one thing; for America, which possesses some of the most undisciplined parties in the world, it might be something quite different. The United States, it is true, has enjoyed a longer history of two-party competition than Britain, but this stability may be due precisely to the lack of discipline in American parties. Change the system and there is no guarantee that American parties would become disciplined or, if they did, that there would be only two of them.[8]

If one were to suppose, however, that constitutions could be put on and taken off as easily as articles of clothing, would it be wise for the United States to adopt the British system? The answer to such a question is not easy. The British system, for all its undoubted virtues, has certain defects: it frequently gives almost complete power to a party enjoying well less than the support of a majority; it has an executive force, increasingly embodied in a single individual (the prime minister) and not the cabinet, that many feel is far too powerful (an "elective dictatorship"); it has a civil service that exerts an extraordinary degree of control over policy; and it greatly exaggerates the pressure for change, forcing swings from one extreme to another with shifts in government.[9]

The American system also, of course, possesses serious defects, which its critics never tire of pointing out. No doubt in both nations certain defects might be partially remedied by reforms that would not touch the basic character of the system. But some of the defects in each regime, one can be certain, are inseparable from the system itself and thus could not be remedied without also destroying the entire system, its virtues included. No political system, in short, is perfect. The question whether the American or the British system is superior is certainly one on which sensible people can disagree but on which no sensible person would probably spend very much time. What counts for any system in place that "has answered in any tolerable degree the common purposes of society" is how it can be maintained and improved, not how it can serve as a plaything to satisfy the curiosity of children of the Enlightenment.

The American Political System

The contemporary attack on separation of powers is not the first of its kind. Criticism of the basic system enjoys a long history, dating back at least as far as Woodrow Wilson's earliest writings. Regrettably, however, this long tradition of criticism has served more to obscure than to clarify the fundamental issues of our political system. Critics, with few exceptions, have ignored the problem of the essential executive power and focused on the secondary question of the character of the policy-making, or leadership, function. Their fundamental complaint has been that the American system lacks a strong, unitary policy-making system situated in some kind of executive officer. Yet, by attacking our system for having a weak executive (when, in fact, it is strong on the essential point), they have skewed the entire debate on constitutional issues. They have defined their version of the strong executive against the theory that underlies the Constitution and, by so doing, have torn the presidency from its constitutional moorings, leaving it vulnerable to attacks that today threaten to undermine its essential properties.

Although it is impossible here to present a complete picture of the American system, we need at least a rough sketch of its basic outline.

The American system must be viewed as operating on three basic levels, each successive level being influenced, but not fully determined, by the levels that precede it. These levels are (1) fundamental sovereignty, (2) the exercise of primary powers, and (3) the policy-making process.

Level 1: fundamental sovereignty. The first level consists of the power to form and modify the basic character of the government, determining its powers and its structure. This power lies, in a primitive sense, with the body of the people in the right of revolution; in its legalized form, it lies with the Constitution and with the process spelled out in Article V for adding amendments. It is this sovereign power, and this power alone, that in theory can alter the basic governmental structure. Separation of powers, it should be observed, is not applicable at this level, for neither the president nor the Supreme Court has any formal role to play in the amending process.

Level 2: the exercise of primary powers. The second level consists of the arrangement of the primary powers of the federal government. The Constitution divides the three primary powers (legislative, executive, and judicial) among three institutions (the Congress, the president, and the Supreme Court). Each of these institutions is given respectively the major part of each of the three powers, but in some instances the powers are shared by more than one institution.

The general idea of assigning the major powers to different institutions, each to be arranged structurally to perform its particular task in the most effective way, was one that enjoyed almost universal support in 1787. The founders' plan to mix or share certain of the powers generated some controversy, particularly in those instances in which some deemed this mix to be prejudicial to the power of the Congress. The founders, however, managed to justify these deviations from what some considered to be a pure separation of powers on the grounds that they would help maintain the basic division of powers over the long run or that, in specific cases, they would promote better government.

Yet, if there was basic agreement on the abstract principle of separation of powers, there were profound differences on what that doctrine should mean in practice. Americans of the founding era were divided between two fundamentally different interpretations: a Whig, or prolegislative, view and a Federalist, or proexecutive, view. Each side to this controversy understood differently the nature of the three powers and the correct relationship or hierarchy that should exist among them (and hence among the three institutions).

According to the Whig view, the legislative was the supreme

power and should hold most of the discretionary power vested in the government. This view reflected not only a deep fear of the executive force inherited from the opposition to the British monarch but also a conviction that the nature of governing was such that nearly all important tasks could be dealt with by law. The role of the executive could be—and ought to be—limited to the modest task of carrying out the will of the legislative power expressed in laws. In addition, the Whigs had a populist streak that favored the concentration of power in the most "popular" of the branches—the popular assembly of the legislature (the House). In fact, since Whigs regarded the executive power as inherently monarchic or nonpopular, the question of who should rule was for them intimately bound up with the question of the division of powers. Seeking more democracy, they could not countenance a strong executive.[10]

The leading founders differed from the Whigs both about the wisdom of concentrating all the legislative power in the Congress (in particular, in the popular branch) and about the possibility of conducting all the affairs of state by law. Most commentators on the founders' thought have emphasized the first point, claiming that the founders regarded the doctrine of separation of powers chiefly as a device to prevent the House from gaining too much power. Yet this is only part of the story. For many of the founders, it was more important to establish the presidency as a distinct and separate institution of the government to protect the integrity of the executive power in its primary sense. It was this objective that led them to reconstruct the doctrine of separation of powers as it had been understood before its transformation by Whigs in the late colonial era.

The doctrine of separation of powers was devised by Locke and Montesquieu in an attempt to solve a fundamental problem in the thought of Thomas Hobbes. Hobbes, who was the first modern thinker to limit the purpose of government to the protection of fundamental rights, argued that to secure those rights required an immense and unchecked political authority. This authority, called the "sovereign," must have unlimited discretion—the sum of the powers we know as law making, executing, and adjudicating. Such an awesome concentration of power was needed, according to Hobbes, because the possible threats to the community, from both within and without, were such that nothing less than a potentially absolute power—free, if need be, of the constraints of written rules—could meet them. The frightful paradox created by this solution was that the sovereign's power was so great that it jeopardized the very rights that government was intended to protect in the first place.

Locke and Montesquieu, the originators of modern constitutionalism, sought to elaborate certain qualifications or checks on the Hobbesian sovereign. These included a right of revolution, limitations on governmental authority, and the separation of powers. But in regard to providing government with an executive power to act with discretion under threatening circumstances, Locke and Montesquieu were hardly less forthcoming than Hobbes. For Locke no less than for Hobbes, there are challenges to the existence of society that do not admit of resolution by law, in the strict sense of a clear rule that is known in advance. Although the legislative power may pass "laws" that grant broad discretion to the executive, these instances only confirm that law, in its ordinary sense, is not sufficient; and even such unlawlike laws cannot solve the entire problem, for the executive may have to act in certain circumstances without a specific grant of discretion or even in contravention of an existing law. The assumption of such extraordinary powers by the executive, reminiscent of the power of Hobbes's sovereign, was known by Locke as "prerogative."

The establishment of constitutionalism, however, did mark a change from Hobbes's understanding of the executive power in two significant respects. First, Locke and Montesquieu (along with the founders) began with a different presumption about the importance of the need for prerogative. If it is true that the state has need of such power, it is also true that it will need it only infrequently, and the exception or extreme case need not define the rule. Most government actions can be defined by law, or at any rate be sanctioned by provisional grants of authority made by the legislative power. Second, the executive power, although it cannot always be subject to precise limitations, can still be watched, checked, and supervised by other institutions possessing an equal or greater regard among the people. Following this theory, the founders placed the greater part of the law-making power in Congress, thereby reducing the prospect that the prerogative power would ever be carried over into normal governance. Moreover, the very presence of institutions as powerful as the Congress and the Supreme Court could serve to check the executive power. Finally, there is a sense in which the founders made the legislative power supreme not so much by giving it the law-making power as by giving it the power to impeach and convict the president. By this means the legislature can dismiss the person exercising the executive power, even though it cannot exercise that power itself.[11]

Although much of the public debate over separation of powers at the time of the founding focused on the specific powers and makeup of the institutions, a more important question, which never received nearly as much attention, concerned the nature of each of the three powers, particularly the dangerous, but necessary, executive power.

From what has been argued already, it is clear that the leading founders considered the executive power to include the function of acting with the force of the community during moments of threat or crisis. This power is contained in the Constitution in the explicit grant of the "executive power" to the president, as well as in such specific grants as the pardoning power, the "take care" clause, and the commander-in-chief role. Presidents from Jefferson to Lincoln to Nixon have relied on this reservoir of executive power in an effort to justify actions that have gone beyond the normal scope of presidential authority.

Locke identified a fourth primary power, which he called the "federative" (that is, the foreign-policy-making) power.[12] Locke considered this power analytically separable from the executive except in moments of crisis. Yet, since the conduct of foreign affairs takes place in an arena in which law cannot normally prevail, in which discretion is required, and in which decisive and swift action is often needed, Locke gave the federative power to the executive officer. For Locke the character of the federative power made it in a sense a necessary adjunct of the executive power. The founders deviated from Locke on this point in that they divided up certain elements of the federative power, giving some to the president, some to the president and one or both houses of Congress, and some to the Congress. These modifications reflected a more democratic spirit among the founders and a greater desire to limit executive power. Nevertheless, following Locke, the founders assigned the greater part of the conduct of foreign affairs to the president, and presidents have generally asserted—and been accorded—a wide range of discretion in this area. Their claim has been that any aspect of the foreign-policy-making power not explicitly assigned to Congress in the Constitution rests with the president as a natural part of the executive power.[13]

Level 3: the policy-making process. The third level of our political system refers to the policy-making process. In the fullest sense policy making includes the tasks of planning, initiating, mobilizing support, legislating, and carrying out.[14] The last two tasks, which are "covered" by the separation of powers and regulated by the Constitution, are important to the policy-making function, but they obviously do not exhaust it. If one looks at where and how other aspects of this process are performed today, one sees a number of institutions acting in a variety of ways. Planning, initiating, and mobilizing for policies are carried out by the parties, the bureaucracy, Congress, presidential candidates, and—above all—presidents. In addition, the courts have set up their own policy-making shop and exercise authority over broad areas under the fig leaf of constitutional and statutory interpretation. Even the constitutionally defined processes of law making and executing are conducted in ways that are not clear from the Constitution alone. Practical influence and power in these areas ebb and flow between the president and Congress, and certain policy-making functions, such as control of monetary policy, have been given by law to independent administrative bodies.

This brief sketch of the present mechanisms for performing the policy-making function barely scratches the surface of a complex arrangement that no one could have envisioned in 1787. Although it can be argued that a few elements of this process rest on shaky constitutional grounds, most present no such problem, even though they are not expressly located or defined in the Constitution. We are thus left with the question of deciding the constitutional status of the policy-making process and, in particular, of determining its relation to the central constitutional doctrine of separation of powers.

Separation of powers, it should now be clear, was a doctrine designed chiefly to allocate the primary powers on what I have identified as the second level of governance. It is not a doctrine, as already noted, that applies to the first level (sovereignty), where power is given to the people, legislatures, and conventions. It applies to the policy-making process (the third level) only partially and indirectly, because of the consequences that flow from the division of the primary powers. The doctrine of separation of powers thus does not define fully—nor was it ever intended to define fully—the exact character of the policy-making process. The Constitution is not completely silent or neutral about the character of the policy-making process, but in the final analysis there is not one single constitutional model for the policy-making function but only constitutional limits within which models must be constructed.

One can only speculate on why the founders never devised a precise policy-making model. Four possible explanations come to mind: (1) they did not understand the policy-making function; (2) they disagreed on how it should be performed and decided not to decide; (3) they did not believe that the precise character of the policy-making process could be settled by fundamental law; or (4) they thought it best to allow the precise character of the policy-making process to change with time and circumstances. Not all these possible explanations are in conflict; indeed, all at some level are compatible. My own reading of the limited evidence on this issue is that, although a case can be made for the first and second possibilities, the more likely explanation is that the founders did not think that the Constitution either could or should determine the regime at this level of specificity.[15]

178

The view that the Constitution does not specify a particular policy-making model is supported not only by the theory of separation of powers but by practice and precedent. For the almost 200 years during which the government has operated under the Constitution, there have been a number of policy-making systems, ranging from the dominant congressional model of the nineteenth century to the strong presidential model of most of the postwar period. In addition, the party system was engrafted onto the regime in the 1820s, in part to resolve certain difficulties in the policy-making process. Given the existence of different policy-making models under the same Constitution, only two possible interpretations on this point are possible: either one must accept that the doctrine of separation of powers allows for significant variation in the structure of policy making, or one must claim that we have abandoned a separation of powers system for long periods of our history. Since almost no one has been willing to adopt the second position, it seems more reasonable to assume that the major historical systems for policy making have been constitutionally permissible. Some systems may have been better conceived than others or better adapted to the particular needs of their time, but these are not considerations that bear on their constitutionality.

This analysis of the different levels of the American political system leads to some important implications for the current debate on institutional change. First, critics of separation of powers tend to collapse the entire task of governance to that of policy making. This tendency may be explained by the fact that their critique was conceived by Woodrow Wilson at a time when Congress was the dominant power in the policy-making structure and the nation lacked a unitary initiating force to clarify policy options. To create such a force, Wilson called for an executive with formidable rhetorical skills who would bring to the nation's attention the chief policy issues of the day. In so doing, however, Wilson (as a theorist) identified the executive power almost exclusively with the policy-making function and thus with the elements of persuasion appropriate to that role. Critics of separation of powers have tended to follow in his footsteps. Forgotten is the tougher side of the executive's role—the exercise of the executive power—wherein persuasion is not as important as the executive's discretion to act as he sees fit.

While it is no doubt true that policy making is the most common task of government and that it has loomed larger as a governmental function since the advent of the welfare state, the issues of governance addressed by separation of powers are no less important today than in 1787 and perhaps are more important, given the role that the United States now plays in international politics. Commentators may

179

fill as many pages as they please about major government policies, such as economic programs and industrial policy, but this talk in no way diminishes either the need to use political power with energy and discretion at critical moments or the necessity of watching and checking that same power. A policy-making perspective slides too easily over these fundamental problems and tends to reduce the problem of governing to that of large-scale management.

Second, critics of separation of powers have engaged in an over-interpretation of the founding and the Constitution. Throughout their long history of criticism, they have tended to attribute to the founders a specific model of the policy-making process, which is always the model in existence at the time any particular attack is made. Dissatisfied with that model, they either criticize the founders directly or patronize them as being wise "for their time." For all their hostility toward the founders, however, they demonstrate a strong dependence on the founders' thought by constantly searching for an original constitutional intention for policy making. Curiously, they seem unwilling to assume responsibility for a task the founders left to subsequent generations: establishing the theories and institutional mechanisms, within the limits of separation of powers, that can produce a viable policy-making structure.

Third, critics of separation of powers have made the Constitution an enemy of what many of them seem to want—a strong executive. To be sure, the Constitution does not permit anything like a total concentration of the policy-making power in the executive. Nothing in the Constitution, however, precludes—and, in fact, much supports—the notion of the so-called modern president, whose task, according to Arthur Maass, is "leadership . . . to initiate and impel."[16] It is unfortunate that so many critics of separation of powers, demanding a whole loaf and unwilling to settle for one slice less, have based their case for a strong executive on an anticonstitutional foundation. Although some of their arguments have served to add strength to the presidency, the same arguments have also saddled it with unnecessary burdens and complications. By assigning to the president more policy-making responsibility than our system will allow, the critics of separation of powers have created expectations for the office that it cannot possibly meet. More important, however, these critics have undermined the constitutional foundation for the executive power and allowed it to be weakened by those who had some temporary advantage to gain. Can it merely be a coincidence that a generation of the intelligentsia, educated on these critics' nonconstitutional understanding of executive power, should have turned so violently against the executive power when certain writers and politicians found that they could promote their short-term policy goals by attacking the presidency?

Finally, an understanding of the different levels of our political system enables us to avoid the false dilemma of either attacking the principle of separation of powers or defending the current policy-making structure. If the current structure has problems—as I believe it does—our constitutional framework offers a great deal of room for criticism and modification. Opponents of separation of powers possess no monopoly on the right of criticism. In fact, most of the arguments they make today about excessive fragmentation in the policy-making process were made long ago by defenders of the system, who warned against the consequences of various schemes of reform that have been enacted over the past two decades.

Comparison of the Parliamentary and Separation of Powers Systems

The level of thought about institutions in much of our public discourse has fallen to a deplorable condition. How often, for instance, do we hear the following chain of reasoning: we face serious problems that politicians have been unable to solve; therefore, there must be some new institutional arrangement that we can adopt to assure us of better results. The notion that there is an institutional solution for every problem overlooks the elementary point that institutions do not solve problems; they only establish the structures within which fallible human beings attempt to solve them. Institutions may be judged good or bad insofar as they provide adequate structures to address problems and insofar as they lessen the probability that decision makers will make grave errors. Since, however, many political problems are unsolvable (in relation to expectations) and since political leaders are bound to make mistakes, even the best institutions may leave many feeling dissatisfied.

Another defect of institutional analysis today is the practice of judging institutions not by the general capacities they promote (such as energy or deliberation) but by their predicted effect on public policies in the near future. This kind of "partisan" or instrumental perspective on institutions enables many commentators in good conscience to shift from being critics of separation of powers on one day to proponents on the next, all the while proclaiming that they are offering detached institutional analysis. Such seeming dishonesty is (privately) justified by the supposedly higher status of the partisan cause, whether liberal or conservative. Although there may in fact be rare instances in which an instrumental perspective is justifiable, tinkering with institutions to suit policy aims is a dangerous game.

181

The effects of institutional change almost always outweigh in importance immediate policy objectives. From a purely practical standpoint, moreover, institutional changes usually outlast the period for which they serve their specific partisan purpose and often begin to serve other purposes. This leaves partisans in the awkward position of scrambling to explain how they can attack what they once defended and defend what they once attacked.

The study of political institutions requires a method that can avoid some of these defects. A first step is to clarify the meaning of the term "institution." I define institution here as a structure designed to endure for a relatively long time, which, through grants and limitations of powers and structural incentives and disincentives, provides or denies discretion for decision makers and influences their behavior in patterned ways.

A second step in considering institutional change is to assess the performance of an existing institution against the expected performance of a proposed alternative. The evaluation must be made in light of the full range of functions or values affected by the institution. It is pointless to condemn an institution without an alternative in mind or to isolate one or two criteria on which an alternative may appear superior. This proves nothing, for no institutional arrangement can simultaneously maximize all the values that might ideally be desired. Choices among different institutional possibilities always involve weighing a mixture of relevant values.

A final step, after evaluating the expected performances of the alternatives, is to consider the costs entailed by the process of change itself. These costs are of three sorts: (1) proponents of a given plan can never be certain that they will be able to control the process of change and obtain the plan they want; (2) proponents of a given plan cannot be certain that their plan will function as they expect or hope, for the unanticipated consequences of change often outweigh in number and significance the anticipated consequences; and (3) the example of change may lead to calls for more changes in the future, opening up matters of constitutional arrangement to constant meddling.

This method cannot be applied in full here, but I can say something about the characteristics expected of the system proposed by critics of the doctrine of separation of powers and about how that system compares with the system now in place. Proponents of the parliamentary system seek to concentrate all policy-making authority in a hierarchic arrangement at one point in the political system. To ensure that this authority would be compatible with democracy, they further stipulate that it must be democratically selected. They rely on an electoral check, rather than on institutional checks, to guarantee against abuses of power. Because political power in this system is both concentrated and democratic, proponents argue that it provides for greater accountability than a separation of powers system, since the public can know who are in charge and hold them responsible for their record. To avoid the problem of accountability to a minority, proponents of the parliamentary system favor the formation of two nationally oriented parties, either of which, after being voted into power, could claim to own a national mandate and to represent the general will of the nation.

The underlying purpose held by the proponents of this new system has shifted over the years. Originally they had in mind facilitating the extension of the scope of activity of the federal government to promote a modern welfare state. The multiple checks of the so-called Madisonian system, particularly the behavior of a retrograde Congress, prevented government, in their view, from being able to exercise greater control over society. Active government would require the concentration of power at one point. This plan was openly liberal in its assumption that liberty in the modern world was threatened more by the forces of society than by government.

This initial purpose has lost much of its appeal, for the welfare state has become the status quo. It is the opponents, if it is anyone, not the proponents, of the welfare state who may be dreaming of concentrated authority, as a way either of implementing a socialist system or alternatively of reducing the role of government in society.[17] Meanwhile, many liberals seem to have made their peace with the current system and can be found happily entrenched in one subcommittee or another of Congress, singing the praises of that retrograde institution. The case against separation of powers today thus rests less on partisan considerations and more on a "pure" institutional argument. Advocates of change emphasize the ever-growing complexity of modern government and argue that this new situation requires greater hierarchy and coordination in formulating and implementing public policy. Modern critics may be praised for their greater sincerity, but they may also have forsaken any realistic chance of finding political support for their proposal.

In comparing the expected performance of the parliamentary model with that of the separation of powers system, we should recall that the separation of powers system only sets the outer limits for the policy-making structure. To avoid identifying its properties with any particular structure, I must speak, for the moment only, of the general properties associated with these limits.

The first and most obvious characteristic of the separation of powers system is the division of policy-making authority among more

183

than one institution. One should be very careful, however, in claiming that this arrangement necessarily leads to stalemate or deadlock. A condition of stalemate refers, strictly speaking, to a situation in which nothing can be done, which critics claim results naturally from our system of divided power. Yet much policy making does not assume the form of a zero-sum game among the institutions. The existence of policy-making authority in more than one institution can allow each to initiate policies that the others may have thought unimportant or better left untouched. Once one institution begins to deal with certain policies, the others may join the process, either willingly or by necessity. In the modern policy arena, we have not only ambition counteracting and thwarting ambition but ambition vying with ambition. The vice of the separation of powers system may sometimes be not stalemate but too much policy making.

The second general characteristic of the separation of powers system is its peculiar way of calculating the public interest. In this respect the system must be distinguished from another effort in the history of political science to divide power, the mixed regime, in which the interests of different classes or estates are represented in different institutions. In the American system, by contrast, powers are divided by function, not by social class, and all the institutions claim legitimacy in the final analysis for representing the same entity, the people. Still, the institutions represent the people in different ways. Although the claims are by no means exclusive, the executive will speak for the whole nation grasped in a direct sense, whereas Congress, while it may deliberate on the same basis, also represents the various parts and specific interests, including the vital interests of other levels of government. It is in the dialogue between these two perspectives—between generality and particulars—that our policy-making system attempts to discover the public interest.

The third characteristic of the separation of powers system is its effect on how the American people think of national majorities. The American people have learned to live comfortably with the idea that at any time there may be no general will or mandate in the nation on policy matters. This assumption, so different, for example, from how people think in France, is central to the operation of our scheme of representative government and to its capacity to engage in deliberation. The American constitutional system entails no theory of a "general will" on policy matters outside or above the decisions reached by constituted authorities. Presidents, of course, may claim mandates for themselves or their parties, and these mandates may receive more or less credence according to the size of a president's majority and the number of seats gained or lost by his party in Congress. But these claims are known to be assertions only, for congressional elections are multidimensional races that turn only partly on considerations of national political issues. The president will keep his mandate as long as he can, but the system can work without it.

The final characteristic of the separation of powers system relates to the practice of administration that has built up around it. By constitutional law members of the legislature are banned from serving simultaneously as members of the executive branch; moreover, the independence of the executive allows presidents to choose cabinet officers from among those not having previous careers in Congress. The patterns of recruitment for cabinet officers give the American bureaucracy a distinctive cast of mind in comparison with the parliamentary system, where almost all the cabinet officials come from Parliament. In addition, the separation of powers system means that administrative entities serve two masters. This gives them some room for maneuvering and some opportunity to exercise power. By and large, however, the separation of powers subjects the bureaucracy in the United States to more political control than is found in parliamentary systems. Administrative agencies not only have two masters to please but have incentives (or can be compelled) to divulge a great deal of information, giving political leaders the opportunity to make decisions that in parliamentary systems often come under the de facto control of administrators.

With these properties of the two systems in mind, let us look briefly at the criteria for judging them.

- *Security.* No democratic system better meets the objective of security than the separation of powers system, for it ensures, no matter what else happens, the integrity of the essential executive power.
- *Liberty.* The debate between separation of powers and its critics has been as much about what liberty means as about how it can be obtained. The critics have taken the view that liberty is threatened more by society than by government, while some, but not all, defenders have taken the opposite position. This debate has now been overtaken by historical developments: we now have a welfare state that was built under a separation of powers system. Given the existence of liberty in systems that do not have a separation of powers system in the precise form in which it is found in America, it would clearly be foolish to assert that separation of the executive and the legislative powers is essential for the preservation of liberty. That is not to say, however, that it is not helpful as an additional check; and it may be precisely in welfare state systems, where political control is already so great, that this additional check is most needed.

185

• *Accountability.* Critics claim that a parliamentary system provides greater democratic accountability because of the concentration of power. Yet this accountability can be fictitious where the government rests on a party having the support of less than a majority. Furthermore, except in the rare cases in which governments in stable parliamentary systems fall, the voters may be compelled to live with government "mandates" for a period of up to five years. In the United States, by contrast, although the president holds his term for four years, a new sounding is taken every two years, and a president can lose influence in policy matters if his party suffers a severe setback in the midterm election.

• *Satisfaction of ambition.* A political system is more than a cold mechanism that processes inputs and outputs. It is made up of live human beings, some of whom seek the honor and recognition of being able to serve as powerful political figures. Under a parliamentary system power is held by a relatively small number of officials. In the United States, by contrast, the existence of an independent legislature provides an institution that can satisfy the desire for political honor for a much larger number of people. The United States is the world's second largest democracy, and the number of people yearning for a place in the sun is accordingly much greater than in Britain, France, or Denmark.

• *Efficiency.* Efficiency consists of at least two elements: (1) the capacity to act energetically to put a program or idea into effect; and (2) the ability to make decisions with as much of the relevant information at hand as possible. A parliamentary system (under certain circumstances) certainly possesses greater efficiency in the first sense than the American system. In the second sense, however, the opposite may well be true. The growth of complexity in government in recent years, involving more interests and more trade-offs in most decisions, has been such that the relevant information may not be discernible by someone "studying the facts" from on high. On the contrary, it may well be that the information relevant to making decisions can best become known under a system of multiple checks and diverse points of entry that allows the effects of any proposed policy to be gauged in an intensely political process. The existence of greater complexity in governing today seems to cut both ways: it creates a need for both more hierarchy and less hierarchy, and it is by no means clear that the separation of powers system is, on balance, less efficient than a parliamentary system.

• *Capacity for change.* Every system must have a capacity to avoid stagnation or deadlock. Although this capacity may be less important in policy matters than in crises, stalemate in the policy process can have harmful consequences that can lead to genuine crises. A political system that responds too quickly to proposed changes or initiates changes when they are unnecessary can itself become the source of problems and crises. To say what constitutes the proper mean between these two extremes would obviously require an essay of its own. What can be said, however, is that the separation of powers system, as modified by the advent of political parties, has enabled strong presidents, backed by coherent parties and impressive electoral mandates, to institute relatively coherent changes in the direction of public policy. That happened after the elections of 1932, 1964, and 1980, as well as after some of the realigning elections in the nineteenth century. The critics of separation of powers, it would seem, have overlooked the phenomenon of critical elections and realignments as not only instances of electoral change but also mechanisms to effect minirevolutions in the direction of public policy.

The Causes of Fragmentation

In the late 1970s a number of commentators began to speak of a "new American political system."[18] By this term they meant to identify a fundamental change in the operation of the government from what had become the norm in previous decades. The distinguishing feature of the new system, it was said, was an extreme fragmentation of the policy-making process. This fragmentation led either to policy stalemate (the incapacity to implement broad new initiatives) or to policy hypersensitivity and incoherence (the enactment of many new initiatives, but in piecemeal fashion and without any attention to the full scope of governmental activity).

The election of 1980 and the first two years of the Reagan presidency called this assessment into question by demonstrating that the system was not so new or different that a strong president leading a unified party could not pursue a relatively coherent program of governance. Still, the structural changes identified by these observers were more than idle speculation. Although such short-term factors as a politically unskilled president and a majority party without a common program exaggerated tendencies toward fragmentation in the late 1970s (just as opposite short-term factors concealed them in 1981 and 1982), the tendencies toward fragmentation remain, implicit in the arrangement of the policy-making structure. Yet what produced this "new" system, to the extent it exists, was certainly not separation of powers, which has existed since 1789, but four new isms: reformism, collectivism, whigism, and judicial activism.

Reformism. The reform movement, launched on the national political scene at the 1968 Democratic convention, gave rise to a populist philosophy opposed to all hierarchic structures of authority. Reformers favored various measures to substitute popular decision making for decision making by representative assemblies; to open deliberations of representative assemblies to public scrutiny; and to provide greater rank-and-file participation in assemblies at the expense of the prerogatives of leadership. Under the sway of reformist ideas, major changes were made both in the party system and in Congress. The presidential nominating process was transformed into a plebiscitary contest, which eliminated the need for presidential candidates to forge links with other party leaders and encouraged demagogic strategies of appeal in pursuing the office.[19] In Congress, with a few exceptions, power was divided into smaller pieces and dispersed more widely to the subcommittees. At the same time, many of the institutional norms that had developed in Congress during the previous half-century were either further eroded or altogether eliminated.

It is impossible, of course, at this early date to evaluate all the consequences of reformism. But many scholars have already observed that one important change has been a "deinstitutionalizing" of the policy-making structure. This has undermined procedures that produced predictable and patterned behavior in favor of procedures that open the process to the influence of short-term and evanescent factors. A harsher assessment would say that in the rush to destroy all the evils of hierarchy, reformers eliminated a number of subtle and important institutional mechanisms that served to channel the ambition of politicians in ways that tended to promote, or at any rate not to conflict with, the public interest. Today, in contrast, politicians seem increasingly to be trapped in the nasty dilemma of being able to help themselves only by compromising the public interest.

Collectivism. The policy-making process of the modern era, at least until the shock of Reagan's electoral victory of 1980, took place in the context of the positive state, in which many more people came to depend on government for their livelihood and well-being and in which government was held responsible for many more activities. It is no wonder, then, that more and more people began to identify governing with policy making. The advent of this new role for government produced a series of dysfunctions that Samuel Beer has called the "subsidy and benefits scramble" of the collectivist state: "Because so many are making claims, the claim of no single group can make much difference to the level of public expenditure. Self-restraint by a particular group, therefore, would bring no discernible benefit to it or to any other group."[20] The paradoxical result of this scramble, especially in the era of diminished economic growth of the 1970s, was government that did more but that was weaker and unable to demand the discipline to keep society within limits it could afford. Government not only yielded to unrealistic demands but actually stimulated those demands by bidding up entitlements to win electoral support.

The problems of "ungovernability" under the conditions just sketched are real enough, but they were (or are) not unique to the United States. Indeed, Beer's description was made specifically in reference to Great Britain during the 1960s and 1970s. It is, accordingly, sheer parochialism to ascribe all the stresses and strains of governing in the United States to separation of powers when these problems clearly have a different origin. Indeed, no form of democratic government in a large system may be able to deal successfully with the demands of collectivism, although until quite recently very few were prepared to entertain the thesis that the problem of ungovernability might lie more with the philosophy of collectivism itself than with any defects in the arrangements of the institutions of government.

Whether the difficulties of managing the conduct of politics under the philosophy of collectivism are magnified by a separation of powers system in comparison with various parliamentary regimes is a difficult question to answer. The "corruption" of a separation of powers system has assumed the form of piecemeal advantages won by interests that the general public may hardly see; the corruption of the British parliamentary system has assumed the form of a more open and blatant bidding for group support by the parties. It is difficult to choose between these vices. One advantage that a separation of powers system may possess, however, is that it does not completely mortgage the executive power to the problems of ungovernability endemic to such systems.

Whigism. The frustrations with the Vietnam War and the events of Watergate led to a powerful attack in the 1970s on the office of the presidency. The animus against the presidency was sustained well beyond its original passionate impulse by a new scholarly interpretation that rivals the Whigs of the 1780s in its jealousy of executive power. Erstwhile supporters of the presidency faded away or became born-again proponents of congressional government. For a brief time in 1974, many in Congress, academia, and the media began to speak of a fundamental shift in the existing policy-making structure in which Congress would replace the president as the usual initiating force in domestic policy and would become an equal partner with the president in making foreign policy.

In the sphere of domestic policy making, this new assertiveness posed no constitutional problems. Congress would only have been reasserting a role that it had played throughout much of the nineteenth century. Nevertheless, the constitutional permissibility of this plan could not obviate its practical implausibility. The complexity of modern policy making calls for at least some effort by a unified initiating force to view policy comprehensively so that trade-offs can be seen clearly and priorities assessed directly. But the fragmented power structure within Congress—made even more fragmented by the 1970 reforms—left Congress even more unsuited to assume the role of principal initiator. After 1975 talk of full-fledged congressional government quietly began to die out. Congress today is surely as powerful in domestic affairs as it was before the 1970s, and probably even more powerful, but in no sense has it assumed the primary responsibility for planning and initiating.

In the sphere of foreign affairs, by contrast, the new assertiveness of Congress does raise constitutional questions, in regard both to the letter and to the underlying theory of the Constitution. Although Congress has not literally taken the lead in foreign policy making, it has taken many steps to fulfill the objective of becoming an equal partner. In one area after another, it has imposed constraints on presidential discretion in foreign affairs. Today, in the House no less than in the Senate, foreign policy issues that would formerly have been considered primarily executive in nature have become matters for routine congressional attention and action. The assumption of many in Congress, all the more dangerous for being held with such sincerity, is that Congress performs its proper duty in a separation of powers system only when it ties the executive's hands and attempts to force the nation to run its foreign policy through the instrument of law. This view, reflective of modern Whig scholarship, is based on a narrow and legalistic understanding of the Constitution and on a failure to recognize the real purpose for which the founders adopted the theory of separation of powers.

Judicial Activism. Critics of separation of powers complain that we suffer not only from an absence of centralized leadership but from a lack of political accountability. On the latter point, at least, their contention is unassailable. The source of this problem lies chiefly not with the branches these critics identify—the presidency and the Congress—but with the branch they never seem to mention: the judiciary. Anyone concerned with policy accountability must give attention to the courts, which have become policy-making institutions not only incidentally, in consequence of the performance of judicial duties, but by deliberate design. Perhaps because critics of separation of powers have traditionally favored a growth in federal responsibilities and greater equality, they have chosen for instrumental reasons to treat the courts' policy-making role with benign neglect. Meanwhile, allies of the political positions taken by the courts have adopted a pious theory of constitutionalism that elevates judicial power far beyond anything originally contemplated. This theory has served successfully to prevent the other branches from summoning the political will to check the judiciary and to assume responsibility for policy matters that ought to be under their control.

The four isms discussed here, much more than the theory of separation of powers, may help to explain many of the problems that seem (to some) to make American government unworkable. If there are changes needed, we ought to begin by realizing that the doctrine of separation of powers imposes on us the responsibility of constructing, within certain limits, the policy-making structure. Before attacking the limits, we would do well to accept our responsibility to examine carefully the elements of the system that have recently been constructed. Change there must always be, but let us approach it prudently, with a disposition to preserve and a willingness to improve.

Notes

1. The fall of the Fourth Republic in the spring of 1958 followed a thirty-eight-day ministerial crisis in the winter during which no government could be formed. Finally a weak prime minister was appointed who could do nothing to quell the spreading insurgency in the armed forces. For an account of these events and a discussion of the influence of the American Constitution on the founders of the Fifth Republic, see William Safran, *The French Polity* (New York: David McKay, 1977), pp. 50–59.

2. Lloyd N. Cutler, "To Form a Government," *Foreign Affairs* (Fall 1980), p. 127, reprinted as chapter 1 in this volume.

3. Ibid., p. 126.

4. Charles M. Hardin, *Presidential Power and Accountability* (Chicago: University of Chicago Press, 1974), p. 2.

5. See, for example, Gabriel A. Almond and G. Bingham Powell, Jr., *Comparative Politics Today*, 2d ed. (Boston: Little, Brown, 1980). The insights of this modern approach were already developed and employed by Montesquieu in *The Spirit of the Laws*.

6. Most of these regimes have parliamentary governments of one sort or another. One (France) combines presidential and parliamentary features, and the United States possesses a pure presidential or separation of powers

system. From this formal perspective, the American system might seem to be the most "extreme" in that it goes further than any of the others in dividing the executive and legislative powers into two distinct institutions—and, partly as a consequence, in giving greater power to the judicial branch.

7. The statement is by Lord Hailsham; it is cited and discussed in Geoffrey Smith and Nelson W. Polsby, *British Government and Its Discontents* (New York: Basic Books, 1981), pp. 137–39.

8. The American policy-making process since the 1820s has rested on a fine balance in which political parties can be neither too strong nor too weak. If parties were too strong, the division of policy-making authority between the president and Congress might be overcome in practice; if parties were too weak or if they should collapse, an important connective web between the executive and the legislature would be lost. In recent years many observers have argued that parties have become too weak.

9. See Smith and Polsby, *British Government and Its Discontents*.

10. For a discussion of the Whig tradition in the colonial and revolutionary period, see Bernard Bailyn, *The Ideological Origins of the American Revolution* (Cambridge, Mass.: Harvard University Press, 1967).

11. For a more extended account of the origins of the executive power, see Gary J. Schmitt, "Executive Privilege: Presidential Power to Withhold Information from Congress," and Robert Scigliano, "The War Powers Resolution and the War Powers," in Joseph M. Bessette and Jeffrey Tulis, eds., *The Presidency and the Constitutional Order* (Baton Rouge: Louisiana State University Press, 1981); and Jeffrey Poelvoorde (Ph.D. diss., University of Virginia, 1985).

12. For a discussion of the federative power, see John Locke, *The Second Treatise on Government*, secs. 146–48, 153. In interpreting Locke's claim that the legislative is supreme (sec. 153) and the executive ministerial and subordinate, one should keep two facts in mind: (1) Locke modifies this claim in his discussion of prerogative (158 and 159); and (2) in the United States the legislative power in its highest sense rests not with Congress and its lawmaking capacity but with the Constitution. The supreme legislature in Lockean terms refers to the first level of government (sovereignty) that I have defined above.

13. See Schmitt, "Executive Privilege"; see also Justice Sutherland's opinion in *United States v. Curtiss-Wright Export Corporation*, 229 U.S. 304 (1936).

14. In referring to the policy-making process here, I mean to exclude the making of policy decisions on matters of sovereignty and matters that fall within the executive's crisis or prerogative authority. Policy making refers to the residue of governmental decision making.

15. That is not to say that they were entirely neutral on this issue. In relation to the prevailing Whig ideas, many founders clearly preferred a stronger executive role in the policy process. This disposition would explain their decision to give the president not just the veto but the right to inform the legislature and make recommendations (Art. 2, sec. 3). Yet even the most liberal reading of this last clause cannot be taken as establishing the president as the system's policy initiator; at most it creates a presumption for that role.

16. Arthur Maass, *Congress and the Common Good* (New York: Basic Books, 1983), p. 13.

17. Modern socialist-minded critics of separation of powers, such as Walter Dean Burnham and Robert Dahl, make the same kind of attack on the so-called Madisonian system that was formerly made by liberals. They argue that the separation of powers system prevents the kind of concentration of power at a single point needed to create a radical change in the relations of government to society. See Walter Dean Burnham, "The Constitution and the Protection of Capitalism," in Robert A. Goldwin and William A. Schambra, eds., *How Capitalistic Is the Constitution?* (Washington, D.C.: American Enterprise Institute, 1982); and Robert Dahl, "Removing Certain Impediments to Democracy in the United States," in Robert Horowitz, ed., *The Moral Foundations of the American Republic* (Charlottesville: University of Virginia Press, 1977).

18. The term is taken from the title of the widely read work, Anthony King, ed., *The New American Political System* (Washington, D.C.: American Enterprise Institute, 1978).

19. For the effects of party reform on the governing process, see Nelson W. Polsby, *Consequences of Party Reform* (New York: Oxford University Press, 1983).

20. Samuel Beer, *Britain against Itself* (New York: W. W. Norton, 1982), pp. 24–33.

A Note on the Book

This book was edited by
Gertrude Kaplan of the AEI Publications staff.
Pat Taylor designed the cover and format.
The text was set in Palatino, a typeface designed by Hermann Zapf.
Exspeedite Printing Service, Inc., of Silver Spring, Maryland,
set the type, and
R.R. Donnelley & Sons Company, of Harrisonburg, Virginia,
printed and bound the book, using
permanent, acid-free paper made by the S.D. Warren Company.

Selected AEI Publications

How Does the Constitution Secure Rights? Robert A. Goldwin and William A. Schambra, eds. (1985, 125 pp., cloth $13.95, paper $5.95)

How Capitalistic Is the Constitution? Robert A. Goldwin and William A. Schambra, eds. (1982, 172 pp., cloth $14.25, paper $6.25)

How Democratic Is the Constitution? Robert A. Goldwin and William A. Schambra, eds. (1980, 150 pp., cloth $12.25, paper $5.25)

Selected Writings and Speeches of Alexander Hamilton, Morton J. Frisch, ed. (1985, 524 pp., cloth $25.95, paper $14.95)

War Powers and the Constitution, Dick Cheney, Lee H. Hamilton, Charles McC. Mathias, Jr., Brent Scowcroft, John Charles Daly, mod. (1984, 29 pp., $3.75)

Religion and the Constitution, Walter Berns, Edd Doerr, Henry J. Hyde, Barry William Lynn, John Charles Daly, mod. (1984, 34 pp., $3.75)

• *Mail orders for publications to:* AMERICAN ENTERPRISE INSTITUTE, 1150 Seventeenth Street, N.W., Washington, D.C. 20036 • *For postage and handling, add 10 percent of total; minimum charge $2, maximum $10 (no charge on prepaid orders)* • *For information on orders, or to expedite service, call toll free 800-424-2873 (in Washington, D.C., 202-862-5869)* • *Prices subject to change without notice.* • *Payable in U.S. currency through U.S. banks only*

AEI Associates Program

The American Enterprise Institute invites your participation in the competition of ideas through its AEI Associates Program. This program has two objectives: (1) to extend public familiarity with contemporary issues; and (2) to increase research on these issues and dissem. .:te the results to policy makers, the academic community, journalists, and others who help shape public policies. The areas studied by AEI include Economic Policy, International Policy, and Political and Social Processes. For the $49 annual fee, Associates receive

• a subscription to *Memorandum,* the newsletter on all AEI activities
• the AEI publications catalog and all supplements
• a 30 percent discount on all AEI books
• a 40 percent discount for certain seminars on key issues
• subscriptions to the following publications: *Public Opinion,* a bi-monthly magazine exploring trends and implications of public opinion on social and public policy questions; and the *AEI Economist,* a monthly newsletter analyzing current economic issues and evaluating future trends.

Call 202/862-7170 or write: AMERICAN ENTERPRISE INSTITUTE
1150 Seventeenth Street, N.W., Suite 301, Washington, D.C. 20036